S0-BYJ-897

NORTH AMERICAN
AIRLINES HANDBOOK

SECOND EDITION

by Tom Norwood & John Wegg

With thanks to:
Glen Etchells (Canada)
Jorge Seguí Martin (México)
Joe Wolf and Brian Rynott (Caribbean & Central America)

COVER: United Airlines Airbus A319-131. (Airbus Industrie)

© Airways International Inc 1999

Desktop publishing: Thinking Cap Communications & Design
Production coordinator/editorial assistant: Gretchen Bender

Printed in Singapore

Published by
Airways International Inc
PO Box 1109, Sandpoint, ID 83864-0872, USA

First edition 1997
Second edition 1999

ISBN 0-9653993-5-4

INTRODUCTION

Welcome to the second edition of our comprehensive guide to the airlines of North America. All information has been updated, and in many cases increased, 99% of the photos are new, and—because of user demand—we have added indexes to radio call-signs and aircraft types illustrated.

In addition, we have expanded our definition of North America to include Central America. All 50 states of the USA—plus the commonwealth of Puerto Rico and the territory of the Virgin Islands, Canada, Greenland (part of the Danish realm), Saint-Pierre et Miquelon (a French *collectivité territoriale*, or territorial collectivity, off the coast of eastern Canada), México, and the island nations of the Caribbean are also included. American Samoa and the Federated States of Micronesia in the Pacific, associated with the USA, are omitted (although Continental Micronesia is incorporated in the listing for Continental Airlines).

With some exceptions, all regularly scheduled passenger airlines operating turbine-powered aircraft of not less than 19 seats, and charter passenger and all-cargo operators of heavy pure-jet equipment receive a one-page entry, including a color photograph depicting a current type.

Other airlines which operate regularly scheduled passenger and/or cargo services, plus selected charter operators, are recorded in the relevant addenda.

Because of the speed of development and changes in the air transport industry, inevitably some of the information recorded will be out of date by the time this book is printed. All route network and detailed fleet changes, plus other airline news items, are recorded by *Airways News Online* at www.airwaysnews.com, which is updated at least twice a month. Feature articles on North American airlines appear every month in *Airways* magazine, along with a selection of news photos.

Any corrections, updates, suggestions, and new slides and photographs will be welcomed by the compilers for the next edition.

John Wegg

Airways International Inc
PO Box 1109
Sandpoint ID 83864-0872
USA

Tel: + 1 208 263 2098
Fax: + 1 208 263 5906
Email: airways@nidlink.com
URL: www.airwaysmag.com

EXPLANATION OF ENTRIES & ABBREVIATIONS
(in order of appearance)

IATA Two-letter designator ('airline code') assigned by the International Air Transport Association and used for ticketing and other purposes

ICAO Three-letter designator ('airline code') assigned by the International Civil Aviation Organization and used for air traffic control and other purposes

IATA/ARC Three-digit code assigned by IATA or the Airlines Reporting Corp (USA) for accounting purposes

RADIO Radio call-sign assigned by ICAO

CONTACTS Admin = Administrative, Info = Information, PR = Public/Press/ Media Relations, Res = Reservations

OPERATION It has been assumed that many primarily scheduled carriers also operate charters and primarily passenger airlines also carry cargo

Cities/airports served on a scheduled or regular charter basis are listed alphabetically by IATA three-letter codes (*see City and Airport Decode*) and, if the territory served includes areas outside of the airline's home section, then separate entries are made for Canada, Caribbean, México, Central America, South America, Europe, Asia, and Oceania

FFP Frequent Flyer Program

HISTORY/STRUCTURE CEO = Chief Executive Officer, COO = Chief Operating Officer, GM = General Manager

OWNERSHIP Publicly traded companies stock market abbreviations: AMEX = American Stock Exchange, IPC = Indice de Precios y Cotizaciones, NASDAQ = National Association of Securities Dealers Automated Quotations, NYSE = New York Stock Exchange, TSE = Toronto Stock Exchange, VSE = Vancouver Stock Exchange

FLEET Listed in order of size of aircraft

Seating configurations: C or J = Business-Class, F = First-Class, Y = Economy-Class (Coach)

Engine Manufacturer prefixes: AE = Allison, ALF = AlliedSignal, AN = Allison, ASh = Shvetsov, BR = BMW Rolls-Royce, CFM = CFM International (SNECMA/General Electric), CO = Teledyne Continental, GA = Garrett (AlliedSignal), GE = General Electric, IAE = International Aero Engines (Rolls-Royce/Pratt & Whitney/Japanese Aero Engines/FIAT), IV = Ivchyenko Progress, KL = Klimov, LY = Textron Lycoming, NK = NK Engines, PW = Pratt & Whitney, PWC = Pratt & Whitney Canada, RM = Rybinsk Motors (Perm), RR = Rolls-Royce, TU = Turboméca, WA = Walter, WR = Wright

ADDENDA Information for companies is listed in the sequence: name, IATA/ICAO/ARC/Radio, mail address, telephone, fax, email, Internet URL, name of CEO/president, type of operation, fleet information

BOEING 767-200 (F)

ABX AIR (dba AIRBORNE EXPRESS)

IATA: GB   **ICAO:** ABX   **IATA/ARC:** 382   **RADIO:** Abex

CONTACTS:

Mail	Telephone/Fax
145 Hunter Drive	Admin: +1 937 382 5591
Wilmington, OH 45177	Fax: +1 937 382 2452
	Info: 1 800 247 2676

Internet: www.airborne-express.com

OPERATION:

Type: Scheduled/charter cargo
Cities Served: US: ABE ABQ ALB ANC ATL ATW AUS BDL BFI BHM BIL BNA BOI BOS BTV BUF BWI CAE CHA CID CLE CLT CNW COS COU CWF DAL DEN DFW DSM DTW ELP EWR FAR FAT FLL FNT FSD GEG GRR GSO GSP HRL HSV IAD IAH ICT ILN ISP JAN JAX JFK LAS LAX LBB LGB LIT MCI MCO MDT MDW MEM MHR MHT MIA MKE MLI MSN MSP MSY OAK OKC OMA ONT ORD ORF PDX PHL PHX PIA PIT PNS PVD PWM RDU RFD RIC RNO ROA ROC RST SAN SAT SBN SEA SGF SHV SJC SLC STL SWF SYR TPA TRI TUL TYS TYS **Canada:** YEG YYZ **Caribbean:** SJU
Other markets served by contract carriers

HISTORY/STRUCTURE:

Founded: April 17, 1980
Start Date: 1980
President/CEO: Carl Donaway
Ownership: Airborne Freight Corp

FLEET:

Type	No	Engines
DC-9-15	2	PW JT8D-7A/-7B
DC-9-30	43	PW JT8D-7A/-7B/-9/-9A/-11
DC-9-40	28	PW JT8D-11/-15
DC-8-61F	13	PW JT3D-3B
DC-8-62F	6	PW JT3D-7
DC-8-63F	17	PW JT3D-7
Boeing 767-200F	7	GE CF6A-80
Ordered		
Boeing 767-200F	20 plus 1 option	

BOEING 737-200 (ADVANCED)

ACCESS AIR

IATA: ZA   **ICAO:** CYD   **IATA/ARC:** 144   **RADIO:** Cyclone

---

CONTACTS:

Mail	Telephone/Fax
601 Locust Street	Admin: +1 515 245 3745
Suite 330	Fax: +1 515 247 2216
Des Moines, IA 50309-3738	Res: +1 877 462 2237
Internet: www.accessair.com	

OPERATION:

Type: Scheduled passenger
Cities Served: COS DSM LAX LGA MLI PIA
FFP: AccessAwards Plus

HISTORY/STRUCTURE:

Founded: 1997
Start Date: February 3, 1999
President/CEO: Roger Pearson
Ownership: Closely held

FLEET:

Type	No	Seats	Engines
Boeing 737-200 (Advanced)	4	C51Y66	PW JT8D-15
Ordered			
Boeing 737-200	2		

RAYTHEON BEECH 1900D

AIR MIDWEST

IATA: ZV   **ICAO:** AMW   **IATA/ARC:** 471   **RADIO:** Air Midwest

---

CONTACTS:

Mail
2230 Air Cargo Road
Wichita, KS 67209

Internet: www.mesa-air.com

Telephone/Fax
Admin: +1 316 942 8137
Fax: +1 316 945 0947
Res: 1 800 428 4322

OPERATION:

Type: Scheduled passenger
Cities Served: APF ART BFD CBE CID CKB DCA DDC DSM DUJ EYW FKL
FOE FYV GBD GCK HYS ICT JAN JAX JHW LBE LIT LNK MBS MCI MCO
MGW MHK MSS MSY OGS OMA PBI PFN PIT PKB PNS SGF SHV SLN TLH
TPA VPS YNG
All service operated as US Airways Express using only US flight numbers
(5500-5749)
FFP: US Airways Dividend Miles

HISTORY/STRUCTURE:

Founded: May 1965 (as Aviation Services)
Start Date: April 1967
President: Dick Paquette
Ownership: Mesa Air Group

FLEET:

Type	No	Seats	Engines
Beech 1900D	40	Y19	PWC PT6A-67D

BOEING 717-200

AIRTRAN AIRWAYS

IATA: FL   **ICAO:** TRS   **IATA/ARC:** 332   **RADIO:** Citrus

CONTACTS:

Mail
9955 AirTran Boulevard
Orlando, FL 32827

Internet: www.airtran.com

Telephone/Fax
Admin: +1 407 251 5600
Fax: +1 407 251 5727
Res: 1 800 247 8726

OPERATION:

Type: Scheduled passenger
Cities Served: ATL BDL BMI BNA BOS BUF CAK DAY DFW EWR FLL FNT GPT GSO HOU IAD JAX LGA MCO MDW MEM MIA MLI MSY PHF PHL RDU RSW SAV TPA TYS VPS
FFP: A-Plus Rewards

HISTORY/STRUCTURE:

Founded: 1992 (as ValuJet Airlines)
Start Date: October 26, 1993
Chairman/CEO: Joseph Leonard
President: Robert Fornaro
Ownership: Airtran Holdings Inc (NASDAQ: AAIR)

FLEET:

Type	No	Seats	Engines
DC-9-32	40	C20Y95	PW JT8D-7B/-9/-9A
Boeing 737-200	8	Y126	PW JT8D-9A/-15/-17
Ordered			
Boeing 717-200	50 plus 50 options		

DOUGLAS DC-8-71F

AIR TRANSPORT INTERNATIONAL

IATA: 8C   **ICAO:** ATN   **IATA/ARC:** 346   **RADIO:** Air Transport

CONTACTS:

Mail	Telephone/Fax
2800 Cantrell Road	Admin: +1 501 615 3500
Little Rock, AR 72202-2046	Fax: +1 501 603 2093

OPERATION:

Type: Charter passenger/cargo
Operates contract services, with several aircraft operated for BAX Global

HISTORY/STRUCTURE:

Founded: 1978 (as US Airways)
Start Date: 1979
General Manager: Charles Adami
Ownership: BAX Global

FLEET:

Type	No	Seats	Engines
DC-8-61F	1	Freighter	PW JT3D-3B
DC-8-62F	6	Freighter or P10Y32	PW JT3D-3B/-7
DC-8-63F	8	Freighter	PW JT3D-7
DC-8-71F	11	Freighter	CFM56-2C1

AIR WISCONSIN

IATA: ZW   **ICAO:** AWI   **IATA/ARC:** none   **RADIO:** Wisconsin

CONTACTS:

Mail	Telephone/Fax
W6390 Challenger Drive, Suite 203	Admin: +1 920 739 5123
Appleton, WI 54915-9120	Fax: +1 920 749 4158
	Res: 1 800 241 6522

Internet: www.airwis.com

OPERATION:

Type: Scheduled passenger
Cities Served: ASE ATW BIL BOI COS CPR DEN DRO EUG FAR GEG GJT GUC HDN ICT JAC JAN LEX MEM MKE MLI MSN MTJ ORD PIA RAP SBA SDF SGF (seasonal: EGE LAX)
All service operated as United Express using only UA flight numbers (5500-5699, 7050-7149)
FFP: United Airlines Mileage Plus

HISTORY/STRUCTURE:

Founded: 1965
Start Date: August 23, 1965
President/CEO: Geoffrey Crowley
Ownership: CJT Holdings

FLEET:

Type	No	Seats	Engines
Dornier 328	11	Y30	PWC PW119C
Canadair RJ 200LR	4	Y50	GE CF34-3A1
BAe 146-100A	1	Y86	ALF502R-5
BAe 146-200A	12	Y86/Y88	ALF502R-5
BAe 146-300A	5	Y100	ALF502R-5
Ordered			
Canadair RJ 200LR	5		

BOEING 737-400

ALASKA AIRLINES

IATA: AS **ICAO:** ASA **IATA/ARC:** 027 **RADIO:** Alaska

CONTACTS:

Mail	Telephone/Fax	
PO Box 68900	Admin:	+1 206 433 3200
Seattle, WA 98168	Fax:	+1 206 433 3366
	Res:	1 800 426 0333
Internet: www.alaskaair.com	PR:	+1 206 433 3170/3134

OPERATION:

Type: Scheduled passenger/cargo
Cities Served: US: ADQ AKN ANC BET BRW BUR CDV DLG DUT FAI GEG JNU KTN LAS LAX OAK OME ONT OTZ PDX PHX PSG PSP RNO SAN SCC SEA SFO SIT SJC SMF SNA WRG YAK **Canada:** YVR **México:** LAP MZT PVR SJD
Code-Share: American Eagle, Canadian, Continental, ERA Aviation, Harbor Airlines, Horizon Air, Northwest, Peninsula Airways, Trans States Airlines
FFP: Alaska Airlines Mileage Plan

HISTORY/STRUCTURE:

Founded: 1932 (as McGee Airways)
Start Date: June 6, 1944
Chairman: John F Kelly
President/CEO: William Ayer
Ownership: Alaska Air Group (NYSE: ALK)

FLEET:

Type	No	Seats	Engines
Boeing 737-200C (Advanced)	8	Y111 or Combi	PW JT8D-17/-17A
Boeing 737-400	40	F8Y132	CFM56-3C1
MD-82	7	F12Y128	PW JT8D-217/-217A
MD-83	32	F12Y128	PW JT8D-219
Ordered			
Boeing 737-700	8	plus 4 options	
Boeing 737-900	10	plus 10 options	

BOMBARDIER DHC-8-102 DASH 8

ALLEGHENY AIRLINES

IATA: none   **ICAO:** ALO   **IATA/ARC:** 395   **RADIO:** Allegheny

CONTACTS:

Mail
1000 Rosedale Avenue
Middletown, PA 17057

Internet: www.usairways.com

Telephone/Fax
Admin: +1 717 948 5400
Fax: +1 717 948 4714
Res: 1 800 428 4322

OPERATION:

Type: Scheduled passenger
Cities Served: ABE ALB AVP BDL BGM BOS BTV BUF BWI CLE ERI EWR HTS HPN IAD ISP ITH LEX LGA MDT MHT PHL PIT RDG ROC SCE SWF SYR TOL (seasonal: ACK MVY)
All service operated as US Airways Express using only US flight numbers (3500-3999)
FFP: US Airways Dividend Miles

HISTORY/STRUCTURE:

Founded: 1957 (as Reading Airlines)
Start Date: August 1957
President: Keith Houk
Ownership: US Airways Group

FLEET:

Type	No	Seats	Engines
DHC-8-102	42	Y37	PWC PW120A

ALLEGIANT AIR

IATA: G4   **ICAO:** AAY   **IATA/ARC:** none   **RADIO:** Allegiant

CONTACTS:

Mail
4955 East Anderson, Suite 120
Fresno, CA 93726

Telephone/Fax
Admin: +1 559 454 7781
Fax: +1 559 454 7708

OPERATION:

Type: Charter passenger

HISTORY/STRUCTURE:

Founded: 1997 (as WestJet Express)
Start Date: 1998
President/CEO: James Patterson
Ownership: Closely held

FLEET:

Type	No	Seats	Engines
DC-9-21	1	Y89	PW JT8D-11
Ordered			
DC-9-51	3		

BOEING 737-200 (ADVANCED)

ALOHA AIRLINES

IATA: AQ   **ICAO:** AAH   **IATA/ARC:** 327   **RADIO:** Aloha

CONTACTS:

Mail	Telephone/Fax
PO Box 30028	Admin: +1 808 836 4101
Honolulu, HI 96820	Fax: +1 808 836 0303
	Res: 1 800 367 5250
Internet: www.alohaair.com	PR: +1 808 836 5247

OPERATION:

Type: Scheduled passenger/cargo
Cities Served: HNL ITO KOA LIH OGG
Code-Share: IslandAir
FFP: AlohaPass

HISTORY/STRUCTURE:

Founded: June 1946 (as Trans-Pacific Airlines)
Start Date: July 26, 1946
President/CEO: Glenn Zander
Ownership: Aloha Airgroup

FLEET:

Type	No	Seats	Engines
Boeing 737-200 (Advanced)	12	F10Y111 or F6Y110	PW JT8D-9A/15
Boeing 737-200QC (Advanced)	5	F10Y103 or F6Y107	PW JT8D-9A/15
Boeing 737-200 (Advanced)	1	Freighter	PW JT8D-15

AIRBUS A319-132

AMERICA WEST AIRLINES

IATA: HP   **ICAO:** AWE   **IATA/ARC:** 401   **RADIO:** Cactus

CONTACTS:

Mail	Telephone/Fax	
4000 East Sky Harbor Boulevard	Admin:	+1 480 693 0800
Phoenix, AZ 85034	Fax:	+1 480 693 5546
	Res:	1 800 235 9292
	PR:	+1 480 693 5729
Internet: www.americawest.com	Job Hotline:	1 800 228 8713

OPERATION:

Type: Scheduled passenger
Cities Served: US: ABQ ATL AUS BOS BUR BWI CLE CMH COS DCA DEN DFW DTW ELP EWR FLL IAD IAH ICT IND JFK LAS LAX LGA LGB MCI MCO MDW MIA MKE MSP OAK OMA ONT ORD PDX PHL PHX RNO SAN SAT SEA SFO SJC SLC SMF SNA STL TPA TUS (seasonal: ANC) **Canada:** YVR
México: ACA MEX MZT PVR SJD ZIH (seasonal: ZLO)
Code-Share: Continental, Continental Express, Mesa
FFP: FlightFund

HISTORY/STRUCTURE:

Founded: February 1981
Start Date: August 1, 1983
President/CEO: William Franke
Ownership: America West Holding Corp (NYSE: AWA)

FLEET:

Type	No	Seats	Engines
Boeing 737-100	1	F8Y87	PW JT8D-9A
Boeing 737-200	17	F8Y105	PW JT8D-9A/-15
Boeing 737-300	46	F8Y118/Y120/Y121	CFM56-3B1/-3B2
Airbus A319-100	3	F12Y112	IAE V2522-A5
Airbus A320-200	33	F12Y138	IAE V2500-A1/V2527-A5
Boeing 757-200	13	F14Y176 or F14Y175	RR RB211-535E4
Ordered			
Airbus A320	9	plus 20 options	
Airbus A319	19	plus 20 options	

BOEING 777-200 (ER)

AMERICAN AIRLINES

IATA: AA   **ICAO:** AAL   **IATA/ARC:** 001   **RADIO:** American

---

CONTACTS:

Mail	Telephone/Fax
PO Box 619616	Admin: +1 817 963 1234
Dallas/Ft Worth Airport, TX 75261	Fax: +1 817 967 4318
	Res: 1 800 433 7300
Internet: www.aa.com	PR: +1 817 967 1575

OPERATION:

Type: Scheduled passenger

Cities Served: US: ABQ ALB AMA ATL AUS BDL BFL BHM BNA BOS BUF BUR BWI CLE CLT CMH CVG DAY DCA DEN DFW DSM DTW ELP FAT FLL GSO HNL HPN HSV IAH ICT IND ISP JAX JFK LAS LAX LGA LGB LIT MCI MCO MDT MEM MIA MKE MSP MSY OAK OGG OKC OMA ONT ORD ORF PBI PDX PHL PHX PIT PSP PVD RDU RIC RNO ROC RST RSW SAN SAT SDF SEA SFO SJC SLC SMF SNA STL SWF SYR TPA TUL TUS (seasonal: DRO EGE GUC HDN JAC) **Canada:** YOW YUL YVR YYC YYZ **Caribbean:** ANU AUA BDA BGI CUR GCM KIN LRM MBJ PAP PLS POP POS SDQ SJU STT STX SXM (seasonal: UVF) **México/Central America:** ACA BJX BZE CUN GDL GUA MEX MGA MTY PTY PVR SAL SAP SJD SJO TGU **South America:** ASU BAQ BOG CCS CLO CNF EZE GIG GRU GYE LIM LPB MVD SCL UIO VVI **Europe:** ARN BHX BRU FRA LGW LHR MAD MAN MXP ORY ZRH (seasonal: GLA) **Asia:** KIX NRT

Global Alliance: oneworld

Code-Share: Aero California, Air Liberté, Air Pacific, American Eagle, Asiana, British Midland, Business Express, Canadian, China, China Eastern, Finnair, Grupo TACA, Gulf Air, Hawaiian, Iberia, Japan Airlines, LOT, QANTAS, Singapore, South African, TAM

FFP: AAdvantage

HISTORY/STRUCTURE:

Founded: January 25, 1930 (as American Airways)

Start Date: May 5, 1934

President: Donald Carty

Ownership: AMR Corp (NYSE: AMR)

BOEING 737-800

FLEET:

Type	No	Seats	Engines
Fokker 100	75	F8Y89	RR Tay 650-15
MD-82	226	F14Y125 or F20Y113	PW JT8D 217A/ 217C
MD-83	33	F14Y125 or F20Y113	PW JT8D-219
Boeing 727-200 (Advanced)	76	F12Y138	PW JT8D-9/-9A/-15
Boeing 737-800	10	F20Y126	CFM56-7B26
Boeing 757-200	102	F22Y166	RR RB211-535E4B
Boeing 767-200	8	F14C30Y128	GE CF6-80A
Boeing 767-200ER	22	F9C30Y126	GE CF6-80A2
Boeing 767-300ER	49	F14C30Y163	GE CF6-80C2B6
Boeing 777-200ER	8	F18C56Y163	RR Trent 892
A300B4-605R	35	F16Y251/Y250 or F10C34Y148	GE CF6-80C2A5
DC-10-10	8	F28C52Y157 or F34Y256	GE CF6-6K
DC-10-30	5	F30Y243	GE CF6-50C2
MD-11	11	F19C35Y201 or F19C56Y163	GE CF6-80C2D1F
Ordered			
Boeing 737-800	93	plus 400 options (any 737 series)	
Boeing 757-200	3	plus 38 options	
Boeing 767-300ER	1	plus 26 options	
Boeing 777-200ER	26	plus 26 options	

NOTES:

EMBRAER EMB-145ER

AMERICAN EAGLE AIRLINES

IATA: none   **ICAO:** EGF   **IATA/ARC:** none   **RADIO:** Eagle Flight

CONTACTS:

Mail	Telephone/Fax
PO Box 619616	Admin: +1 817 967 1295
MD5475	Fax: +1 817 967 0977
DFW Airport, TX 75261	Res: 1 800 433 7300
Internet: www.aa.com	

OPERATION:

Type: Scheduled passenger
Cities Served: US: ABI ACT AEX ALB AMA APF AZO BDL BFL BMI BNA BOS BPT BTR BUF BWI CID CLE CLL CMH CMI CRP CVG DAY DCA DBQ DFW DLH DSM EVV EYW FAT FLL FSM FWA GGG GRB GRR HOU HRL ICT ILE IND JAN JAX JFK LAN LAS LAW LAX LBB LCH LFT LIT LRD LSE MAF MCO MEM MIA MGM MKE MRY MSN MTH OKC OMA ORD PHL PIA PIT PSP PVD RDU ROC RSW SAN SBA SBN SBP SGF SHV SJT SPI SPS SRQ SYR TOL TVC TXK TYR TYS XNA **Canada:** YUL **Caribbean:** ANU BGI DOM EIS FDF FPO GHB GND LRM MAZ MHH NAS POP PSE PTP PUJ SDQ SJU SKB SLU STI STT STX TAB
All service operated using only AA flight numbers (3200-5899)
Code-Share: Hawaiian
FFP: AAdvantage

HISTORY/STRUCTURE:

Founded: 1998	**Start Date:** April 30, 1998
President: Peter Bowler	**Ownership:** AMR Corporation

FLEET:

Type	No	Seats	Engines
SAAB 340B	110	Y34	GE CT7-9B
ATR42-300	35	Y46	PWC PW120
ATR72-200	43	Y64	PWC PW123/PW126
EMB-145	31	Y50	AE3007
Ordered			
EMB-135	75 plus 95 options		
EMB-145	19 plus 17 options		
Canadair RJ 700	25		

Note: Executive Airlines, which was expected to be merged into American Eagle by the end of 1999, is included

LOCKHEED L-1011-385-3 TRISTAR 500

AMERICAN TRANS AIR

IATA: TZ   **ICAO:** AMT   **IATA/ARC:** 366   **RADIO:** Amtran

---

CONTACTS:

Mail	Telephone/Fax	
PO Box 51609	Admin:	+1 317 247 4000
Indianapolis, IN 46251	Fax:	+1 317 243 4165
	Res:	1 800 435 9282
	Job Hotline:	+1 317 240 7106

Internet: www.ata.com

OPERATION:

Type: Scheduled/charter passenger
Cities Served: US: DEN DFW FLL HNL IND JFK LAS LAX LGA MCO MDW MKE OGG PHL PHX PIE RSW SFO SRQ **Caribbean:** MBJ SJU **México:** CUN **Europe** (seasonal): DUB SNN
Code-Share: Chicago Express
FFP: none

HISTORY/STRUCTURE:

Founded: August 1973 (as Ambassadair)
Start Date: March 1981
President/CEO: John Tague
Ownership: Amtran (NASDAQ: AMTR)

FLEET:

Type	No	Seats	Engines
Boeing 727-200 (Advanced)	24	Y168	PW JT8D-15/-15A/ -17/-17A/-17R
Boeing 757-200	9	Y216	RR RB211-535E4
L-1011-50	11	Y362	RR RB211-22B
L-1011-100	2	Y362	RR RB211-22B
L-1011-150	1	Y362	RR RB211-22B
L-1011-500	5	Y307	RR RB211-524B4

BOEING 727-200 (ADVANCED) (F)

AMERIJET INTERNATIONAL

IATA: JH   **ICAO:** AJT   **IATA/ARC:** 810   **RADIO:** Amerijet

CONTACTS:

Mail
498 SW 34th Street
Ft Lauderdale, FL 33315

Internet: www.amerijet.com

Telephone/Fax
Admin: +1 954 359 0077
Fax: +1 954 359 7871
Info: 1 800 927 6059

OPERATION:

Type: Scheduled cargo
Cities Served: US: MIA **México:** CUN GDL MEX MID **Caribbean:**
ANU BGI BQN DOM GND PAP POP SDQ SKB SLU SVD SXM UVF

HISTORY/STRUCTURE:

Founded: 1974
Start Date: 1974
President/CEO: David Bassett
Ownership: Bassett Enterprises

FLEET:

Type	No	Engines
Boeing 727-200F (Advanced)	12	PW JT8D-9A/-15/-15A

DOUGLAS DC-8-62 (F)

ARROW AIR

IATA: JW **ICAO:** APW **IATA/ARC:** 404 **RADIO:** Big A

CONTACTS:

Mail
PO Box 026062
Miami, FL 33102-6062

Telephone/Fax
Admin: +1 305 526 0900
Fax: +1 305 874 1432

Internet:www.arrowair.com

OPERATION:

Type: Scheduled/charter cargo
Cities Served: US: ATL IAH MIA **Caribbean:** SJU **South America:** AGT ASU GYE LIM PTY UIO

HISTORY/STRUCTURE:

Founded: 1947
Start Date: May 26, 1981
President: Barry Fine
Ownership: Fine Air Services

FLEET:

Type	No	Engines
DC-8-62F	11	PW JT3D-3B/-7
DC-8-63F	1	PW JT3D-7
DC-8-63	1	PW JT3D-7
L-1011-200F	3	RR RB211-524B4
L-1011-500	1	RR RB211-524B4

BOMBARDIER CANADAIR CL-600-2B19 REGIONAL JET SERIES 200ER

ATLANTIC COAST AIRLINES

IATA: DH   **ICAO:** BLR   **IATA/ARC:** 480   **RADIO:** Blue Ridge

---

CONTACTS:

Mail
515A Shaw Road
Sterling, VA 20166

Internet: www.atlanticcoast.com

Telephone/Fax
Admin: +1 703 925 6000
Fax: +1 703 925 6299
Res: 1 800 241 6522
PR: +1 703 925 6019

OPERATION:

Type: Scheduled passenger
Cities Served: ABE ALB AVP BGM BNA BOS BTV BUF BWI CAE CHO CHS
CLE CMH CRW DAY DTW EWR FAR FSD GSO GSP HPN ILM IND JAX JFK
LGA LYH MDT MHT ORD ORF PHF PHL PIA PIT PVD PWM RDU RIC ROA
ROC RSW SAV SCE SGF SWF SYR TYS
All service operated as United Express using only UA flight numbers
(7100-7899)
FFP: United Mileage Plus

HISTORY/STRUCTURE:

Founded: 1989
President/CEO: Kerry Skeen

Start Date: December 15, 1989
Ownership: Publicly traded company
(NASDAQ: ACAI)

FLEET:

Type	No	Seats	Engines
Jetstream Super 31	28	Y19	GA TPE331-12UAR-701H
Jetstream 41	32	Y29	GA TPE331-14HR-805H
Canadair RJ 200ER	20	Y50	GE CF34-3B1
Ordered			
Canadair RJ 200ER	24 plus 27 options		

BOMBARDIER CANADAIR CL-600-2B19 REGIONAL JET SERIES 200ER

ATLANTIC SOUTHEAST AIRLINES (ASA)

IATA: EV   **ICAO:** CAA   **IATA/ARC:** 862   **RADIO:** Candler

---

CONTACTS:

Mail
100 Hartsfield Center Parkway, Suite 800
Atlanta, GA 30354-1356

Telephone/Fax
Admin: +1 404 766 1400
Fax: +1 404 209 0162
Res: 1 800 221 1212

Internet: www.asa-air.com

OPERATION:

Type: Scheduled passenger
Cities Served: ABY AEX AGS ATL AUS AVL BPT BQK CHA CLE CRP CRW
CSG DAB DFW DHN DSM EVV FAY FLO FSM FWA GNV GPT GSP GTR HOU
IAH ICT ILE ILM ISP JAN JFK LAW LBB LEX LFT LYH MCN MEI MGM MLB
MYR OAJ OKC PFN ROA SAT SDF SHV SPS SWF TLH TOL TRI TUL TXK VLD
VPS XNA
All service operated as Delta Connection using only DL flight numbers
(4000-4999)
FFP: Delta SkyMiles

HISTORY/STRUCTURE:

Founded: March 1979
Start Date: June 27, 1979
President: Skip Barnette
Ownership: Delta Air Lines

FLEET:

Type	No	Seats	Engines
EMB-120ER Brasilia	58	Y30	PWC PW118
ATR72-212	12	Y64	PWC PW127
Canadair RJ 200ER	22	Y50	GE CF34-3B1
Ordered			
Canadalr RJ 200ER	23 plus 45 options		
Canadair RJ 700	12 plus 8 options		

BOEING 747-400F

ATLAS AIR

IATA: 5Y   **ICAO:** GTI   **IATA/ARC:** 369   **RADIO:** Giant

---

CONTACTS:

Mail
538 Commons Drive
Golden, CO 80401-5705

Telephone/Fax
Admin: +1 303 526 5050
Fax: +1 303 526 5051

Internet: www.atlasair.com

OPERATION:

Type: Charter cargo
Areas Served: Worldwide freight services for major airlines on an ACMI
(Aircraft, Crew, Maintenance, Insurance) basis

HISTORY/STRUCTURE:

Founded: April 1992
Start Date: February 1993
CEO: Michael Chowdry
President: Mickey Foret
Ownership: Atlas Holdings (NYSE: CGO)

FLEET:

Type	No	Engines
Boeing 747-200F	23	PW JT9D-7J or GE CF6-50E2
Boeing 747-400F	6	GE CF6-80C2B1F
Ordered		
Boeing 747-400F	6 plus 8 options	

FAIRCHILD SA227-AC METRO III

BIG SKY AIRLINES

IATA: GQ   **ICAO:** BSY   **IATA/ARC:** 387   **RADIO:** Big Sky

CONTACTS:

Mail	Telephone/Fax
1601 Aviation Place	Admin: +1 406 245 9449
Billings, MT 59105	Fax: +1 406 259 8750
	Res: 1 800 237 7788

Internet: www.bigskyair.com

OPERATION:

Type: Scheduled passenger
Cities Served: BIL BIS BWD DFW ELD FCA GDV GEG GGW GTF HLN HOT HRO HVR JBR LWT MLS MSO OLF PNC SDY STL WDG WMH
FPP: Northwest Worldperks

HISTORY/STRUCTURE:

Founded: 1978
Start Date: September 15, 1978
President/CEO: Terry Marshall
Ownership: Big Sky Transportation

FLEET:

Type	No	Seats	Engines
Metro III	11	Y19	GA TPE331-11U-612G
Metro 23	3	Y19	GA TPE331-12U-701G

SAAB 340B

BUSINESS EXPRESS AIRLINES (BEX)

IATA: HQ   **ICAO:** GAA   **IATA/ARC:** 357   **RADIO:** Bizex

CONTACTS:

Mail
55 Washington Street, Suite 300
Dover, NH 03820

Telephone/Fax
Admin: +1 603 740 3000
Fax: +1 603 740 3058

OPERATION:

Type: Scheduled passenger
Cities Served: US: ALB BGR BOS BTV BWI HPN ISP LGA MHT PHL PQI PVD
PWM ROC SYR (seasonal: ACK) **Canada:** YHZ YOW YQB
Operates as American Eagle, Delta Connection, and Northwest Airlink using AA,
DL (6200-6599), and NW flight numbers, respectively
FFP: AAdvantage, Delta SkyMiles, Northwest WorldPerks

HISTORY/STRUCTURE:

Founded: 1979 (as Atlantic Air)
Start Date: May 22, 1981
President: Gary Ellmer
Ownership: AMR Eagle

FLEET:

Type	No	Seats	Engines
SAAB 340A	22	Y34	GE CT7-5A2
SAAB 340B	20	Y34	GE CT7-9B
Ordered			
EMB-135	20 plus 20 options		

NOTES: BEX is expected to be merged into American Eagle in 2000

BOEING 727-200 (ADVANCED) (F)

CAPITAL CARGO INTERNATIONAL AIRLINES

IATA: PT   **ICAO:** CCI   **IATA/ARC:** none   **RADIO:** Cappy

CONTACTS:

Mail
6200 Hazletine National Drive
Orlando, FL 32822

Internet: www.capitalcargo.com

Telephone/Fax
Admin: +1 407 855 2004
Fax: +1 407 855 6620
Info: 1 800 593 9119

OPERATION:

Type: Charter cargo

HISTORY/STRUCTURE:

Founded: September 1995
Start Date: April 1996
President/CEO: Peter Fox
Ownership: Privately held

FLEET:

Type	No	Engines
Boeing 727-200F (Advanced)	8	PW JT8D-7B/-15

BRITISH AEROSPACE 3101 JETSTREAM 31

CASINO AIRLINES

IATA: none   **ICAO:** CSO   **IATA/ARC:** none   **RADIO:** Casair

CONTACTS:

Mail
1500 Airport Drive, Suite 1500
Shreveport, LA 71107

Telephone/Fax
Admin: +1 318 227 2121
Fax: +1 318 424 0000
Res: 1 888 227 1177

Internet: www.shreve.net/casinoair

OPERATION:

Type: Scheduled passenger
Cities Served: ABI BTR DAL DTN

HISTORY/STRUCTURE:

Founded: 1996
Start Date: December 17, 1997
President/CEO: Brad Galbraith
Ownership: Privately held

FLEET:

Type	No	Seats	Engines
Jetstream 31	2	Y19	GA TPE331-10UR-513H

BOEING 737-200

CASINO EXPRESS

IATA: XP   **ICAO:** CXP   **IATA/ARC:** none   **RADIO:** Casino Express

---

CONTACTS:

Mail
976 Mountain City Highway
Elko, NV 89801-2728

Telephone/Fax
Admin: +1 775 738 6040
Fax: +1 775 738 1881
Res: 1 800 258 8800

OPERATION:

Type: Charter passenger
Areas Served: Midwestern/western US and Canadian cities to Elko

---

HISTORY/STRUCTURE:

Founded: 1987
Start Date: 1989
General Manager: Arthur Moses
CEO: Norval Nelson
Ownership: TEM Enterprises (Todd E McClasky)

FLEET:

Type	No	Seats	Engines
Boeing 737-200	5	Y124	PW JT8D-15

BRITISH AEROSPACE 3201 JETSTREAM 32EP

CCAIR

IATA: ED   **ICAO:** CDL   **IATA/ARC:** 354   **RADIO:** Carolina

CONTACTS:

Mail
PO Box 19929
Charlotte, NC 28219-9929

Internet: www.ccairinc.com

Telephone/Fax
Admin: +1 704 359 8990
Fax: +1 704 359 0351
Res: 1 800 428 4322

OPERATION:

Type: Scheduled passenger
Cities Served: AGS AHN AVL CHS CLT CSG CVG GNV GSP HKY HTS INT ISO LEX LYH MIA MYR OAJ ORF PGV RDU RWI SOP TLH
All service operated as US Airways Express using only US flight numbers (5000-5249)
FFP: US Airways Dividend Miles

HISTORY/STRUCTURE:

Founded: 1979 (as Sunbird Airlines)
Start Date: November 15, 1979
President/CEO: Kenneth W Gann
Ownership: Mesa Air Group

FLEET:

Type	No	Seats	Engines
Jetstream 31	1	Y19	TPE331-10UGR-514H
Jetstream 32EP	19	Y19	GA TPE331-12UAR-704H
DHC-8-102	11	Y37	PWC PW120A

GRUMMAN G-73 FRAKES TURBO MALLARD

CHALK'S INTERNATIONAL AIRLINE

IATA: OP   **ICAO:** none   **IATA/ARC:** 370   **RADIO:** none

CONTACTS:

Mail
1000 MacArthur Causeway
Miami, FL 33132

Telephone/Fax
Admin: +1 305 373 1120
Fax: +1 305 371 7968
Res: 1 800 359 7262

OPERATION:

Type: Scheduled passenger
Cities Served: US: FLL MPB   **Caribbean:** NSB PID

HISTORY/STRUCTURE:

Founded: July 1919 (as Chalk's Flying Service)
Start Date: 1919
President: William Jones
Ownership: Air Alaska, World Pacific Air Lease (70%)

FLEET:

Type	No	Seats	Engines
Turbo Mallard	3	Y17	PWC PT6A-34

NOTES: Currently operating under bankruptcy supervision by Gulfstream
International Airlines

McDONNELL DOUGLAS DC-10-40 (F)

CHALLENGE AIR CARGO

IATA: WE   **ICAO:** CWC   **RADIO:** Challenge Cargo

CONTACTS:

Mail	**Telephone/Fax**
PO Box 523979	Admin: +1 305 869 8333
Miami, FL 33152-3979	Fax: +1 305 869 8299
	Info: 1 800 242 5536

Internet: www.challengeaircargo.com

OPERATION:

Type: Scheduled cargo
Cities Served: US: DFW MIA **Caribbean:** SDQ
Central America/South America: BOG CCS GUA GYE LIM LPB MGA PTY
SAL SAP SJO TGU UIO VCP VVI

HISTORY/STRUCTURE:

Founded: 1978 (as Challenge Air Transport)
Start Date: December 1986
President: William F Spohrer
Ownership: Airline Holding Co (Bill Spohrer & Associates)

FLEET:

Type	No	Engines
Boeing 757-200PF	3	RR RB211-535E4
DC-10-40F	4	PW JT9D-59A

NOTE: Challenge has agreed to be purchased by United Parcel Service

BOEING 727-200 (ADVANCED)

CHAMPION AIR

IATA: MG   **ICAO:** CCP   **IATA/ARC:** none   **RADIO:** Champion

---

CONTACTS:

Mail
8009 34th Avenue South, Suite 700
Bloomington, MN 55425

Telephone/Fax
Admin: +1 612 814 8700
Fax: +1 612 814 8799

Internet: www.championair.com

OPERATION:

Type: Charter passenger

HISTORY/STRUCTURE:

Founded: July 1995
Start Date: 1995
President: Michael Gerend
Ownership: GHI-CA (Carl Pohlad 60%, NWA 40%)

FLEET:

Type	No	Seats	Engines
Boeing 727-200 (Advanced)	8	Y173	PW JT8D-9A/-17/-17A

SAAB SF340A

CHAUTAUQUA AIRLINES

IATA: none   **ICAO:** CHQ   **IATA/ARC:** 363   **RADIO:** Chautauqua

CONTACTS:

Mail
2500 South High School Road, Suite 160
Indianapolis, IN 46241

Internet: www.flychautauqua.com

Telephone/Fax
Admin: +1 317 484 6000
Fax: +1 317 484 6040
Res: 1 800 428 4322

OPERATION:

Type: Scheduled passenger
Cities Served: US: AOO BNA BTV BUF CAE CHS CLE CMH CMI DAY EVV
EWR FNT FWA GRR HGR IND JST LGA LNS MKE PIT ROC SAV SHD SYR
Canada: YHM YXU YYZ
All service operated as US Airways Express using only US flight numbers
(4200-4449)
FFP: US Airways Dividend Miles

HISTORY/STRUCTURE:

Founded: May 3, 1973
Start Date: August 1, 1974
President/CEO: Bryan K Bedford
Ownership: Wexford Management

FLEET:

Type	No	Seats	Engines
Jetstream 31	19	Y19	GA TPE331-10UG-513H
SAAB 340A	14	Y30	GE CT7-5A2
EMB-145	2	Y50	AE3007A1
Ordered			
EMB-145	8 plus 20 options		

BRITISH AEROSPACE 3101 JETSTREAM 31

CHICAGO EXPRESS AIRLINES

IATA: C8   **ICAO:** WDY   **IATA/ARC:** 488   **RADIO:** Windy City

CONTACTS:

Mail
5333 South Laramie Avenue
Chicago, IL 60638

Internet: www.chicagoexpress.com

Telephone/Fax
Admin: +1 773 585 0585
Fax: +1 773 585 4877
Res: 1 800 264 3929

OPERATION:

Type: Scheduled passenger
Cities Served: DAY DSM GRR IND LAN MDW MKE MSN
All service operated as ATA Connection using only TZ flight numbers
(3100-3399)
Code-Share: American Trans Air
FFP: none

HISTORY/STRUCTURE:

Founded: 1993
Start Date: August 9, 1993
President: Courtney Anderson
Ownership: AmTran Inc

FLEET:

Type	No	Seats	Engines
Jetstream 31	7	Y19	GA TPE-331-10UG-513H

RAYTHEON BEECH 1900D

COLGAN AIR

IATA: 9L   **ICAO:** CJC   **IATA/ARC:** 426   **RADIO:** Colgan

CONTACTS:

Mail
PO Box 1650
Manassas, VA 22110

Telephone/Fax
Admin: +1 703 368 8880
Fax: +1 703 331 3116
Res: 1 800 272 5488

Internet: www.colganair.com

OPERATION:

Type: Scheduled passenger
Cities Served: ACK ATL AUG BHB BKW BLF BOS CHO HHH HYA IAD LGA RKD RUT
All service operated as Continental Connection using only CO flight numbers (4700-4899)

HISTORY/STRUCTURE:

Founded: 1991 (as National Capital Airways)
Start Date: December 1, 1991
President/CEO: Charles Colgan
Ownership: Michael and Charles Colgan

FLEET:

Type	No	Seats	Engines
Beech 1900C-1	6	Y19	PWC PT6A-65B
Beech 1900D	1	Y19	PWC PT6A-67D

BOMBARDIER CANADAIR CL-600-2B19 REGIONAL JET SERIES 100ER

COMAIR

| **IATA:** OH | **ICAO:** COM | **IATA/ARC:** 886 | **RADIO:** Comair |

CONTACTS:

Mail	Telephone/Fax
PO Box 75021	Admin: +1 606 767 2550
Cincinnati, OH 45275	Fax: +1 606 767 2278
	Res: 1 800 221 1212

Internet: www.comair.com

OPERATION:

Type: Scheduled passenger
Cities Served: US: ABE ATW AVL AVP AZO BGR BHM BNA BOS BUF CAE CAK CHA CHO CID CLE CLT CMH COS CRW CVG DAY DSM DTW EVV EWR EYW FLL FWA GRR GSO GSP HPN HSV HTS IAD IAH ICT IND ISP JAN LAN LEX LIT MCI MCO MDT MDW MEM MHT MIA MKE MSN MSP MSY MYR OMA PBI PIT PNS RDU RIC ROA ROC RSW SBN SDF SRQ STL SWF SYR TLH TOL TPA TRI TUL TYS **Canada:** YUL YYZ **Caribbean:** FPO NAS
All service operated as Delta Connection using only DL flight numbers (5000-5749)
FFP: Delta SkyMiles

HISTORY/STRUCTURE:

Founded: 1976 (as Wings Airways)
Start Date: April 1977
CEO: David R Mueller
President: David Siebenburgen
Ownership: Comair Holdings (NASDAQ: COMR)

FLEET:

Type	No	Seats	Engines
EMB-120RT Brasilia	27	Y30	PWC PW118
Canadair RJ 100ER	78	Y50	GE CF34-3A1
Ordered			
Canadair RJ 100	32 plus 65 options		
Canadair RJ 700	20 plus 70 options		

RAYTHEON BEECH 1900D

COMMUTAIR

IATA: TH   **ICAO:** UCA   **IATA/ARC:** none   **RADIO:** Commutair

CONTACTS:

Mail
518 Rugar Street
Plattsburgh, NY 12901

Telephone/Fax
Admin: +1 518 562 2700
Fax: +1 518 562 8030
Res: 1 800 428 4322

OPERATION:

Type: Scheduled passenger
Cities Served: ALB BGM BOS BTV BUF ELM EWR GSO HPN IAD ILM ISP ITH LGA ORH PHL PLB POU PVD PWM RIC ROA ROC SLK SYR UCA
All service operated as US Airways Express using only US flight numbers (4450-4699)
FFP: US Airways Dividend Miles

HISTORY/STRUCTURE:

Founded: 1989
Start Date: August 1, 1989
President: John A Sullivan Jr
CEO: Tony von Elbe
Ownership: Champlain Enterprises

FLEET:

Type	No	Seats	Engines
Beech 1900D	30	Y19	PWC PT6A-67D

BOEING 777-200 (ER)

CONTINENTAL AIRLINES

IATA: CO   **ICAO:** COA   **IATA/ARC:** 005   **RADIO:** Continental

CONTACTS:

Mail
1600 Smith Street
Houston, TX 77002

Internet: www.flycontinental.com

Telephone/Fax
Admin: +1 713 324 5000
Fax: +1 713 324 2087
Res: 1 800 523 3273
PR: +1 713 324 5080

OPERATION:

Type: Scheduled passenger
Cities Served: US: ABQ ANC ATL AUS BDL BHM BNA BOS BUF BWI CHS CLE CLT CMH COS CRP CVG DAB DCA DEN DFW DTW ELP EWR FLL GSO HNL IAD IAH IND JAX LAS LAX LBB LGA MAF MCI MCO MDW MEM MFE MHT MIA MKE MSP MSY MYR OKC OMA ONT ORD ORF PBI PDX PHL PHX PIT PNS PVD PWM RDU RIC RNO ROC RSW SAN SAT SDF SEA SFO SJC SLC SNA SRQ STL TPA TUL TUS (seasonal: HDN MTJ) **Canada:** YUL YVR YYC YYZ **Caribbean:** ANU BDA SDQ SJU SXM **México/Central America:** ACA BJX BZE CUN CZM GDL GUA MEX MGA MID MTY PTY PVR SAL SAP SJD SJO TGU VER ZIH **South America:** BOG CCS GIG GRU GYE LIM SCL UIO **Europe:** AMS BHX BRU CDG DUB DUS FCO FRA GLA LGW LIS MAD MAN MXP SNN ZRH **Asia:** CTS DPS FUK KIJ MNL NGO NRT OKJ OSA SDJ SEL TPE **Oceania:** CNS GUM JON KSA KWA MAJ NOU PNI ROR SPN TKK YAP
Global Alliance: Wings
Code-Share: Air France, Alaska Airlines, America West, ASERCA, British Midland, China Airlines, Colgan Air, Continental Express, Continental Micronesia, COPA, ĆSA, EVA Airways, Gulfstream International, Northwest, Virgin Atlantic
FFP: OnePass

HISTORY/STRUCTURE:

Founded: 1934 (as Varney Speed Lines)
Start Date: July 15, 1934 (July 1, 1937 as Continental)
CEO: Gordon M Bethune
President: Greg Brenneman
Ownership: Publicly traded company (NYSE: CAL)

BOEING 737-500

FLEET:

Type	No	Seats	Engines
DC-9-30	16	F8Y95	PW JT8D-9A/-15
Boeing 737-500	67	F10Y94	CFM56-3B1
Boeing 737-300	65	F12Y116	CFM56-3B1
Boeing 737-700	24	F12Y112	CFM56-7B24
Boeing 737-800	19	F14Y141	CFM56-7B26
MD-81	5	F14Y127	PW JT8D-217
MD-82	61	F14Y127	PW JT8D-217/-217A/-219
MD-83	3	F14Y127	PW JT8D-219
Boeing 727-200 (Advanced)	28	F14Y137	PW JT8D-9A/-15
Boeing 757-200	36	C16Y156 or C24Y159 or C12Y177	RR RB211-535E4-B
DC-10-30	31	C38Y204 or C28Y254 or C18Y269	GE CF6-50C2/-50C2B
Boeing 777-200ER	8	C48Y235	GE GE90-92B
Ordered			
Boeing 737-700/800	44 plus 52 options		
Boeing 737-900	15 plus 25 options		
Boeing 757-200	6		
Boeing 767-200ER	10		
Boeing 767-400	26 plus 10 options		
Boeing 777-200	8 plus 18 options		

NOTES: Cities/fleet include Continental Micronesia

EMBRAER EMB-145ER

CONTINENTAL EXPRESS

IATA: none   **ICAO:** BTA   **IATA/ARC:** none   **RADIO:** Jetlink

CONTACTS:

Mail	Telephone/Fax
Gateway Two, Suite 600	Admin: +1 281 985 2700
15333 John F Kennedy Boulevard	Fax: +1 281 590 3820
Houston, TX 77032	Res: 1 800 523 3273

Internet: www.flycontinental.com

OPERATION:

Type: Scheduled passenger
Cities Served: US: ABE ACT AEX ALB AMA ATL AVP AZO BDL BGR BNA BPT BRO BTR BTV BUF BWI CAE CAK CLE CLL CLT CMH CRP CVG DAY DCA DTW EFD ERI EWR FNT FWA GPT GRR GSO GSP HOU HPN HRL IAD IAH ICT ILE IND JAN LAN JAX LBB LCH LEX LFT LIT LRD MBS MDT MFE MEM MHT MKE MLU MOB MSP OMA ORF PHL PIT PVD PWM RDU RIC ROC SAV SBN SDF SHV STL SYR TOL TYR TYS VCT (seasonal: ACK MVY)
Canada: YHZ YOW YUL YYZ **México:** CUU TAM
All service operated using only CO flight numbers (3001-4399)
FFP: OnePass

HISTORY/STRUCTURE:

Founded: 1956 (as Vercoa Air Service)
Start Date: 1968 (as commuter, became Britt Airlines)
President: David Siegel   **Ownership:** Continental Airlines

FLEET:

Type	No	Seats	Engines
Beech 1900D	25	Y19	PWC PT6A-67D
EMB-120RT Brasilia	26	Y30	PWC PW118
ATR42-320	30	Y46	PWC PW121
ATR42-512	8	Y46	PWC PW127E
ATR72-212	2	Y64	PWC PW127
EMB-145	43	Y50	AE3007A
Ordered			
EMB-135	25 plus 50 options		
EMB-145	31 plus 125 options		

BRITISH AEROSPACE 3201 JETSTREAM 32EP

CORPORATE AIRLINES

IATA: 3C **ICAO:** CEA **IATA/ARC:** 310 **RADIO:** Corp-X

CONTACTS:

Mail
PO Box 270487
Nashville, TN 37227

Telephone/Fax
Admin: +1 615 275 3950
Fax: +1 615 275 3039
Res: 1 800 446 4392

Internet: www.midwayair.com/corpair.html

OPERATION:

Type: Scheduled passenger
Cities Served: ATL BWI CAE CHS GSP ILM MYR ORF RDU
Code-Share: Midway Airlines (JI 1500-1649 flight numbers)
FFP: AAdvantage

HISTORY/STRUCTURE:

Founded: 1996 (as Corporate Express Airlines)
Start Date: December 16, 1996
President/CEO: Charles Howell IV
Ownership: division of Corporate Flight Management/privately held

---

FLEET:

Type	No	Seats	Engines
Jetstream 32EP	9	Y19	GA TPE331-12UAR-704H

BOEING 727-100C

CUSTOM AIR TRANSPORT

IATA: DG   **ICAO:** CTT   **IATA/ARC:** none   **RADIO:** Catt

CONTACTS:

Mail	Telephone/Fax
3305 Southwest 9th Avenue, Floor 2	Admin: +1 954 523 4211
Ft Lauderdale, FL 33315	Fax: +1 954 523 6811
	Info: 1 800 473 9131

Internet: www.customair.qpg.com

OPERATION:

Type: Charter cargo

HISTORY/STRUCTURE:

Founded: 1995
Start Date: December 9, 1995
President/CEO: Richard Wellman
Ownership: Brent Aviation

FLEET:

Type	No	Engines
Boeing 727-100C	4	PW JT8D-7B
Boeing 727-200F	3	PW JT8D-9A/-15

NOTES: Some aircraft operated in colors of Charter America, an affiliated company

McDONNELL DOUGLAS MD-11

DELTA AIR LINES

IATA: DL   **ICAO:** DAL   **IATA/ARC:** 006   **RADIO:** Delta

CONTACTS:

Mail	Telephone/Fax
PO Box 20706	Admin: +1 404 715 2600
Atlanta, GA 30320	Fax: +1 404 715 2596
	Res: 1 800 221 1212
Internet: www.delta-air.com	PR: +1 404 715 5162

OPERATION:

Type: Scheduled passenger
Cities Served: US: ABE ABQ AGS ALB ANC ATL AUS BDL BHM BIL BNA BOI BOS BTR BUF BWI BZN CAE CHS CLE CLT CMH COS CVG DAB DAY DCA DEN DFW DTW ELP EWR FAI FCA FLL GEG GRR GSO GSP GTF HLN HNL HOU HSV IAD IAH IND ISP JAN JAX JFK LAS LAX LEX LGA LIT MCI MCO MDT MDW MEM MGM MIA MKE MLB MLU MOB MSO MSP MSY OAK OGG OKC OMA ONT ORD ORF PBI PDX PHL PHX PIT PNS PSC PVD PWM RDU RIC RNO ROC RSW SAN SAT SAV SBN SDF SEA SFO SHV SJC SLC SMF SNA SRQ STL SYR TLH TPA TUL TUS TYS (seasonal: EGE GUC) **Canada:** YUL YYZ **Caribbean:** BDA GCM NAS SJU STT STX **México/Central America:** GDL GUA MEX PTY SAL SJO **South America:** CCS GIG GRU LIM **Europe:** AMS ARN ATH BCN BRU CDG DUB FCO FRA HAM IST LGW MAD MAN MUC MXP NCE SNN STR SVO VIE ZRH **Asia:** BOM FUK NGO NRT
Code-Share: AeroMexico, Air France, Air Jamaica, ASA, Austrian, Business Express, Comair, MALÉV, SABENA, SkyWest, Swissair, TAP-Air Portugal, TransBrasil, Trans States
FFP: SkyMiles

HISTORY/STRUCTURE:

Founded: 1924 (as Huff-Daland Dusters)
Start Date: June 17, 1929
President/CEO: Leo Mullin
Ownership: Publicly traded company (NYSE: DAL)

BOEING 737-200 (ADVANCED)

FLEET:

Type	No	Seats	Engines
Boeing 737-200 (Advanced)	54	F12Y95 or Y119	PW JT8D-15/-15A
Boeing 737-300	26	F8Y120 or F8Y114	CFM56-3B1
Boeing 737-800	7	F16Y138	CFM56-7B26
MD-88	121	F14Y128	PW JT8D-219
MD-90-30	16	F12Y138	IAE V2525-D5
Boeing 727-200 (Advanced)	121	F12Y137 or Y157	PW JT8D-9A/-15
Boeing 757-200	100	F24Y159	PW2037
Boeing 767-200	15	F18Y186	GE CF6-80A2
Boeing 767-300	28	F24Y228	GE CF6-80A2 or PW4060
Boeing 767-300ER	50	F10C28Y174 or F10C28Y165 or C48Y142/147	PW4060
L-1011-1	16	F32Y270	RR RB211-22B/-524B
L-1011-250	6	F30Y265	RR RB211-524B4
L-1011-500	11	F24Y217	RR RB211-524B4
MD-11	15	F18C40Y168 or F18C40Y188 or F18C40Y200 or C50Y211/219	PW4460
Boeing 777-200ER	2	C52Y225	RR Trent 892
Ordered			
Boeing 737-800	117 plus 54 options		
Boeing 757-200	25 plus 19 options		
Boeing 767-300ER	11 plus 8 options		
Boeing 767-400	21 plus 24 options		
Boeing 777-200ER	14 plus 20 options		

BOEING 727-100 (F)

DHL AIRWAYS

IATA: ER   **ICAO:** DHL   **IATA/ARC:** 423   **RADIO:** Dahl

---

CONTACTS:

Mail
PO Box 75122
Cincinnati, OH 45275

Internet: www.dhl.com

Telephone/Fax
Admin: +1 606 283 2232
Fax: +1 606 525 1998
Info: 1 800 345 7775

OPERATION:

Type: Scheduled cargo
Cities Served: US: ATL AUS BDL BOS BWI CVG DEN DFW DTW EWR IAH
JFK LAX MCI MCO MIA MSP ORD PHL PHX SEA SFO SLC SMF TPA
Caribbean: SJU **México:** GDL MEX **Europe:** BRU EMA LHR
All service operated as DHL Worldwide Express; additional cities served by
contract carriers.

HISTORY/STRUCTURE:

Founded: 1969 (as DHL, by Dalsye, Hillblom & Lynn)
Start Date: 1982
VP Airline Operations: Richard Cozzi
Ownership: DHL Corp (Japan Airlines (1%), Hillbloom Trust, Nissho Iwai (7.5%))

FLEET:

Type	No	Engines
Boeing 727-100F	11	PW JT8D-7
Boeing 727-200F	8	PW JT8D-7/15/-17/-17R
DC-8-73F	8	CFM56-2/-2C5
Airbus A300B4 (F)	2	GE CF6-50C2
Ordered		
Airbus A300B4 (F)	5	

EASTWIND AIRLINES

IATA: W9   **ICAO:** SGR   **IATA/ARC:** 175   **RADIO:** Stinger

---

CONTACTS:

Mail
8642 West Market Street
Suite 134
Greensboro, NC 27409

Telephone/Fax
Admin: +1 336 393 0111
Fax: +1 336 393 0277
Res: 1 800 644 3592

Internet: www.eastwindairlines.com

OPERATION:

Type: Scheduled passenger
Cities Served: BOS GSO LGA MCO PHL PIT TTN

HISTORY/STRUCTURE:

Founded: 1993
Start Date: August 16, 1995
President/CEO: Terry Hallcom
Ownership: United Medical Holdings of New Jersey

FLEET:

Type	No	Seats	Engines
Boeing 737-200	3	Y120	PW JT8D-9A
Boeing 737-700	2	Y132	CFM56-7B24

McDONNELL DOUGLAS DC-10-10 (F)

EMERY WORLDWIDE AIRLINES

IATA: EB   **ICAO:** EWW   **IATA/ARC:** 591   **RADIO:** Emery

CONTACTS:

Mail
1 Emery Plaza
Vandalia, OH 45377

Telephone/Fax
Admin: +1 937 264 1212
Fax: +1 937 264 1566
Info: 1 800 227 1981

Internet: www.emeryworld.com

OPERATION:

Type: Scheduled cargo
Cities Served: US: ABQ ATL AUS BDL BHM BNA BOS BRO BUF BWI CAE
CLE CLT DAY DEN DFW DTW EFD ELP EWR FLL FNT GRR GSO GSP HSV
IAD ICT IND JAN JAX JFK LAX LRD MCI MCO MDT MHR MIA MKE MSP MSY
OAK OKC ONT ORD ORF PDX PHL PHX PIA PSM RDU RIC ROA ROC SAN
SAT SEA SFO SHV SJC SLC STL SWF SYR TPA TUL TUS
Canada: YYZ **Caribbean:** SJU **México:** GDL MTY **Europe:** BRU
Operates US Postal Service flights from Indianapolis

HISTORY/STRUCTURE:

Founded: 1987 (as Air Train)
Start Date: May 1987
President: Roger Piazza
Ownership: CNF Transportation

FLEET:

Type	No	Engines
DC-8F-54	2	PW JT3D-3B
DC-8-62F	7	PW JT3D-3B
DC-8-63F	8	PW JT3D-7
DC-8-71F	10	CFM56-2C/-2C1
DC-8-73F	16	CFM56-2C1
DC-10-10 (F)	1	GE CF6-6D
Ordered		
DC-10-10 (F)	4	

Boeing 727s operated by Express One and Ryan International
(see separate entries)

CONVAIR 580

ERA AVIATION

IATA: 7H   **ICAO:** ERH   **IATA/ARC:** 808   **RADIO:** Erah

CONTACTS:

Mail
6160 Carl Brady Drive
Anchorage, AK 99502-9987

Telephone/Fax
Admin: +1 907 248 4422
Fax: +1 907 266 8350
Res: 1 800 866 8394

Internet: www.era-aviation.com

OPERATION:

Type: Scheduled/charter passenger/cargo
Cities Served: US: ADQ ANC BET CDV CYF EEK ENA GNU HOM HPB ILI
KKH KPN KWK KWN MYU NME OOK PTU SCM TNK VAK VDZ WTL WWT
Canada: YXY
Some scheduled service operated as Alaska Airlines Commuter using AS flight
numbers (4800-4899)
FFP: Alaska Airlines Mileage Plan

HISTORY/STRUCTURE:

Founded: 1948
Start Date: 1948
CEO: Charles Johnson
Ownership: Rowan Companies (RDC)

FLEET:

Type	No	Seats	Engines
DHC-6-200/-300	9	Y15 or Y19	PWC PT6A-20/-27
DC-3	2	Y21	PW R-1830-90
operated by ERA Classic Airlines			
DHC-8-100	2	Y37	PWC PW120A/PW121
Convair 580	6	Y50	AN 501-D13H

BOEING 747-200C

EVERGREEN INTERNATIONAL AIRLINES

IATA: EZ   **ICAO:** EIA   **IATA/ARC:** 494   **RADIO:** Evergreen

CONTACTS:

Mail
3850 Three Mile Lane
McMinnville, OR 97128-9496

Telephone/Fax
Admin: +1 503 472 0011
Fax: +1 503 434 4210

Internet: www.evergreenaviation.com

OPERATION:

Type: Scheduled/charter cargo
Areas Served: Operates US Postal Service flights in western US from Oakland hub and worldwide contract and charter cargo services

HISTORY/STRUCTURE:

Founded: 1975
Start Date: November 28, 1975
President: Larry Lane
Ownership: Evergreen International Aviation

FLEET:

Type	No	Engines
DC-9-15F	2	PW JT8D-7A/-7B
DC-9-32/33F	8	PW JT8D-9
Boeing 747-100/200F	13	PW JT9D-7A/-7J

SAAB SF340A

EXPRESS AIRLINES I

IATA: 9E   **ICAO:** FLG   **IATA/ARC:** 430   **RADIO:** Flagship

---

CONTACTS:

Mail
1689 Nonconnah Boulevard, Suite 111
Memphis, TN 38132

Telephone/Fax
Admin: +1 901 348 4100
Fax: +1 901 348 6896
Res: 1 800 225 2525

Internet: nwairlink.com

OPERATION:

Type: Scheduled passenger
Cities Served: AEX BTR CSG CVG DHN EVV FSM GLH GSP GTR HOU JAN
JLN MEI MEM MGM MKL MLU MOB MSL OKC OWB PAH PFN PIB PNS SDF
SHV TUL TUP XNA
All service operated as Northwest Airlink using only NW flight numbers
(5600-5899)
FFP: Northwest WorldPerks

HISTORY/STRUCTURE:

Founded: February 1985
Start Date: June 1986
President/CEO: Philip Trenary
Ownership: NWA Inc

FLEET:

Type	No	Seats	Engines
SAAB 340A	18	Y33	GE CT7-5A2
SAAB 340B	11	Y33	GE CT7-9B
Ordered			
Canadair RJ 200LR	54 plus 70 options		

BOEING 727-200 (ADVANCED) (F)

EXPRESS ONE INTERNATIONAL

IATA: EO   **ICAO:** LHN   **IATA/ARC:** none   **RADIO:** Longhorn

CONTACTS:

Mail
3890 Northwest Highway, Suite 700
Dallas, TX 75220

Telephone/Fax
Admin: +1 214 902 2500
Fax: +1 214 350 1399

OPERATION:

Type: Charter passenger/cargo
Areas Served: Operates freight services in the US for Emery Worldwide and other forwarders, and for TNT in Europe, plus *ad hoc* passenger charters

HISTORY/STRUCTURE:

Founded: 1975 (as Jet East International Airlines)
Start Date: 1975
CEO: James Wikert
Ownership: Alinda and James Wikert (Wikert International)

FLEET:

Type	No	Seats	Engines
DC-9-31	5	Y115	PW JT8D-9
Boeing 727-100F	2	Freighter	PW JT8D-7B
Boeing 727-200F	22	Freighter	PW JT8D-9/-15/-17R

BOEING 727-200

FALCON AIR EXPRESS

IATA: F2   **ICAO:** FAO   **IATA/ARC:** none   **RADIO:** Panther

---

CONTACTS:

Mail
7270 NW 12th Street, Suite 680
Miami, FL 33126

Telephone/Fax
Admin: +1 305 592 5672
Fax: +1 305 592 7298

Internet: www.falconairexpress.com

OPERATION:
Type: Charter passenger

HISTORY/STRUCTURE:
Founded: 1995
Start Date: March 1996
President: Emilio Dirube
Ownership: Emilio Dirube

FLEET:

Type	No	Seats	Engines
Boeing 727-200	4	Y164	PW JT8D-7B/-91/-15

DE HAVILLAND CANADA DHC-7-102 DASH 7

FARWEST AIRLINES

IATA: none   **ICAO:** none   **IATA/ARC:** none   **RADIO:** none

CONTACTS:

Mail
1201 W Route 66, Suite 200
Flagstaff, AZ 86001

Internet: www.farwestairlines.com

Telephone/Fax
Admin: +1 520 773 1976
Fax: +1 520 773 1610
Res: 1 800 843 8724

OPERATION:

Type: Scheduled/charter passenger
Cities Served: FLG GCN PHX

HISTORY/STRUCTURE:

Founded: 1998
Start Date: June 23, 1999
President: James Jeffries
Ownership: Privately held

FLEET:

Type	No	Seats	Engines
DHC-7-102	2	Y50	PWC PT6A-50

McDONNELL DOUGLAS DC-10-30 (F)

FEDEX

IATA: FX   **ICAO:** FDX   **IATA/ARC:** 023   **RADIO:** Fedex

---

CONTACTS:

Mail
PO Box 727
Memphis, TN 38194

Internet: www.fedex.com

Telephone/Fax
Admin: +1 901 369 3600
Fax: +1 901 395 4928
Info: 1 800 463 3339
PR: +1 901 395 3460

OPERATION:

Type: Scheduled cargo
Cities Served: US: ABE ABQ ALB AFW ANC ATL ATW AUS BDL BFM BHM
BOI BOS BUF BTV BUR BWI CAE CHS CID CLE CLT COS CPR CVG DAY
DEN DFW DLH DSM DTW ELP EWR FLL FNT FSD FWA GEG GFK GRR GSO
GSP GTF HNL HRL IAD IAH ICT IND JAX JFK LAS LAX LBB LCK LGB MCI
MCO MDT MEM MIA MHT MKE MSN MSP MSY OAK OKC OMA ONT ORD
ORF PDX PHL PHX PIA PIT PVD PWM RDU RIC ROA RNO ROC RST RSW
SAN SAT SAV SBN SDF SEA SFO SHV SJC SLC SNA STL SWF SYR TLH
TPA TUL TUS TYS **Canada:** YMX YVR YWG YYC YYZ **Caribbean:** BQN SJU
México/Central America GDL MTY PTY TLC **South America:** EZE SCL VCP
VLN **Europe:** ARN BSL CDG FRA IST MUC MXP PIK STN VKO **Asia:** BKK
BOM DXB HKG KHH KIX KUL MNL NRT PEK PEN SEL SFS SHA SIN TPE TLV
Oceania: NAN SYD
Other cities served by FedEx Feeder contract carriers

HISTORY/STRUCTURE:

Founded: 1971 (as Federal Express)
Start Date: April 17, 1973
President/CEO: Theodore Weise
Ownership: Federal Express Corp (NYSE: FDX)

SHORTS SD3-60 VARIANT 300 (F)

FLEET:

Type	No	Engines
Cessna 208A/B	261	PWC PT6A-114/-114A
Shorts SD3-60 (300)	11	PWC PT6A-67B
F27 Mk 500/600	32	RR Dart 532-7/552-7R
Boeing 727-100F	68	PW JT8D-7B
Boeing 727-200F	95	PW JT8D-9A/-15/-17/-17A/-217C
Airbus A310F-200	39	PW JT9D-7R4D1/E1 or GE CF6-80A3
Airbus A300F-600	33	GE CF6-80C2A5
DC-10-10 to be converted to MD-10F	30	GE CF6-6D
DC-10-10F	22	GE CF6-6D/-6D1A
DC-10-30F	22	GE CF6-50C2
MD-11F	29	GE CF6-80C2D1F
Cessna 208 Caravans, Shorts 360s, and Fokker F27s operated as FedEx Feeder under contract by Baron Aviation, Corporate Air (US and Philippines), CSA Air, Empire Airlines, ERA Aviation, Morningstar Air Express (Canada—which also operates three 727-100Fs), Mountain Air Cargo, WestAir, and Wiggins Airlines		
Ordered		
Ayres LM200	50 plus 150 options	
Airbus A300F-600	4	
DC-10-10	21 (ex-American/United, to be MD-10F)	
MD-11	30 (ex-American/Swissair, to be MD-11F)	

NOTES:

DOUGLAS DC-8F-54 JET TRADER

FINE AIR

IATA: FB   **ICAO:** FBF   **IATA/ARC:** none   **RADIO:** Fine Air

---

CONTACTS:

Mail
PO Box 523726
Miami, FL 33152-3726

Telephone/Fax
Admin: +1 305 871 6606
Fax: +1 305 871 4232

Internet: www.fineair.com

OPERATION:

Type: Scheduled/charter cargo
Cities Served: US: MIA **Caribbean:** POP SDQ SJU **Central/South America:** BOG CCS GUA GYE MAR MGA PTY SAL SAP SJO UIO VCP

HISTORY/STRUCTURE:

Founded: 1992
Start Date: November 10, 1992
President/CEO: Barry Fine
Ownership: Frank & Barry Fine

FLEET:

Type	No	Engines
DC-8-50F	12	PW JT3D-3B
DC-8-61F	2	PW JT3D-3B
L-1011-200F	1	RR RB211-524B4

DOUGLAS DC-8-61 (F)

FLORIDA WEST INTERNATIONAL AIRWAYS

IATA: RF **ICAO:** FWL **IATA/ARC:** 330 **RADIO:** Florida West

---

CONTACTS:

Mail
7500 NW 25th Street, Suite 237
Miami, FL 33122-1714

Telephone/Fax
Admin: +1 305 591 9161
Fax:　+1 305 591 2385

OPERATION:

Type: Scheduled/charter cargo
Cities Served: US: ATL IAH MIA **Caribbean:** POS **South America:** BOG EZE
IQT LIM SCL

HISTORY/STRUCTURE:

Founded: 1981 (as Florida West Airlines)
Start Date: 1983
President/CEO: Richard Haberly
Ownership: Haberly, Fast Air Group

FLEET:

Type	No	Engines
DC-8-61F	1	PW JT3D-3B
DC-8-71F	1	CFM56-2C1
Additional DC-8-71F aircraft leased from Fast Air as required		

BOEING 737-300

FRONTIER AIRLINES

IATA: F9   **ICAO:** FFT   **IATA/ARC:** 422   **RADIO:** Frontier Flight

---

CONTACTS:

Mail
12015 East 46th Avenue
Denver, CO 80239

Internet: www.flyfrontier.com

Telephone/Fax
Admin: +1 303 371 7400
Fax: +1 303 371 7007
Res: 1 800 432 1359

OPERATION:

Type: Scheduled passenger
Cities Served: ABQ ATL BMI BOS BWI DEN DFW ELP LAS LAX MDW MSP
OMA PDX PHX SAN SEA SFO SLC
FFP: Continental OnePass

HISTORY/STRUCTURE:

Founded: 1994
Start Date: July 5, 1994
President/CEO: Samuel Addoms
Ownership: Publicly traded company (NASDAQ: FRNT)

FLEET:

Type	No	Seats	Engines
Boeing 737-200	5	Y108	PW JT8D-9A/-17
Boeing 737-300	11	Y136/Y138	CFM56-3B1/-3B2/-3C1
Ordered			
Boeing 737-300	1		

FRONTIER FLYING SERVICE

IATA: 2F   **ICAO:** FTA   **IATA/ARC:** 517   **RADIO:** Frontier Air

CONTACTS:

Mail
3820 University Avenue
Fairbanks, AK 99709

Telephone/Fax
Admin: +1 907 474 0014
Fax: +1 907 474 0774

Internet: www.frontierflying.com

OPERATION:

Type: Scheduled/charter passenger/cargo
Cities Served: AET AKP ANC ARC BTI BTT FAI FYU GAL HSL KAL NUI NUL OME OTZ RBY SCC TAL VEE WBQ

HISTORY/STRUCTURE:

Founded: 1959
Start Date: 1959
President/CEO: John Hajdukovich
Ownership: Privately held

FLEET:

Type	No	Seats	Engines
Cessna 207	1	Y5	CO IO-520-F
PA-31-310 Navajo	1	Y7	LY TIO-540-A2C
PA-31-350 Chieftain/T-1020	5	Y9	LY TIO-540-J2B/-J2BD
Beech 1300	2	Y13	PWC PT6A-42
Beech 99	1	Y15	PWC PT6A-27
Beech 1900C-1	4	Y19	PWC-PT6A-65B
DC-3	1	Freighter	PW R-1830

McDONNELL DOUGLAS DC-10-30 (F)

GEMINI AIR CARGO

IATA: GR   **ICAO:** GCO   **IATA/ARC:** 358   **RADIO:** Gemini

---

CONTACTS:

Mail
44965 Aviation Drive, Suite 300
Washington Dulles Intl Airport
Dulles, VA 20166

Telephone/Fax
Admin: +1 703 260 8100
Fax: +1 703 260 8102

Internet: www.gac-cargo.com

OPERATION:

Type: Charter cargo
Areas Served: Operates worldwide freight services on behalf of other carriers

---

HISTORY/STRUCTURE:

Founded: 1995
Start Date: October 24, 1996
President: Bill Stockbridge
Ownership: William D Carlyle Group

FLEET:

Type	No	Engines
DC-10-30F	8	GE CF6-50C2
Ordered		
DC-10-30F	3	

RAYTHEON BEECH 1900D

GREAT LAKES AIRLINES

IATA: ZK   **ICAO**: GLA   **IATA/ARC**: 846   **RADIO**: Lakes Air

CONTACTS:

Mail
1965 330th Street
Spencer, IA 51301

Telephone/Fax
Admin: +1 712 262 1000
Fax: +1 712 262 1001
Res: 1 800 241 6522

Internet: www.greatlakesav.com

OPERATION:

Type: Scheduled passenger, charter cargo
Cities Served: AIA ALO ALS AMA BFF BIL BIS BKX BRL CDR CEZ CGX CPR CYS DBQ DDC DEC DEN DIK DRO DVL EGE FAR FMN FRM FSD GBD GCC GCK GJT GLD GRI GUC HDN HON HUF HYS IMT ISN IWD JMS LAA LAF LAN LAR LBF LBL MBL MCK MKG MSO MSP MTO MVN OFK ORD OSH OTM PIR PUB RHI RIW RKS SAF SHR SLN SPI SPW TEX TVC UIN WRL YKN
All service operated as United Express using only UA flight numbers (6300-6799)
FFP: United Mileage Plus

HISTORY/STRUCTURE:

Founded: April 5, 1977 (as Spirit Lake Airways)
Start Date: October 12, 1981
President/CEO: Douglas G Voss
Ownership: Great Lakes Aviation (NASDAQ: GLUX)

FLEET:

Type	No	Seats	Engines
Beech 1900D	40	Y19	PWC PT6A-67D
EMB-120ER/RT Brasilia	8	Y30	PWC PW118/118A

DE HAVILLAND CANADA DHC-7-102 DASH 7

GULFSTREAM INTERNATIONAL AIRLINES

IATA: 3M   **ICAO:** GFT   **IATA/ARC:** 449   **RADIO:** Gulf Flight

---

CONTACTS:

Mail
1815 Griffin Road, Suite 400
Dania, FL 33004

Telephone/Fax
Admin: +1 954 266 3000
Fax: +1 954 266 3030
Res: 1 800 525 0280

Internet: www.gulfstreamair.com

OPERATION:

Type: Scheduled passenger
Cities Served: US: EYW FLL GNV JAX MCO MIA PBI RSW TLH TPA
Caribbean: ELH FPO MHH NAS PID TCB
All service operated as Continental Connection or United Express using only CO
(9100-9549) and UA flight numbers
FFP: Continental OnePass, United Mileage Plus

HISTORY/STRUCTURE:

Founded: October 1988
Start Date: December 1, 1990
President/CEO: Thomas L Cooper
Ownership: G-Air Holdings Corp

FLEET:

Type	No	Seats	Engines
Beech 1900C	25	Y19	PWC PT6A-65B
DHC-7-100	4	Y50	PWC PT6A-50

McDONNELL DOUGLAS DC-10-30

HAWAIIAN AIRLINES

IATA: HA   **ICAO:** HAL   **IATA/ARC:** 173   **RADIO:** Hawaiian

---

CONTACTS:

Mail
PO Box 30008
Honolulu, HI 96820

Internet: www.hawaiianair.com

Telephone/Fax
Admin: +1 808 835 3700
Fax: +1 808 835 3690
Res: 1 800 367 5320
PR: +1 808 838 6778

OPERATION:

Type: Scheduled/charter passenger
Cities Served: US: ANC (charter) HNL ITO KOA LAS LAX LIH LNY MKK OGG
PDX SEA SFO **Oceania:** PPG PPT (charter)
Code-Share: American Eagle
FFP: AAdvantage, HawaiianMiles, One Pass, WorldPerks

HISTORY/STRUCTURE:

Founded: January 30, 1929
Start Date: November 11, 1929
President/CEO: Paul Casey
Ownership: Public (AMEX: HA)

FLEET:

Type	No	Seats	Engines
DC-9-51	15	F8Y125	PW JT8D-17/-17A
DC-10-10	10	F34Y270	GE CF6-6K
DC-10-30	2	F34Y270	GE CF6-50C2

BOMBARDIER DHC-8-202 DASH 8

HORIZON AIR

IATA: QX   **ICAO:** QXE   **IATA/ARC:** 481   **RADIO:** Horizon Air

CONTACTS:

Mail
PO Box 48309
Seattle, WA 98148

Internet: www.horizonair.com

Telephone/Fax
Admin: +1 206 241 6757
Fax: +1 206 431 4696
Res: 1 800 547 9308
PR: +1 206 431 4672

OPERATION:

Type: Scheduled passenger
Cities Served: US: ACV ALW BIL BLI BOI BTM BZN CLM EAT EUG FAT FCA
GEG GTF HLN IDA LAX LMT LWS MFR MSO MWH OTH PDT PDX PIH PSC
PUW RDD RDM SEA SJC SMF SUN YKM **Canada:** YEG YLW YVR YYC YYJ
Operates as an Alaska Airlines Commuter using AS flight numbers (2000-2999),
and partners with American, Canadian, Continental, and Northwest
FFP: AAdvantage, Alaska Airlines Mileage Plan, Continental OnePass,
Northwest WorldPerks

HISTORY/STRUCTURE:

Founded: May 1981
Start Date: September 1, 1981
President/CEO: George D Bagley
Ownership: Horizon Air Industries/Alaska Air Group

FLEET:

Type	No	Seats	Engines
DHC-8-100	13	Y37	PWC PW120A
DHC-8Q-200	25	Y37	PWC PW123D
F28 Mk 4000	20	Y69	RR Spey 555-15P
Ordered			
DHC-8Q-200	3		
Canadair RJ 700	25 plus 25 options		
DHC-8Q-400	15 plus 15 options		

DE HAVILLAND CANADA DHC-6-300 TWIN OTTER

ISLAND AIR (dba ALOHA ISLAND AIR)

IATA: WP   **ICAO:** PRI   **IATA/ARC:** 347   **RADIO:** Princeville

CONTACTS:

Mail
99 Kapalulu Place
Honolulu, HI 96819

Telephone/Fax
Admin: +1 808 833 7108
Fax: +1 808 833 5498
Res: 1 800 323 3345

OPERATION:

Type: Scheduled passenger
Cities Served: HNL HNM JHM LNY MKK OGG
All service operated for Aloha using only AQ flight numbers (1100-1699)
Code-Share: none
FFP: AlohaPass

HISTORY/STRUCTURE:

Founded: 1980 (as Princeville Airways)
Start Date: September 9, 1980
President: Neil M Takekawa
Ownership: Aloha Airgroup

FLEET:

Type	No	Seats	Engines
DHC-6-300	3	Y18	PWC PT6A-27
DHC-8-100	3	Y37	PWC PW120A

DOUGLAS DC-9-15F

KITTY HAWK AIR CARGO

IATA: KR   **ICAO:** KHA   **IATA/ARC:** none   **RADIO:** Kitty Hawk

---

CONTACTS:

Mail
PO Box 612787
Dallas/Ft Worth Airport, TX 75261

Telephone/Fax
Admin: +1 972 456 6000
Fax: +1 972 456 2277

Internet: www.kha.com

OPERATION:

Type: Scheduled/charter cargo
Cities Served: (Kitty Hawk Cargo) BWI DEN HUF IAH MCO MSP
Operates contract charters for several forwarders in the US, Europe, and the Pacific

---

HISTORY/STRUCTURE:

Founded: 1976 (as Kitty Hawk Airways)
Start Date: 1985
CEO: M Tom Christopher
President: Tilmon Reeves
Ownership: Kitty Hawk Group

FLEET:

Type	No	Engines
DC-9-15F	5	PW JT8D-7B
Boeing 727-100C	1	PW JT8D-7B
Boeing 727-200F	32	PW JT8D-9/-9A/-15/-15A

BOEING 747-200B (F)

KITTY HAWK INTERNATIONAL

IATA: CB   **ICAO:** CKS   **IATA/ARC:** 571   **RADIO:** Connie

CONTACTS:

Mail
842 Willow Run Airport
Ypsilanti, MI 48198

Telephone/Fax
Admin: +1 734 484 0088
Fax: +1 734 484 3630

Internet: www.kha.com

OPERATION:

Type: Scheduled/charter cargo
Cities Served: (Kitty Hawk Cargo) ATL BDL BOS DFW ELP EWR HUF LAX
MIA PHL SEA SFO YIP
Several aircraft based at Miami for charter contracts to Latin America

HISTORY/STRUCTURE:

Founded: 1972 (as Kalitta Flying Service)
Start Date: November 1972
CEO: M Tom Christopher
President: Tillman Reeves
Ownership: Kitty Hawk Group

FLEET:

Type	No	Engines
DC-8F-50	3	PW JT3D-3B
DC-8-61F	3	PW JT3D-3B
DC-8-62F	4	PW JT3D-3B/-7
DC-8-63F	2	PW JT3D-7
L-1011-200F	6	RR RB211-524B-02
Boeing 747-100F	2	PW JT9D-7A
Boeing 747-200F	5	PW JT9D-7F

McDONNELL DOUGLAS DC-10-10

LAKER AIRWAYS

IATA: 6F   **ICAO:** LKR   **IATA/ARC:** 385   **RADIO:** Laker

CONTACTS:

Mail	Telephone/Fax
6261 NW 61st Way, Suite 201	Admin: +1 954 202 0444
Ft Lauderdale, FL 33309	Fax: +1 954 772 7153

OPERATION:
Type: Charter passenger

HISTORY/STRUCTURE:
Founded: 1995
Start Date: April 6, 1996
President: James Kenney
Ownership: Sir Freddie Laker, Oscar Wyatt

FLEET:

Type	No	Seats	Engines
Boeing 727-100	1	F54	PW JT8D-7B
Boeing 727-200 (Advanced)	2	F59	PW JT8D-15
DC-10-10	1	Y353	GE CF6-6D
DC-10-30	3	Y353	GE CF6-50C2

LOCKHEED 382G (L-100-30) HERCULES

LYNDEN AIR CARGO

IATA: L2   **ICAO:** LYC   **IATA/ARC:** 344   **RADIO:** Lynden

---

CONTACTS:

Mail
4000 West 50th Street
Anchorage, AK 99502

Telephone/Fax
Admin: +1 907 243 0215
Fax: +1 907 245 0213

OPERATION:

Type: Scheduled/charter cargo
Cities Served: AKN ANC BET DLG KSM OME OTZ UNK

HISTORY/STRUCTURE:

Founded: 1995
Start Date: August 31, 1995
President: Mike Hart
Ownership: Lynden Inc

FLEET:

Type	No	Engines
L-100-30 Hercules	4	AN 501-D13A

RAYTHEON BEECH 1900D

MESA AIRLINES

IATA: YV   **ICAO: ASH**   **IATA/ARC** 533   **RADIO:** AirShuttle

CONTACTS:

Mail
410 North 44th Street
Suite 700
Phoenix, AZ 85008

Telephone/Fax

Admin:	+1 602 685 4000
Fax:	+1 602 685 4350
Res:	1 800 637 2247 (Mesa)
Res:	1 800 235 9292
	(America West Express)
Res:	1 800 428 4322
	(US Airways Express)

Internet: www.mesa-air.com

OPERATION:

Type: Scheduled passenger
Cities Served: US: ABQ ACK ACY ALM ASE AVP BDR BFL BGR BHM BOS
BNA BWI CLD CMH CNM COS CRW CVG CVN DCA DEN DRO DSM EUG FAT
FHU FLG FMN GJT GON GUP HII HOB HSV HYA IAD IFP IGM IPT ITH LEB
LGA LNS LRU MAF MDW MHT MKE MTJ MVY PHF PHL PHX PQI PRC PSP
RDG RDU ROC ROW SBA SBP SDF STL SVC SWF SYR TEX TYS YUM
México: GYM HMO
Some service operated as America West Express (HP5000-6799) and
US Airways Express (US5250-5499, 5850-5999)
FFP: America West FlightFund, US Airways Dividend Miles

HISTORY/STRUCTURE:

Founded: 1980
Start Date: October 12, 1980
President/CEO: Jonathan Orenstein
Ownership: Mesa Air Group (NASDAQ: MESA)

FLEET:

Type	No	Seats	Engines
Beech 1900D	38	Y19	PWC PT6A-67D
DHC-8-200	12	Y36	PWC PW123
Canadair RJ 200ER	26	Y50	GE CF34-3B1
Ordered			
Canadair RJ 200ER	6 plus 16 options		

SAAB 340B*PLUS*

MESABA AIRLINES

IATA: XJ   **ICAO**: MES   **IATA/ARC**: 582   **RADIO**: Mesaba

CONTACTS:

Mail	**Telephone/Fax**
7501 26th Avenue South	Admin: +1 612 726 5151
Minneapolis, MN 55450	Fax: +1 612 725 4901
	Res: 1 800 225 2525
Internet: www.mesaba.com	PR: +1 612 725 4915

OPERATION:

Type: Scheduled passenger
Cities Served: US: ABE ABR ALO APN ATL ATW ATY AZO BEH BGM BIS BJI
BMI BRD CAK CID CIU CLE CMH CMI CMX CRW CVG CWA DAY DBQ DFW
DLH DSM DTW EAU ELM ERI ESC EVV FAR FNT FOD FSD FWA GFK GPZ
GRB GSO HIB HPN ICT INL LAF LAN LEX LNK LSE MBS MCW MDT MEM
MKG MLI MQT MSN MSP OMA PIA PIR PIT PLN PWM RAP RHI ROA ROC
RFD RST SBN SCE SDF STC STL SUX TOL TVC TVF TYS XNA YNG (season-
al: ASE FCA LYU) **Canada:** YOW YQT YUL YWG YXU (seasonal: YQK)
All service operated as Northwest Airlink using only NW flight numbers (2700-
3699). Some flights additionally code-share with Continental
FFP: Northwest WorldPerks

HISTORY/STRUCTURE:

Founded: 1944 (as Mesaba Aviation)
Start Date: February 4, 1973
President/CEO: John Fredericksen (interim)
Ownership: Mesaba Holdings (NASDAQ: MAIR)

FLEET:

Type	No	Seats	Engines
SAAB 340A	23	Y30	GE CT7-5A2
SAAB 340B	50	Y34	GE CT7-9B
AVRO RJ85	27	F16Y53	ALF507-1F
Ordered			
AVRO RJ85	5		

BOEING 727-200 (ADVANCED)

MIAMI AIR INTERNATIONAL

IATA: GL **ICAO:** BSK **IATA/ARC:** none **RADIO:** Biscayne

---

CONTACTS:

Mail
PO Box 660880
Miami, FL 33266-0880

Telephone/Fax
Admin: +1 305 876 3600
Fax: +1 305 871 4222

Internet: www.miamiair.com

OPERATION:

Type: Charter passenger

HISTORY/STRUCTURE:

Founded: August 1990
Start Date: October 15, 1991
President: D Ross Fischer
Chairman: George A Lyall
Ownership: Fischer, Lyall & Kornmeyer

FLEET:

Type	No	Seats	Engines
Boeing 727-200 (Advanced)	7	Y172	PW JT8D-15/-15A

BOMBARDIER CANADAIR CL-600-2B19 REGIONAL JET SERIES 200LR

MIDWAY AIRLINES

IATA: JI   **ICAO:** MDW   **IATA/ARC:** 878   **RADIO:** Midway

CONTACTS:

Mail
2801 Slater Road, Suite 200
Morrisville, NC 27560

Internet: www.midwayair.com

Telephone/Fax
Admin: +1 919 595 6000
Fax: +1 919 595 6480
Res: 1 800 446 4392

OPERATION:

Type: Scheduled passenger
Cities Served: ATL BDL BOS CHS CMH DCA EWR FLL JAX LGA MEM MCO MSY MYR PBI PHL RDU SWF TPA
Code-Share: Corporate Airlines
FFP: AAdvantage

HISTORY/STRUCTURE:

Founded: 1993
Start Date: November 15, 1993
President: Robert Ferguson
Ownership: Publicly traded company (NASDAQ: MDWY)

FLEET:

Type	No	Seats	Engines
Canadair RJ 200ER	12	Y50	GE CF34-3A1
Fokker 100	8	F8Y90	RR Tay 650-15
Ordered			
Canadair RJ 200ER	12 plus 14 options		
Boeing 737-700	17 plus 10 options		

DOUGLAS DC-9-32

MIDWEST EXPRESS

IATA: YX   **ICAO:** MEP   **IATA/ARC:** 453   **RADIO:** Midex

---

CONTACTS:

Mail
6744 South Howell Avenue
Oak Creek, WI 53154-1402

Telephone/Fax
Admin: +1 414 570 4000
Fax: +1 414 570 0199
Res: 1 800 452 2022
PR: +1 414 570 3640

Internet: www.midwestexpress.com

OPERATION:

Type: Scheduled passenger
Cities Served: US: ATL ATW BDL BOS CLE CMH DCA DEN DFW EWR FLL
GRR IAD LAS LAX LGA MCI MCO MKE MSN OMA PHL PHX RDU RSW SFO
TPA **Canada:** YYZ
Code-Share: Skyway Airlines
FFP: Midwest Express Frequent Flyer

HISTORY/STRUCTURE:

Founded: 1983
Start Date: April 29, 1984
President/CEO: Timothy Hoeksema
Ownership: Midwest Express Holdings (NYSE: MEH)

FLEET:

Type	No	Seats	Engines
DC-9-14/15	8	F52 or F60	PW JT8D-7B
DC-9-30	16	F84	PW JT8D-7B/-9A
MD-81	3	F116	PW JT8D-217C
MD-82	2	F116	PW JT8D-217C
MD-88	2	F112	PW JT8D-219
Ordered			
MD-81	2		

BOEING 757-200

NATIONAL AIRLINES

IATA: N7   **ICAO:** none   **IATA/ARC:** 007   **RADIO:** none

CONTACTS:

Mail
PO Box 26598
Las Vegas, NV 89126-6598

Internet: www.nationalairlines.com

Telephone/Fax
Admin: +1 702 944 2800
Res: 1 888 757 5387
PR: +1 702 944 2777

OPERATION:

Type: Scheduled passenger
Cities Served: DFW JFK LAS LAX MDW SFO
FFP: National Comps

HISTORY/STRUCTURE:

Founded: April 1995
Start Date: May 27, 1999
President/CEO: Michael Conway
Ownership: Closely held

FLEET:

Type	No	Seats	Engines
Boeing 757-200	4	F22Y153	RR RB211-535E4
Ordered			
Boeing 747-200	4		

BOEING 737-800

NORTH AMERICAN AIRLINES

IATA: XG   **ICAO:** NAO   **IATA/ARC:** 455   **RADIO:** North American

CONTACTS:

Mail
Suite 250 Building 75
North Hangar Road
JFK International Airport
Jamaica, NY 11430

Telephone/Fax
Admin: +1 718 656 2650
Fax: +1 718 995 3372

Internet: www.northamair.com

OPERATION:

Type: Charter passenger
Areas Served: Worldwide charters including US sub-services for El Al

HISTORY/STRUCTURE:

Founded: 1989
Start Date: January 20, 1990
President/CEO: Dan McKinnon
Ownership: Dan McKinnon (75.1%), El Al (24.9%)

FLEET:

Type	No	Seats	Engines
Boeing 737-800	2	Y169	CFM56-7B26
Boeing 757-200	2	Y215 or F24Y179	RR RB211-535E4

USA

NORTHERN AIR CARGO

IATA: HU   **ICAO:** NAC   **IATA/ARC:** 345   **RADIO:** Northern Air Cargo

---

CONTACTS:

Mail
3900 West International Airport
Anchorage, AK 99502

Telephone/Fax
Admin: +1 907 243 3545
Fax: +1 907 249 5190

Internet: www.nacargo.com

OPERATION:

Type: Scheduled cargo
Cities Served: ADQ ANC ANI BET BRW DLG FAI GAL ILI KSM MCG OME RDB SCC SNP STG UNK

HISTORY/STRUCTURE:

Founded: 1956 (as Sholton & Carlson Inc)
Start Date: 1956
CEO: Rita Sholton
President: Mary Sholton Witte
Ownership: Sholton family

FLEET:

Type	No	Engines
DC-6A/B	12	PW R-2800-CB16
Boeing 727-100F	3	PW JT8D-7B

BOEING 747-400

NORTHWEST AIRLINES

IATA: NW   **ICAO:** NWA   **IATA/ARC:** 012   **RADIO:** Northwest

---

CONTACTS:

Mail	Telephone/Fax	
5101 Northwest Drive	Admin:	+1 612 726 2111
St Paul, MN 55111-3034	Fax:	+1 612 726 6599
	Res:	1 800 225 2525
	PR:	+1 612 726 2331
Internet: www.nwa.com	Job Hot Line:	+1 612 727 7450

OPERATION:

Type: Scheduled/charter passenger/cargo

Cities Served: US: ABE ABQ ALB ANC ATL AUS AZO BDL BHM BIL BIS BNA BOI BOS BTR BUF BWI BZN CID CLE CLT COS CMH CVG DAY DCA DEN DFW DLH DSM DTW EWR FAR FLL FNT FSD FWA GEG GFK GPT GRB GRR GSO GSP GTF HNL HOU HPN IAD IAH ICT IND JAN JAX JFK LAN LAS LAX LGA LIT LSE MBS MCI MCO MDT MDW MEM MHT MIA MKE MOT MSN MSO MSP MSY OKC OMA ONT ORD ORF PBI PDX PHL PHX PIT PVD RAP RDU RIC RNO ROC RST RSW SAN SAT SBN SDF SEA SFO SJC SLC SMF SNA SRQ STL SUX SYR TPA TUS TVC TYS VPS (seasonal: EGE FAI FCA HDN PSP) **Canada:** YEG YUL YVR YWG YXE YYC YYZ **Caribbean:** MBJ SJU (seasonal: POP SXM) **México:** CUN MEX (seasonal: ACA CZM PVR SJD ZIH) **Central America:** (seasonal: Liberia) **Europe:** AMS CDG FRA LGW OSL **Asia:** BKK BOM DEL HKG KIX KUL MNL NGO NRT PEK SEL SHA SIN SPN TPE **Oceania:** GUM

Global Alliance: Wings

Code-Share: Air China, Alaska, America West, Big Sky, Business Express, Continental, Continental Express, Eurowings, Express Airlines I, Hawaiian, Horizon, Japan Air System, KLM, KLM exel, KLM uk, Martinair, Mesaba, Pacific Island Aviation, Trans States

FFP: WorldPerks

HISTORY/STRUCTURE:

Founded: September 1, 1926 (as Northwest Airways)

Start Date: October 1, 1926

President/CEO: John H Dasburg

Ownership: Northwest Airlines Corp (NASDAQ: NWAC)

McDONNELL DOUGLAS DC-10-30

FLEET:

Type	No	Seats	Engines
DC-9-14/15	10	F8Y70	
		or F16Y64	PW JT8D-7B
DC-9-31/32	116	F16Y84	PW JT8D-7B/-9A/-15
DC-9-41	12	F16Y94	PW JT8D-11
DC-9-51	35	F16Y109	PW JT8D-17
DC-9-82	8	F12Y136	PW JT8D-217
Boeing 727-200 (Advanced)	38	F12Y137	
		or F56	PW JT8D-15/-15A/17/-17R
Airbus A320-200	70	F12Y138	CFM56-5A1
Boeing 757-200	48	F14Y176/Y180	PW2037
DC-10-30	20	C34Y247	GE CF6-50C/-50C2/ -50C2B
DC-10-40	21	C34Y256	PW JT9D-20/-20J
		or C34Y247	
Boeing 747-100	2	C34Y416	PW JT9D-7A
Boeing 747-200	21	F8C66Y296	PW JT9D-7F/-7Q/-7R4G2
		or F12C63Y296	
		or F8C63Y296	
Boeing 747-200F	8	Freighter	PW JT9D-7F/-7Q
Boeing 747-400	11	F18C62Y338	PW4056
Ordered			
Airbus A319-100	68		
Airbus A320-200	12		
Airbus A330-300	16		
Boeing 757-200	25		
Boeing 747-400	3		

McDONNELL DOUGLAS DC-10-10

OMNI AIR INTERNATIONAL

IATA: X9   **ICAO:** OAE   **IATA/ARC:** none   **RADIO:** Omni Express

CONTACTS:

Mail	Telephone/Fax
PO Box 582527	Admin: +1 918 836 5393
Tulsa, OK 74158	Fax: +1 918 834 4850

Internet: www.omniairintl.com

OPERATION:

Type: Charter passenger
Areas Served: Worldwide

HISTORY/STRUCTURE:

Founded: 1984 (as Continental Air Transport)
Start Date: 1984
CEO: Sanford P Burnstein
Ownership: Privately held

FLEET:

Type	No	Seats	Engines
DC-10-10	2	Y380	GE CF6-6K
DC-10-30	1	Y370	GE CF6-50C2

BOEING 737-200 (ADVANCED)

PACE AIRLINES

IATA: none   **ICAO:** none   **IATA/ARC:** none   **RADIO:** none

CONTACTS:

Mail
PO Box 525
Winston-Salem, NC 27102
Email: charter@flypiedmont.com

Telephone/Fax
Admin: +1 910 776 6060
Fax: +1 910 776 6061

Internet: www.flypiedmont.com

OPERATION:

Type: Charter passenger
Areas Served: US, Canada, Caribbean, South America; contract carrier for
Charlotte Hornets/Atlanta Hawks/Washington Wizards sports teams

HISTORY/STRUCTURE:

Founded: 1940 (as Piedmont Aviation)
Start Date: January 2, 1996
President/CEO: Jim A Taylor
Ownership: Piedmont Aviation Services

FLEET:

Type	No	Seats	Engines
Boeing 737-200	3	C44/C46	PW JT8D-9A

BOEING 727-200 (ADVANCED)

PANAGRA AIRWAYS

IATA: 7E   **ICAO**: PGI   **IATA/ARC**: none   **RADIO**: Panagra

---

CONTACTS:

Mail
750 SW 34th Street, Suite 201A
Fort Lauderdale, FL 33315

Telephone/Fax
Admin: +1 954 359 9944
Fax: +1 954 359 3075

Internet: www.panagra.com

OPERATION:

Type: Charter passenger
Areas Served: Worldwide

HISTORY/STRUCTURE:

Founded: 1995
Start Date: March 28, 1997
President: Robert Mencel
Ownership: Privately held

FLEET:

Type	No	Seats	Engines
Boeing 727-200	1	Y160	PW JT8D-9A

NOTES: Airline filed Chapter 11 bankruptcy June 1999

BOEING 727-200 (ADVANCED)

PAN AMERICAN AIRWAYS

IATA: PA   **ICAO:** PAA   **IATA/ARC:** none   **RADIO:** Clipper

---

CONTACTS:

Mail
14 Aviation Avenue
Portsmouth, NH 03801

Telephone/Fax
Admin: +1 603 766 2000
Fax: +1 603 766 2094

OPERATION:

Type: Scheduled/charter passenger
Cities Served: US: PSM SFB **Caribbean:** BQU SJU

HISTORY/STRUCTURE:

Founded: 1996
Start Date: September 26, 1996
President/CEO: David A Fink
Ownership: Guilford Transportation Industries

FLEET:

Type	No	Seats	Engines
Boeing 727-200	7	Y173	PW JT8D-7B/-9A/-15/-17R
Boeing 737-200 operated by Nations Air Express	1	Y125	PW JT8D-9A

NOTES: Pan Am recently acquired Nations Air Express

SAAB 340B

PENINSULA AIRWAYS (dba PENAIR)

IATA: KS   **ICAO**: PEN   **IATA/ARC**: 339   **RADIO**: Peninsula

CONTACTS:

Mail
6100 Boeing Avanue
Anchorage, AK 99502

Internet: www.penair.com

Telephone/Fax
Admin: +1 907 243 2485
Fax: +1 907 243 6848
Res: 1 800 448 4226

OPERATION:

Type: Scheduled passenger
Cities Served: ADQ AKN ANC ANI BET CDB DLG DUT KSM MCG OTZ SDP SNP STG UNK
Operates as Alaska Airlines Commuter on selected routes using AS flight numbers (4200-4299)
FFP: Alaska Airlines Mileage Plan

HISTORY/STRUCTURE:

Founded: 1955
Start Date: 1967 (scheduled service)
President: Orin D Seybert
Ownership: Seybert family

FLEET:

Type	No	Seats	Engines
Cessna A185F	1	Y3	CO IO-520-D
PA-32-300/-301	13	Y5	LY IO-540-K1A5/-K1G5/-K1G5D
G-44 Widgeon	2	Y5	LY GO-480-B1D
G-21A Goose	2	Y6	PW R-985
PA-31-350 Chieftain	5	Y9	LY TIO-540-J2BD
PA-31T3-T-1040	1	Y9	PWC PT6A-11
Cessna 208	3	Y9	PWC PT6A-114
Cessna 441	2	Y9	GA TPE331-8-401S
Metro III	5	Y19	GA TPE331-11U-611G/-612G
SAAB 340B	2	Y30	GE CT7-9

BOMBARDIER DHC-8-102 DASH 8

PIEDMONT AIRLINES

IATA: PI   **ICAO**: PDT   **IATA/ARC**: 531   **RADIO**: Piedmont

CONTACTS:

Mail
5443 Airport Terminal Road
Salisbury, MD 21804-1700

Internet: www.piedmont-airlines.com

Telephone/Fax
Admin: +1 410 742 2996
Fax: +1 410 742 4069
Res: 1 800 428 4322

OPERATION:

Type: Scheduled passenger
Cities Served: US: AVL BWI CAE CHA CHO CLT CRW DCA EWN EYW FAY FLO GSO HHH HPN HVN ILM JAX LYH MCO MIA MYR ORF PBI PHF PHL PIT RDU RIC ROA SAV SBY TLH TPA **Canada:** YOW YYZ **Caribbean:** ELH GHB MHH TCB
All service operated as US Airways Express using only US flight numbers (3000-3499)
FFP: US Airways Dividend Miles

HISTORY/STRUCTURE:

Founded: 1964 (as Henson Airlines)
Start Date: October 1, 1964
President/CEO: John F Leonard
Ownership: US Airways Group

FLEET:

Type	No	Seats	Engines
DHC-8-100	45	Y37	PWC PW120A
DHC-8-200	11	Y37	PWC PW123
Ordered			
DHC-8-200	8		

BOEING 747-100 (F)

POLAR AIR CARGO

IATA: PO   **ICAO:** PAC   **IATA/ARC:** 403   **RADIO:** Polar Tiger

CONTACTS:

Mail
100 Ocean Gate, 15th Floor
Long Beach, CA 90802

Telephone/Fax
Admin: +1 562 436 7471
Fax: +1 562 436 9333

Internet: www.polaraircargo.com

OPERATION:

Type: Scheduled/charter cargo
Cities Served: US: ANC ATL HNL JFK LAX LCK MIA ORD SFO
South America: CCS EZE GIG LIM MAO SCL VCP **Europe:** AMS
HEL PIK MAN SNN **Africa:** JNB HRE NBO **Asia:** DEL DXB HKG KHV KIX
MNL NRT SIN TPE **Oceania:** MEL NAN SYD

HISTORY/STRUCTURE:

Founded: June 1990
Start Date: July 1994
CEO: Lou Valerio
Ownership: Closely held

FLEET:

Type	No	Engines
Boeing 747-100F	11	PW JT9D-7A
Boeing 747-200F	3	PW JT9D-7Q

BOEING 737-400

PRO AIR

IATA: XL   **ICAO:** PRH   **IATA/ARC:** none   **RADIO:** Prohawk

CONTACTS:

Mail
101 Elliott Avenue West, Suite 500
Seattle, WA 98119

Internet: www.proair.com

Telephone/Fax
Admin: +1 206 623 2000
Fax: +1 206 623 6612
Res: 1 888 776 2477

OPERATION:

Type: Scheduled passenger
Cities Served: ATL BWI DET EWR IND LGA MDW MCO RSW TPA

HISTORY/STRUCTURE:

Founded: 1995
Start Date: July 4, 1997
CEO: Kevin Stamper
President: Craig Belmondo
Ownership: Privately held

FLEET:

Type	No	Seats	Engines
Boeing 737-300	1	F20Y88	CFM56-3B2
Boeing 737-400	3	F8Y138	CFM56-3C1

DORNIER 328-110

PSA AIRLINES

IATA: none   **ICAO**: JIA   **IATA/ARC**: none   **RADIO**: Blue Streak

CONTACTS:

Mail
3400 Terminal Drive
Vandalia, OH 45377-1041

Telephone/Fax
Admin: +1 937 454 1116
Fax: +1 937 454 0653
Res: 1 800 428 4322

OPERATION:

Type: Scheduled passenger
Cities Served: US: AZO BHM BTV CAE CAK CHS CLT CRW CVG DAY DCA
EVV GRR GSO GSP IAD PIT PWM RIC ROA SBN TRI TYS **Canada:** YOW
All service operated as US Airways Express using only US flight numbers
(4000-4199)
FFP: US Airways Dividend Miles

HISTORY/STRUCTURE:

Founded: 1969 (as Vee Neal Airlines)
Start Date: May 19, 1980
(renamed Jetstream International, December 1, 1983)
President/CEO: Richard Pfenning
Ownership: US Airways Group

FLEET:

Type	No	Seats	Engines
Dornier 328-110	25	Y31/32	PWC PW119B

BOEING 727-100C

REEVE ALEUTIAN AIRWAYS

IATA: RV   **ICAO**: RVV   **IATA/ARC**: 338   **RADIO**: Reeve

---

CONTACTS:

Mail
4700 West International Airport Road
Anchorage, AK 99502

Telephone/Fax
Admin: +1 907 243 1112
Fax: +1 907 249 2317
Res: 1 800 544 2248

OPERATION:

Type: Scheduled passenger/cargo, military contract
Cities Served: ADK AKN ANC BET CDB DLG DUT PTH SDP SNP

HISTORY/STRUCTURE:

Founded: 1932 (as Reeve Airways)
Start Date: November 15, 1932
President/CEO: Richard D Reeve
Ownership: Reeve Corporation

FLEET:

Type	No	Seats	Engines
Lockheed Electra	3	Combi	AN 501-D13A
Boeing 727-100QC	2	Combi	PW JT8D-7B

DOUGLAS DC-9-15F

RELIANT AIRLINES

IATA: none   **ICAO:** RLT   **IATA/ARC:** none   **RADIO:** Reliant

CONTACTS:

Mail
827 Willow Run Airport
Ypsilanti, MI 48198-0899

Telephone/Fax
Admin: +1 734 483 3616
Fax: +1 734 483 2629

Internet: www.reliantairlines.com

OPERATION:

Type: Charter passenger/cargo
Areas served: North America, Central America, Caribbean

HISTORY/STRUCTURE:

Founded: April 1984
Start Date: June 1984
President: Reese Zantop
Ownership: ESOP

FLEET:

Type	No	Seats	Engines
Falcon 10	1	7	GA TFE731-2-1C
Falcon 20	13	Freighter	GE CF700-2D2
DC-9-15F	3	Freighter	PW JT8D-7B

McDONNELL DOUGLAS DC-10-10

RYAN INTERNATIONAL AIRLINES

IATA: none   **ICAO**: RYN   **IATA/ARC**: none   **RADIO**: Ryan

CONTACTS:

Mail
266 North Main Street
Wichita, KS 67202-1504

Telephone/Fax
Admin: +1 316 265 7400
Fax: +1 316 942 7949

Internet: www.flyryan.com

OPERATION:

Type: Charter passenger/cargo
Operates 727 freighters for Emery Worldwide.
Operates 737-400/-500 aircraft for Apple Vacations/Transglobal Vacations
during winter season. A320 aircraft operated in winter season for Apple
Vacations and in summer season for Flying Colours. A320 and DC-10s operate
for Sunquest Tours as SkyService USA

HISTORY/STRUCTURE:

Founded: 1973
Start Date: March 3, 1973
President/CEO: Ronald D Ryan
Ownership: Ryan Aviation Corp

FLEET:

Type	No	Seats	Engines
Boeing 727-100F	22	Freighter	PW JT8D-7B
Boeing 727-200F	8	Freighter	PW JT8D-7B
Boeing 727-200	2	Y160	PW JT8D-9A
A320-200	2	Y180	CFM56-5B4
DC-10-10	2	Y380	GE CF6-6D

FOKKER F27 FRIENDSHIP MK 500

SCENIC AIRLINES

IATA: YR   **ICAO:** TLO   **IATA/ARC:** 398   **RADIO:** Talon

CONTACTS:

Mail
275 E Tropicana Avenue, Suite 220
Las Vegas, NV 89109

Internet: www.scenic.com

Telephone/Fax
Admin: +1 702 736 3333
Fax: +1 702 895 7824
Res: 1 800 634 6801

OPERATION:

Type: Scheduled/charter passenger
Cities Served: GCN LAS

HISTORY/STRUCTURE:

Founded: 1967
Start Date: June 1967
President/CEO: Cliff Evarts
Ownership: Eagle Group

FLEET:

Type	No	Seats	Engines
Cessna 207A/T207A	4	Y7	CO IO-520-F/TSIO-520-M
Cessna 402	5	Y9	CO TSIO-520-E
DHC-6-300	9	Y19	PWC PT6A-27
F27 Mk 500	3	Y48	RR Dart 532-7R
operated using ICAO code EGJ (Eagle Jet)			

BOMBARDIER DHC-8-315 DASH 8

SHUTTLE AMERICA

IATA: S5   **ICAO:** TCF   **IATA/ARC:** none   **RADIO:** Shuttlecraft

---

CONTACTS:

Mail
PO Box 3246
Windsor Locks, CT 06096

Telephone/Fax
Admin: +1 860 386 4200
Fax: +1 860 386 4266
Res: 1 888 999 3273

Internet: www.airshuttle.com

OPERATION:

Type: Scheduled passenger
Cities served: ALB BDL BUF ILG ISP ORF TTN

HISTORY/STRUCTURE:

Founded: 1995
Start Date: November 12, 1998
President: David Hackett
Ownership: Closely held

FLEET:

Type	No	Seats	Engines
DHC-8-300	4	Y50	PWC PW123B
Ordered			
DHC-8-300	2		

BOEING 737-200 (ADVANCED)

SIERRA PACIFIC AIRLINES

IATA: SI   **ICAO:** SPA   **IATA/ARC:** none   **RADIO:** Sierra Pacific

---

CONTACTS:

Mail
7700 North Business Park Drive
Tucson, AZ 85743

Telephone/Fax
Admin: +1 520 744 1144
Fax: +1 520 744 0138

OPERATION:

Type: Charter passenger, operations for US Forestry Service &
US Marshalls Service

HISTORY/STRUCTURE:

Founded: 1976 (as Mountainwest Aviation)
Start Date: February 1976
President: Gar M Thorsrud
Ownership: Sierra Pacific Corp

FLEET:

Type	No	Seats	Engines
Boeing 737-200 (Advanced)	1	Y122	PW JT8D-17

BOEING 727-200

SKY TREK INTERNATIONAL AIRLINES

IATA: none   **ICAO:** PZR   **IATA/ARC:** none   **RADIO:** Phazer

---

CONTACTS:

Mail
67 Scotch Road
Ewing, NJ 08628

Telephone/Fax
Admin: +1 609 671 0200
Fax: +1 609 671 0300

OPERATION:

Type: Charter passenger

HISTORY/STRUCTURE:

Founded: 1995
Start Date: 1997
President: Robert W Iverson II
Ownership: Privately held

FLEET:

Type	No	Seats	Engines
Boeing 727-200	5	Y168-Y173	PW JT8D-7B/17

RAYTHEON BEECH 1900D

SKYWAY AIRLINES

IATA: K8   **ICAO:** SYX   **IATA/ARC:** none   **RADIO:** Skyway Ex

CONTACTS:

Mail
1190 West Rawson Avenue
Oak Creek, WI 53154-1453

Telephone/Fax
Admin: +1 414 570 2300
Fax: +1 414 570 1441
Res: 1 800 452 2022

Internet: www.midwestexpress.com

OPERATION:

Type: Scheduled passenger
Cities Served: US: ATW BNA CLE CMH CVG CWA DAY DSM DTW FNT GRB GRR IND LAN LSE MCI MKG MSN OMA RFD SBN SDF STL
Canada: YYZ
All service operated as Midwest Express Connection using only YX flight numbers (1000-1999)
FFP: Midwest Express Frequent Flyer

HISTORY/STRUCTURE:

Founded: 1993
Start Date: February 3, 1994
President: David Reeve
Ownership: Astral Aviation (subsidiary Midwest Express Holdings)

FLEET:

Type	No	Seats	Engines
Beech 1900D	15	Y19	PWC PT6A-67D
Ordered			
Fairchild 328JET	5 plus 10 options		

EMBRAER EMB-120RT BRASILIA

SKYWEST AIRLINES

IATA: OO   **ICAO**: SKW   **IATA/ARC**: 302   **RADIO**: Skywest

---

CONTACTS:

Mail
444 South River Road
St George, UT 84790

Internet: www.skywest.com

Telephone/Fax
Admin: +1 435 634 3000
Fax: +1 435 634 3505
Res: 1 800 221 1212
PR: +1 435 634 3522

OPERATION:

Type: Scheduled passenger
Cities Served: US: ABQ ACV BFL BIL BLI BOI BTM BUR BZN CDC CEC CIC CLD COD COS CPR EKO EUG FAT GJT HLN IDA IPL IYK JAC LAS LAX MCE MFR MOD MRY MSO OMA ONT OXR PDX PIH PSC PSP RAP RDD RDM RNO SAN SBA SBP SEA SFO SGU SJC SLC SMF SMX SNA STS SUN TWF VEL VIS YKM YUM (seasonal: WYS) **Canada:** YVR YYC
All service operated as Delta Connection or United Express using DL (3600-3999, 5750-6099) or UA (5000-5499, 6800-6999, 7900-7999) flight numbers
FFP: Delta SkyMiles, United Mileage Plus

HISTORY/STRUCTURE:

Founded: 1972
Start Date: June 19, 1972
President/CEO: Jerry C Atkin
Ownership: SkyWest Inc (NASDAQ: SKYW)

FLEET:

Type	No	Seats	Engines
EMB-120ER Brasilia	95	Y30	PWC PW118A
Canadair RJ 100LR	11	Y50	GE CF34-3A1
Ordered			
EMB-120ER Brasilia	4		
Canadair RJ 200LR	35 plus 25 options		

DOUGLAS DC-9-32

SOUTHEAST AIRLINES
(Sun Jet International Inc dba)

IATA: JX   **ICAO:** SNK   **IATA/ARC:** none   **RADIO:** Sun King

---

CONTACTS:

Mail
12552 Belcher Road
Largo, FL 33773

Telephone/Fax
Admin: +1 727 532 1632
Fax: +1 727 530 1515

OPERATION:

Type: Charter passenger
Areas served: US, Caribbean

HISTORY/STRUCTURE:

Founded: 1993 (as Sun Jet International Airlines)
Start Date: July 1993
President: P Thomas Kolfenbach
Ownership: Privately held

FLEET:

Type	No	Seats	Engines
DC-9-32	1	Y115	PW JT8D-9A
Ordered			
DC-9-32	1		

BOEING 737-700

SOUTHWEST AIRLINES

IATA: WN   **ICAO: SWA**   **IATA/ARC:** 526   **RADIO:** Southwest

---

CONTACTS:

Mail	Telephone/Fax	
PO Box 36611	Admin:	+1 214 904 4000
Dallas, TX 75235-1611	Fax:	+1 214 904 5097
	Res:	1 800 435 9792
	PR:	+1 214 792 4847
Internet: www.southwest.com	Job Hot Line:	+1 214 904 4803

OPERATION:

Type: Scheduled passenger
Cities Served: ABQ AMA AUS BHM BNA BOI BUR BWI CLE CMH CRP DAL DTW ELP FLL GEG HOU HRL IAH IND ISP JAN JAX LAS LAX LBB LIT MAF MCO MDW MCI MHT MSY OAK OKC OMA ONT PDX PHX PVD RDU RNO SAN SAT SDF SEA SFO SJC SLC SMF SNA STL TPA TUL TUS
FFP: Rapid Rewards

HISTORY/STRUCTURE:

Founded: 1967
Start Date: June 18, 1971
President/CEO: Herbert (Herb) D Kelleher
Ownership: Publicly traded company (NYSE: LUV)

FLEET:

Type	No	Seats	Engines
Boeing 737-200	39	Y122	PW JT8D-9A/-15
Boeing 737-500	25	Y122	CFM56-3B1
Boeing 737-300	193	Y137	CFM56-3B1
Boeing 737-700	37	Y137	CFM56-7
Ordered			
Boeing 737-700	104 plus 56 options		

McDONNELL DOUGLAS DC-9-87 (MD-87)

SPIRIT AIRLINES

IATA: NK   **ICAO**: NKS   **IATA/ARC**: 487   **RADIO**: Spirit Wings

---

CONTACTS:

Mail
18121 East 8 Mile Road
Eastpointe, MI 48021

Internet: www.spiritair.com

Telephone/Fax
Admin: +1 810 779 2700
Fax: +1 810 779 9332
Res: 1 800 772 7117

OPERATION:

Type: Scheduled/charter passenger
Cities Served: ACY BOS CLE DTW FLL EWR ISP LAX LGA MCO MLB MYR
PBI RSW TPA

HISTORY/STRUCTURE:

Founded: 1989 (as Charter One)
Start Date: June 1990
President: Edward W Homfeld
Ownership: Privately held

FLEET:

Type	No	Seats	Engines
DC-9-30	10	Y117	PW JT8D-7B/-9A/-11
DC-9-40	2	Y127	PW JT8D-17
MD-87	1	Y120	PW JT8D-219
MD-82	5	Y165	PW JT8D-217/-219
MD-83	1	Y165	PW JT8D-219
Ordered			
MD-82	11		

McDONNELL DOUGLAS DC-10-15

SUN COUNTRY AIRLINES

IATA: SY   **ICAO**: SCX   **IATA/ARC**: none   **RADIO**: Sun Country

---

CONTACTS:

Mail
2520 Pilot Knob Road, Suite 250
Mendota Heights, MN 55120

Internet: www.suncountry.com

Telephone/Fax
Admin: +1 651 681 3900
Fax: +1 651 681 3970
Res: 1 800 752 1218

OPERATION:

Type: Scheduled/charter passenger
Cities Served: US: ANC BOS DFW DTW IAD IAH JFK LAS LAX MCO MKE MSP ORD PHX SAT SEA SFO **Caribbean:** AUA

HISTORY/STRUCTURE:

Founded: July 1, 1982
Start Date: January 20, 1983
President/CEO: William LaMacchia Jr
Ownership: New Sun Inc

FLEET:

Type	No	Seats	Engines
Boeing 727-200 (Advanced)	11	Y180	PW JT8D-17/-17A/-17R/-217C
DC-10-15	4	Y360	GE CF6-50C2F
Ordered			
Boeing 737-800	6		

BOEING 727-200 (ADVANCED)

SUNWORLD INTERNATIONAL AIRLINES

IATA: SM   **ICAO**: SWI   **IATA/ARC:** none   **RADIO**: Sunworld

---

CONTACTS:

Mail
207 Grandview Drive
Fort Mitchell, KY 41017

Telephone/Fax
Admin: +1 606 331 0091
Fax: +1 606 331 6383

Internet: www.sunworld-air.com

OPERATION:

Type: Scheduled/charter passenger
Cities Served: US: CVG EWR **Caribbean:** ANU GCM STX UVF

HISTORY/STRUCTURE:

Founded: 1995
Start Date: July 1996
President: William Yung
Ownership: William Yung

FLEET:

Type	No	Seats	Engines
Boeing 727-200 (Advanced)	2	Y167	PW JT8D-15

BOEING 747-100

TOWER AIR

IATA: FF   **ICAO:** TOW   **IATA/ARC:** 305   **RADIO:** Tee Air

CONTACTS:

Mail
Hangar 17
JFK International Airport
Jamaica, NY 11430

Telephone/Fax
Admin: 1 718 553 4300
Fax: +1 718 553 4312
Res: 1 800 348 6937

Internet: www.towerair.com

OPERATION:

Type: Scheduled passenger
Cities Served: US: JFK LAX MIA SFO **Caribbean:** SDQ SJU
Europe: ORY **Asia:** TLV
FFP: Tower Air Frequent Flyer Program

HISTORY/STRUCTURE:

Founded: August 1982
Start Date: November 1, 1983
President/CEO: Morris Nachtomi
Ownership: Publicly traded company (NASDAQ: TOWR)

FLEET:

Type	No	Seats	Engines
Boeing 747-100	4	Y480	PW JT9D-7A
Boeing 747-100F	1	Freighter	PW JT9D-7A
Boeing 747-200	10	Y480	PW JT9D-7F/-7J/-7Q
Boeing 747-200F	2	Freighter	PW JT9D-7Q or GE CF6-80E2

LOCKHEED L-1011-385-1 (F) TRISTAR

TRADEWINDS AIRLINES

IATA: WI   **ICAO:** TDX   **IATA/ARC:** 490   **RADIO:** Tradewinds Express

CONTACTS:

Mail
PO Box 35329
Greensboro, NC 27425

Telephone/Fax
Admin: +1 336 668 7500
Fax: +1 336 668 7517

OPERATION:

Type: Scheduled cargo
Cities Served: US: BDL GSO **Caribbean:** BQN

HISTORY/STRUCTURE:

Founded: 1969 (as Wrangler Aviation)
Start Date: 1973
President/CEO: Larry Scheevel
Ownership: Tropic Communications

FLEET:

Type	No	Engines
L-1011-1F	1	RR RB211-22B

DOUGLAS DC-8-61 (F)

USA

TRANS CONTINENTAL AIRLINES

IATA: none   **ICAO:** TCN   **IATA/ARC:** 837   **RADIO:** Trans Continental

CONTACTS:

Mail
803 Willow Run Airport
Ypsilanti, MI 48198

Telephone/Fax
Admin: +1 734 484 3435
Fax: +1 734 484 3260

OPERATION:

Type: Charter cargo
Areas Served: US, South America

HISTORY/STRUCTURE:

Founded: 1994
Start Date: August 1994
President/CEO: David Clark
Ownership: Privately held

FLEET:

Type	No	Engines
Boeing 727-100C	2	PW JT8D-7B
Boeing 727-200F	2	PW JT8D-15
DC-8F-50	2	PW JT3D-3B
DC-8-62F	1	PW JT3D-7
DC-8-61F	1	PW JT3D-3B

SHORTS SD3-60 VARIANT 300

TRANS INTERNATIONAL EXPRESS
(TIE Aviation)

IATA: 5B **ICAO:** BAP **IATA/ARC:** 336 **RADIO:** Big Apple

---

CONTACTS:

Mail	Telephone/Fax
PO Box 300994	Admin: +1 718 244 8909
Jamaica, NY 11430	Fax: +1 718 244 8912
	Res: 1 888 244 8922

Internet: www.iflytie.com

OPERATION:

Type: Scheduled/charter passenger
Cities Served: ALB BGM JFK

HISTORY/STRUCTURE:

Founded: 1993
Start Date: November 20, 1998
President: Joseph Manor
Ownership: Privately held

FLEET:

Type	No	Seats	Engines
PA-23 Aztec	1	Y5	LY IO-540-C4B5
PA-31-350 Chieftain	1	Y9	LY TIO-540-J2BD
Shorts 360 (300)	2	Y36	PWC PT6A-67B

AIRBUS A320-231

TRANSMERIDIAN AIRLINES

IATA: T9   **ICAO**: TRZ   **IATA/ARC**: none   **RADIO**: Transmeridian

CONTACTS:

Mail
680 Thornton Way
Lithia Springs, GA 30122

Telephone/Fax
Admin: +1 770 732 6900
Fax: +1 770 732 6956

Internet: www.transmeridian-airlines.com

OPERATION:
Type: Charter passenger

HISTORY/STRUCTURE:
Founded: 1995
Start Date: October 30, 1995
President/CEO: Glen Schaub
Ownership: Prime Air (subsidiary of Translift Airways)

FLEET:

Type	No	Seats	Engines
Boeing 727-200 (Advanced)	2	Y160	PW JT8D-15/-15A
Airbus A320-231	3	Y180	IAE V2500-A1

Several additional A320s leased in during northern winter season
One additional A320 operated for DaimlerChrysler in corporate shuttle service

EMBRAER EMB-145ER

TRANS STATES AIRLINES

IATA: 9N   **ICAO**: LOF   **IATA/ARC**: 414   **RADIO**: Waterski

CONTACTS:

Mail	Telephone/Fax
9275 Genaire Drive	Admin: +1 314 895 8700
St Louis, MO 63134	Fax: +1 314 895 1040
	Res: 1 800 221 2000
Internet: www.transstates.net	1 800 428 4322

OPERATION:

Type: Scheduled passenger

Cities Served: ALB ALO BDL BHM BMI BOS BRL BWI CGI CHA CMI COU DCA DEC EVV FAT FWA GRR GSO JFK JLN LAX LEX MEM MLI MRY MSN MWA ORD ORF PAH PHL PIA PIT PSP RDU RIC ROA ROC SAN SBA SBN SFO SGF SMF SPI STL SUX TBN TRI UIN XNA

All service operated as Delta Connection, TW Express, United Express, or US Airways Express using only DL (6800-6999), TW (7000-7799), UA (5775-5799), & US (4700-4824) flight numbers. Additional code-shares on West Coast with Alaska and Northwest

FFP: Delta SkyMiles, TWA Frequent Flight Bonus, United Mileage Plus, US Airways Dividend Miles

HISTORY/STRUCTURE:

Founded: May 1982 (as Resort Air)

Start Date: April 1983

President/CEO: Hulas Kanodia

Ownership: Privately held

FLEET:

Type	No	Seats	Engines
Jetstream Super 31	35	Y19	GA TPE331-12UAR-701H
Jetstream 41	25	Y30	GA TPE331-14HR-805H
ATR42-300	5	Y48	PWC PW120
ATR72-200	3	Y68	PWC PW124B
EMB-145ER	5	Y50	AE3007A
Ordered			
EMB-145	10 plus 10 options		

BOEING 767-300 (ER)

TRANS WORLD AIRLINES

IATA: TW   **ICAO**: TWA   **IATA/ARC**: 015   **RADIO**: TWA

CONTACTS:

Mail
One City Centre
515 North 6th Street
St Louis, MO 63101

Internet: www.twa.com

Telephone/Fax
Admin: +1 314 589 3000
Fax: +1 314 589 3129
Res: 1 800 221 2000
PR: +1 314 589 3213/3214

OPERATION:

Type: Scheduled passenger
Cities Served: US: ABQ ATL AUS BDL BNA BOS BWI CID CLE CLT CMH COS
CVG DAY DCA DEN DFW DSM DTW ELP EWR FLL FSD HNL IAD IAH ICT
IND JAN JAX JFK LAS LAX LGA LIT LNK MCI MCO MDT MFE MIA MKE MLI
MSP MSY OKC OMA ONT ORD ORF PBI PDX PHL PHX PIT PWM RDU RIC
RNO RSW SAN SAT SDF SEA SFO SGF SHV SJC SLC SMF SNA SRQ STL
TPA TUL TYS (seasonal: ANC HDN) **Canada:** YYZ (seasonal: YVR)
Caribbean: AUA MBJ NAS POP SDQ SJU (seasonal: SXM) **México:** CUN MEX
(seasonal: PVR ZIH) **Europe:** BCN CDG FCO LGW LIS MAD MXP
Asia: RUH TLV **Africa:** CAI
Code-Share: Royal Air Maroc, Royal Jordanian, Trans States Airlines
FFP: TWA Frequent Flight Bonus

HISTORY/STRUCTURE:

Founded: July 16, 1925 (as Western Air Express)
Start Date: October 1, 1930 (as Transcontinental & Western Air)
Chairman/CEO: Gerald Gitner
President: Bill Compton
Ownership: Publicly traded company (AMEX: TWA)

McDONNELL DOUGLAS DC-9-83 (MD-83)

FLEET:

Type	No	Seats	Engines
DC-9-15	5	F12Y65	PW JT8D-7B
DC-9-30	35	F16Y84	PW JT8D-9A/-15
DC-9-40	3	F16Y84	PW JT8D-15
DC-9-50	9	F20Y95	PW JT8D-17
MD-82	40	F20Y120	PW JT8D-217A/-217C
MD-83	41	F20Y122	PW JT8D-217C/-219
Boeing 727-200	22	F20Y125	PW JT8D9A/-15
Boeing 757-200	18	F22Y158 or F16Y158	PW2037
Boeing 767-200	12	F24Y168	PW JT9D-7R4D
Boeing 767-300	4	F30Y203	PW4060

Ordered	
Boeing 717-200	50 plus 50 options
Airbus A318	50
Airbus A320 (Family)	25 plus 75 options
MD-83	22
Boeing 757-200	9 plus 16 options
Boeing 767-300	4
Airbus A330-300	10 plus 20 options

NOTES:

BOEING 777-200 (ER)

UNITED AIRLINES

IATA: UA   **ICAO**: UAL   **IATA/ARC**: 016   **RADIO**: United

---

CONTACTS:

Mail	**Telephone/Fax**
PO Box 66100	Admin: +1 847 700 4000
Chicago, IL 60666	Fax: +1 847 700 2214
	Res: 1 800 241 6522
Internet: www.ual.com	PR: +1 847 700 5501

OPERATION:

Type: Scheduled passenger/cargo

Cities Served: US: ABE ALB ANC ATL AUS BDL BHM BIL BNA BOI BOS BTV BUF BUR BWI CID CLE CLT CMH COS CVG DAY DCA DEN DFW DSM DTW EUG EWR FLL FSD GEG GRR GSO HNL HPN IAD IAH ICT IND JAC JAX JFK KOA LAS LAX LGA LIH LNK MBS MCI MCO MDT MEM MFR MHT MIA MKE MRY MSN MSP MSY MTJ OAK OGG OKC OMA ONT ORD ORF PBI PDX PHL PHX PIT PSP PVD PWM RDU RIC RNO ROC RSW SAN SAT SDF SEA SFO SJC SLC SMF SNA STL SYR TPA TUL TUS TYS (seasonal: EGE HDN MTJ) **Canada:** YVR YYC YYZ **Caribbean:** SJU STT **México/Central America/South America:** CCS EZE GIG GRU GUA LIM MEX MVD SAL SCL SJO **Europe:** AMS BRU CDG DUS FRA LHR MUC MXP STR ZRH **Asia:** BKK DEL HKG KIX MNL NRT PEK SEL SHA SIN TPE **Oceania:** AKL MEL SYD

Global Alliance: Star

Code-Share: Aeromar, Air ALM, Air Canada, Air New Zealand, All Nippon, Aloha, Ansett Australia, British Midland, Cayman, Emirates, Gulfstream International, Lufthansa, Mexicana, SAS, Saudi Arabian, THAI International, Trans States, United Express (Air Wisconsin, Atlantic Coast, Great·Lakes, Trans States, UFS), VARIG

FFP: Mileage Plus

HISTORY/STRUCTURE:

Founded: February 1, 1929 (as United Aircraft & Transport Corp)

Start Date: July 1, 1931

Chairman/CEO: James Goodwin

President: Rono Dutta

Ownership: UAL Corp (55% employees) (NYSE: UAL)

BOEING 737-500

FLEET:

Type	No	Seats	Engines
Boeing 737-200	24	F8Y101	PW JT8D-7B/-9A/-17
Boeing 737-500	57	F8Y100 or F8Y108	CFM56-3C1
Boeing 737-300	101	F8Y118 or F8Y126	CFM56-3C1
Airbus A319-100	27	F8Y118	IAE V2522-A5
Airbus A320-200	54	F12Y132	IAE V2527-A5
Boeing 727-200 (Advanced)	75	F12Y135	PW JT8D-15
Boeing 757-200	98	F24Y164	PW2037
Boeing 767-200	19	F10C33Y126 or F10C32Y126	PW JT9D-7R4D
Boeing 767-300ER	28	F10C38Y158 or F34Y217	PW4060/PW4052
DC-10-10	9	F28Y259 or F38Y260	GE CF6-6D
DC-10-30CF	4	F38Y260	GE CF6-50C2
DC-10-30F	4	Freighter	GE CF6-50C2
Boeing 777-200	37	F12C49Y231 or F12C49Y217	PW4077
Boeing 747-100	4	F42Y408	PW JT9D-7A
Boeing 747-200	7	F18C79Y272	PW JT9D-7J
Boeing 747-400	41	F36C123Y142 or F18C80Y320 or F18C84Y270	PW4056
Ordered			
Airbus A319-100	20		
Airbus A320-200	32		
Boeing 767-300ER	9		
Boeing 777-200	15		
Boeing 747-400	10		

UNITED FEEDER SERVICE

IATA: U2   **ICAO:** UFS   **IATA/ARC:** none   **RADIO:** Feeder Flight

---

CONTACTS:

Mail
9275 Genaire Drive
St Louis, MO 63134

Telephone/Fax
Admin: +1 314 895 4500
Fax: +1 314 895 1040
Res: 1 800 241 6522

OPERATION:

Type: Scheduled passenger
Cities Served: AZO CAK CWA FWA GRB ORD PIA SBN YNG
All service operated as United Express using only UA flight numbers
(5700-5774)
FFP: United Mileage Plus

HISTORY/STRUCTURE:

Founded: 1993
Start Date: September 1993
President/CEO: Hulas Kanodia
Ownership: UFS Inc (associated with Trans States Airlines)

FLEET:

Type	No	Seats	Engines
BAe ATP	9	Y64	PWC PW126A

UNITED PARCEL SERVICE (UPS)

IATA: 5X **ICAO**: UPS **IATA/ARC**: 406 **RADIO**: UPS

CONTACTS:

Mail
1400 North Hurstbourne Parkway
Louisville, KY 40223

Internet: www.ups.com

Telephone/Fax
Admin: +1 502 329 6500
Fax: +1 502 329 6550
Info: 1 800 743 5877
PR: +1 502 329 6522

OPERATION:

Type: Scheduled cargo/charter passenger
Cities Served: US: ABQ ABY ALB ANC ATL AUS BDL BFI BFM BHM BIL BOI
BOS BUF BUR BWI CAE CID CLE CLT DEC DEN DFW DSM DTW EFD ELP
EWR FAT FSD FWA GEG GSO HNL IAD ICT JAN JAX JFK KOA LAN LAS LAX
LCK LFT LGB LIT MCI MCO MDT MEM MHR MHT MIA MKE MSP MSY OAK
OGG OKC OMA ONT ORD PBI PDX PHL PHX PIE PIT RDU RFD RIC RNO
ROA RSW SAN SAT SDF SGF SHV SJC SLC SNA STL SWF SYR TUL TYS
Canada: YHM YMX YVR YYC **Caribbean:** SJU **México/Central America/
South America:** CCS GDL MEX SJO VCP **Europe:** CDG CGN EMA MAD NUE
STN VIE **Asia:** BOM HKG KIX KUL MNL NRT PEN SEL SHJ TPE **Oceania:**
NAN SYD
Other cities served by contract air carriers
Code-Share: Nippon Cargo Airlines

HISTORY/STRUCTURE:

Founded: 1907
Start Date: February 1, 1988
President: Thomas H Weidemeyer
Ownership: Trust of 18,000 current and former managers

NORTH AMERICAN AIRLINES HANDBOOK – USA 111

BOEING 757-200PF

USA

FLEET:

Type	No	Engines
Boeing 727-100C (QF)	38	RR Tay 651-54
Boeing 727-100QC (QF)	6	RR Tay 651-54
Boeing 727-200F (Advanced)	8	PW JT8D-15/-17
Boeing 757-200PF	73	PW2040 (35) or RR RB211-535E4
DC-8-71/-73F	49	CFM56-2
Boeing 767-300F (ER)	27	GE CF6-80C2B7F
Boeing 747-100F	12	PW JT9D-7A
Boring 747-200F	4	PW JT9D-7Q

Ordered		
Airbus A300F4-605R	30	
Boeing 757-200PF	2	
Boeing 767-300F (ER)	3	

NOTES:

AIRBUS A320-214

US AIRWAYS

IATA: US   **ICAO**: USA   **IATA/ARC**: 037   **RADIO**: USAir

---

CONTACTS:

Mail
2345 Crystal Drive
Arlington, VA 22227

Internet: www.usairways.com

Telephone/Fax
Admin: +1 703 418 7000
Fax: +1 703 418 5437
Res: 1 800 428 4322
PR: +1 703 418 5100

OPERATION:

Type: Scheduled passenger
Cities Served: US: ABE ALB ATL AVL BDL BGM BHM BNA BOS BTV BUF
BWI CAE CAK CHA CHS CLE CLT CMH CRW DAY DCA DEN DFW DTW ELM
ERI EWR FAY FLL GRR GSO GSP HPN HSV IAD IAH ILM IND ITH JAX LAS
LAX LEX LGA MCI MCO MDT MDW MEM MHT MIA MKE MSP MSY MYR ORD
ORF PHL PHX PIT PNS PVD PWM RDU RIC ROA ROC RSW SAN SAV SBN
SDF SEA SFO SNA SRQ STL SWF SYR TOL TPA TRI TYS (seasonal: LWB)
Canada: YOW YUL YYZ **Caribbean:** BDA GCM MBJ NAS SJU STT STX SXM
México: CUN **Europe:** AMS CDG FCO FRA LGW MAD MUC
Code-Share: Deutsche BA, Trans States, US Airways Express (Air Midwest,
Allegheny, Chautauqua, Commutair, Mesa, Piedmont, PSA), US Airways Shuttle
FFP: US Airways Dividend Miles

HISTORY/STRUCTURE:

Founded: March 5, 1937 (as All American Airways)
Start Date: August 12, 1940
CEO: Stephen M Wolf
President: Rakesh Gangwal
Ownership: US Airways Group (NYSE: USAirGp)

BOEING 737-200 (ADVANCED)

FLEET:

Type	No	Seats	Engines
Fokker 100	40	F12Y85	RR Tay 650-15
DC-9-30	47	F12Y88	PW JT8D-7B/-9A
Boeing 737-200	64	F12Y96 or Y118	PW JT8D-9A/-15/-15A
Boeing 737-300	85	F12Y114	CFM56-3B1/-3B2
Boeing 737-400	54	F12Y132	CFM56-3B2
MD-81/-82	31	F8Y133	PW JT8D-217
Airbus A319-100	10	F12Y108	CFM56-5B6
Airbus A320-200	2	F16Y126	CFM56-5B4
Boeing 757-200	34	F24Y158	RR RB211-535E4
Boeing 767-200ER	12	C24Y192	GE CF6-80C2B2
Ordered			
Airbus A319/A320/A321	228 plus 160 options		
Airbus A330-300	14 plus 16 options		

NOTES:

BOEING 727-200

US AIRWAYS SHUTTLE

IATA: TB   **ICAO**: USS   **IATA/ARC**: 857   **RADIO**: US Shuttle

CONTACTS:

Mail
PO Box 710616
Flushing, NY 11371-0616

Telephone/Fax
Admin: +1 718 397 6000
Fax: +1 718 397 6040

Internet: www.usairways.com

OPERATION:

Type: Scheduled passenger
Cities Served: BOS DCA IAD LGA
Code-Share: US Airways
FFP: US Airways Dividend Miles

HISTORY/STRUCTURE:

Founded: October 1988 (as The Trump Shuttle)
Start Date: June 8, 1989
President: Micheal Sheeringa
Ownership: US Airways Group

FLEET:

Type	No	Seats	Engines
Boeing 727-200	12	Y163	PW JT8D-7B/-9A

DASSAULT FALCON 20D (C)

USA JET

IATA: U7   **ICAO**: JUS   **IATA/ARC**: none   **RADIO**: Jet USA

CONTACTS:

Mail
2064 D Street
Belleville, MI 48111-1278

Internet: www.activeaero.com

Telephone/Fax
Admin: +1 734 483 7833
Fax: +1 734 480 0014
Res: 1 800 877 5387

OPERATION:

Type: Charter cargo
Areas Served: Primarily *ad hoc* charters in US

HISTORY/STRUCTURE:

Founded: 1994
Start Date: December 1994
President: Robert Phelps
Ownership: Active Aero Group

FLEET:

Type	No	Engines
Falcon 20	13	GE CF700-2D2
DC-9-15F	8	PW JT8D-7B

BOEING 737-200

VANGUARD AIRLINES

IATA: NJ   **ICAO**: VGD   **IATA/ARC**: 311   **RADIO**: Vanguard Air

---

CONTACTS:

Mail	Telephone/Fax
7000 Squibb Road	Admin: +1 913 789 1388
Third Floor	Fax: +1 913 789 1779
Mission, KS 66202	Res: 1 800 826 4827

Internet: www.flyvanguard.com

OPERATION:

Type: Scheduled passenger
Cities Served: ATL BUF CVG DEN DFW MCI MDW MSP MYR PIT

HISTORY/STRUCTURE:

Founded: 1994
Start Date: December 2, 1994
President/CEO: Robert Spane
Ownership: Publicly traded company (NASDAQ: VNGD)

FLEET:

Type	No	Seats	Engines
Boeing 737-200	12	Y120	PW JT8D-7/-9A/-15
Ordered			
Boeing 737-200	3		

BOEING 737-200 (ADVANCED)

WINAIR

IATA: none   **ICAO:** WNA   **IATA/ARC:** none   **RADIO:** Winair

---

CONTACTS:

Mail
303 North 2370 West
Salt Lake City, UT 84116

Internet: www.flywinair.com

Telephone/Fax
Admin: +1 801 519 2100
Fax: +1 801 519 2200
Res: 1 800 494 6247

OPERATION:
Type: Charter/scheduled charter passenger
Cities Served: LAS LGB SLC SMF

HISTORY/STRUCTURE:
Founded: 1997
Start Date: January 25, 1998
President: Larry Gelwix
Ownership: Privately held

FLEET:

Type	No	Seats	Engines
Boeing 737-200 (Advanced)	2	Y122	PW JT8D-15A

McDONNELL DOUGLAS MD-11

WORLD AIRWAYS

IATA: WO   **ICAO**: WOA   **IATA/ARC:** 468   **RADIO:** World

---

CONTACTS:

Mail
13873 Park Center Road, Suite 490
Herndon, VA 20171

Telephone/Fax
Admin: +1 703 834 9200
Fax: +1 703 834 9437

Internet: www.worldair.com

OPERATION:

Type: Charter passenger/cargo
Areas Served: Worldwide. Major contracts include sub-services for Malaysia, Garuda, and charters for US military

---

HISTORY/STRUCTURE:

Founded: March 29, 1948
Start Date: May 1948
CEO: Hollis Harris
President: Gil Morgan
Ownership: WorldCorp, MHS Berhad, public (NASDAQ: WLDA)

FLEET:

Type	No	Seats	Engines
DC-10-30	3	Y380	GE CF6-50C2
DC-10-30F	1	Freighter	GE CF6-50C2
MD-11	5	Y409	PW4460/4462
MD-11F	3	Y410/Freighter	PW4460/4462

LOCKHEED 188A (F) ELECTRA

ZANTOP INTERNATIONAL AIRLINES

IATA: none   **ICAO:** ZAN   **IATA/ARC:** none   **RADIO:** Zantop

CONTACTS:

Mail
840 Willow Run Airport
Ypsilanti, MI 48198-0840

Telephone/Fax
Admin: +1 734 485 8900
Fax: +1 734 485 4813

OPERATION:
Type: Charter cargo

HISTORY/STRUCTURE:
Founded: 1972
Start Date: 1972
President: Duane Zantop
Ownership: Zantop family

FLEET:

Type	No	Engines
Lockheed Electra	6	AN 501-D13A
DC-8F-54	1	PW JT3D-3B

US Addenda

AIR CARGO CARRIERS (UN/SNC/Night Cargo) 4984 South Howell Avenue, Milwaukee, WI 53207; +1 414 482 1711, Fax: +1 414 482 2038, www.aircar.com, James Germek. Charter cargo. 1 x Merlin II, 13 x Shorts 330, 7 x Shorts 360

AIR CARGO EXPRESS (3K/FXG/Cargo Express) PO Box 61680, Fairbanks, AK 99706; +1 907 474 3488, Fax: +1 907 474 3002, Robert Everts. Scheduled/charter cargo. 1 x C-46, 7 x DC-6

AIR CARGO MASTERS (RNR/Runner) 701 West National Guard Drive, Sioux Falls, SD 57104; +1 605 373 0303, Fax: +1 605 373 9595, www.aircargomasters.com, Dennis Sherrill. Charter passenger/cargo. 2 x Navajo, 1 x MU-2, 3 x Metro, 2 x Beech 1900

AIR CHARTER EXPRESS (FRG/Freight Runners) 1901 East Layton Avenue, Milwaukee, WI 53207; +1 414 744 5525, Fax: +1 414 744 4850, Charles Zens. Charter passenger/cargo. 2 x Cessna 207, 5 x Cessna 402, 5 x Beech 99

AIR ST THOMAS (ZP/STT/315/Paradise) PO Box 302788, St Thomas, USVI 00803; +1 340 776 2722, Fax: +1 340 776 2992, Res: 1 800 522 3084, www.airstthomas.com, Paul Wikander. Scheduled passenger. 3 x Piper Aztec, 1 x Cessna 402

AIR SUNSHINE (YI/RSI/806/Air Sunshine) PO Box 22237, Ft Lauderdale, FL 33335; +1 954 434 8900, Fax: +1 954 359 8229, Res: 1 800 327 8900, www.airsunshine.com, Allen Adili. Scheduled passenger. 8 x Cessna 402, 2 x Bandeirante

AIR TAHOMA (HMA/Tahoma) 5469 Kearney Villa Road, Suite 201, San Diego, CA 92123; +1 760 560 4544, Fax: +1 760 560 0664, Noel Rude. Charter cargo. 4 x Convair 580

AIR VEGAS (6V/VGA/389/Air Vegas) PO Box 11008, Las Vegas, NV 89111; +1 702 736 3599, Fax: +1 702 896 2906, Res: 1 800 255 7474, www.airvegas.com, James Petty. Scheduled/charter passenger. 1 x Bonanza, 9 x Beech 99

ALASKA CENTRAL EXPRESS (KO/AER/Ace Air) 3551 Postmark Drive, Anchorage, AK 99502; +1 907 245 0253, Fax: +1 907 245 0243, www.acepak.com, Dale Erickson. Scheduled/charter cargo. 3 x Cessna 207, 4 x Beech 1900

ALASKA SEAPLANE SERVICE (UI) 8995 Yandukin Drive, Juneau, AK 99801; +1 907 789 7880, Fax: +1 907 789 3221, Res: 1 800 478 3360, www.akseaplanes.com, Craig Loken. Scheduled/charter passenger. 2 x Cessna 180, 1 x Cessna 207, 2 x Beaver

ALPINE AIR (5A/AIP/511/Alpine Air) 3450 West Mike Jense Parkway, Provo, UT 84601; +1 801 373 1508, Fax: +1 801 373 3781, www.alpineairaviation.com, Bill Distefano. Charter passenger/cargo. 1 x Piper Lance, 3 x Navajo Chieftain, 2 x Cheyenne III, 12 x Beech 99

AMERIFLIGHT (AMF/Amflight) 4700 Empire Avenue, Hangar 1, Burbank, CA 91505; +1 818 980 5005, Fax: +1 818 980 5018, Gary Richards. Charter cargo. 20 x Piper Lance, 11 x Cessna 402, 42 x Navajo/Chieftain, 1 x King Air 200, 40 x Beech 99, 5 x Lear 35, 11 x Beech 1900, 35 x Metro III/Expediter

AMERISTAR JET CHARTER (AJI/Ameristar) PO Box 700548, Dallas, TX 7537-0548; +1 972 248 2478, Fax: +1 972 931 6011, 1 800 368 5387, www.ameristarjet.com, Tom Wachendorfer. Charter passenger/cargo. 1 x JetRanger, 1 x King Air, 17 x Lear 24/25, 12 x Falcon 20

ARCTIC CIRCLE AIR SERVICE (5F/CIR/Air Arctic) PO Box 190228, Anchorage, AK 99706; +1 907 243 1380, Fax: +1 907 248 0042, Ervin Terry. Scheduled/charter passenger/cargo. 1 x Piper Lance, 1 x Cessna 206, 5 x Cessna 207, 2 x Cessna 402, 1 x Cessna 208, 3 x Skyvan

ARCTIC TRANSPORTATION SERVICES (7S/RCT/Arctic Transport) 5701 Silverado Way, Unit L, Anchorage, AK 99518; +1 907 562 2227, Fax: +1 907 563 8177, John Eckels. Scheduled/charter passenger/cargo. 10 x Cessna 207, 1 x Cessna 402, 2 x Beech 18, 2 x CASA 212

AUSTIN EXPRESS (7V/TXX/342/Cowboy) 1901 East 51st Street, Suite 210, Austin, TX 78723; +1 512 236 1100, Fax: +1 512 236 1112, www.austinexpress.com, Jim Echols. Scheduled passenger. 1 x Metro III

BAKER AVIATION (8Q/BAJ/Baker Aviation) PO Box 708, Kotzebue, AK 99752; +1 907 442 3108, Fax: +1 907 442 3018, Marjorie Baker. Scheduled/charter passenger. 1 x Cessna 206, 2 x Cessna 207, 3 x Cessna 208, 2 x King Air, 1 x Navajo, 1 x Chieftain

BARON AVIATION SERVICES (BVN/Show Me) PO Box 518, Vichy, MO 65580; +1 573 299 4744, Fax: +1 573 299 4272, Charles Schmidt. Charter cargo/operates FedEx Feeder flights in Midwest. 40 x Cessna 208

BASLER AIRLINES (BFC/Basler) PO Box 2305, Oshkosh, WI 54903; +1 920 236 7827, Fax: +1 920 236 7833, www.baslerturbo.com, Rod McNeal. Charter cargo. 1 x Beech 58 Baron, 5 x DC-3, 1 x DC-3 Turbo Express

BEMIDJI AIRLINES (CH/BMJ/872/Bemidji) PO Box 624, Bemidji, MN 56601; +1 218 751 1880, Fax: +1 218 759 3552, Res: 1 800 332 7133, Larry Diffley. Scheduled passenger, charter cargo. 3 x Piper Aztec, 2 x Baron, 11 x Queen Air, 1 x King Air, 5 x Beech 99

BERING AIR (8E/BRG/Bering Air) PO Box 1650, Nome, AK 99762; +1 907 443 5422, Fax: +1 907 443 5919, Res: +1 907 443 4564, www.beringair.com, James Rowe. Scheduled passenger/cargo. 4 x Cessna 207, 5 x Navajo Chieftain/T-1020, 2 x Cessna 208B, 4 x Beech 18, 1 x CATPASS 250, 1 x CASA 212

BERRY AVIATION (BYA/Berry) 1807 Airport Drive, San Marcos, TX 78666; +1 512 353 2379, Fax: +1 512 353 2593, Harry Berry III. Charter passenger/cargo. 16 x Merlin IV/Metro II/Metro III

BIGHORN AIRWAYS (BHR/Bighorn Air) PO Box 4037, Sheridan, WY 82801; +1 307 672 3421, Fax: +1 307 674 4468, Bob Eisele. Charter cargo. 2 x Navajo Chieftain, 4 x Dornier 228, 2 x CASA 212

BUSINESS AIRFREIGHT (RLR/Rattler) RR 1 Box 1104, Bennington, VT 05201-9711; +1 802 447 2111, Fax: +1 802 447 2116, www.airnow.com, David Corey. Charter cargo. 3 x Aztec, 2 x Cessna 404, 12 x Bandeirante

BUSINESS AVIATION COURIER (DKT/Dakota) 3501 Aviation Avenue, Sioux Falls, SD 57104; +1 605 336-7791, Fax: +1 605 336 8009, Dale Froelich. Charter passenger/cargo. 5 x Cessna 310, 10 x Cessna 402, 1 x Cessna 404, 1 x Metro III

C&M AIRWAYS 7335 Boeing Drive, El Paso, TX 79925; +1 915 779 3097, Fax: +1 915 779 0479, Bradley Cryderman. Charter cargo. 6 x Convair 640

CAMAI AIR (R9/CAM/451/Air Camai) PO Box 221188, Bethel, AK 99522; +1 907 543 4040, Fax: +1 907 543 2369, Don King. Charter passenger, scheduled cargo. 1 x Cherokee 6, 1 x Cessna 206, 5 x Cessna 207.

CAPE AIR (9K/KAP/306/Cair) 660 Barnstable Road, Hyannis, MA 02601; +1 508 790 3122, Fax: +1 508 778 1870, Res: 1 800 352 0714, www.flycapeair.com, Dan Wolf. Scheduled/charter passenger. 48 x Cessna 402C

CAPE SMYTHE AIR SERVICE (6C/CMY/879/Cape Smythe Air) PO Box 549, Barrow, AK 99723; +1 907 852 8333, Fax: +1 907 852 8332, csas-ome/capesmythe.com, Grant Thompson. Scheduled passenger/cargo. 2 x Cessna 185, 7 x Cessna 207, 3 x Navajo Chieftain, 1 x Cheyenne IIXL, 6 x Piper T-1040, 3 x Beech 99

CHERRY-AIR (CCY/Cherry-Air) 4584 Claire Chennault Road, Dallas, TX 75248, +1 972 248 1707, Fax: +1 972 380 0046, Kenneth Donaldson. 5 x Lear 24/25, 4 x Falcon 20

COASTAL AIR TRANSPORT (DQ/CXT/457/Coastal) PO Box 2985, Christiansted, St Croix, USVI 00822; +1 340 773 6862, Michael Foster. Scheduled passenger. 1 x Cessna 402

COMMUNITY AIR 1100 Hastings Road, Suite A, Ukiah, CA 95482; +1 707 463 1245, Fax: +1 707 473 5888, www.communityair.com, John Mayginnes. Scheduled passenger. 2 x Pilatus PC-12

CONTRACT AIR CARGO (TSU/Trans Auto) 6860 South Service Drive, Waterford, MI 48327; +1 248 666 9630, Fax: +1 248 666 9614, Alan Ross. Charter cargo. 2 x Convair 340, 8 x Convair 580, 2 x Convair 5800

CORPORATE AIR (CPT/Air Spur) PO Box 30998, Billings, MT 59107; +1 406 248 1541, Fax: +1 406 248 7670, Linda Overstreet. Charter cargo/operates FedEx Feeder flights in Rocky Mountain area. 2 x Commander 500, 6 x Commander 680, 43 x Cessna 208, 6 x Beech 99, 4 x Twin Otter, 1 x Beech 200, 3 x Beech 1900, 1 x Falcon 20, 3 x Shorts 330, 2 x Shorts 360, 2 x Brasilia

CSA AIR (IRO/Iron Air) 260 Riverhills Road, Iron Mountain, MI 49801; +1 906 774 3101, Fax: +1 906 779 1304, Harold Ross. Charter cargo/operates FedEx Feeder flights in Midwest. 21 x Cessna 208

DESERT AIR TRANSPORT 180 North 2400 West, Salt Lake City, UT 84116, +1 801 699 9496, Fax: +1 801 539 1923, Dennis Gladwin. Charter cargo. 3 x DC-3

EMPIRE AIRLINES (EM/CFS/464/Empire Air) 2115 Government Way, Coeur d'Alene, ID 83814; +1 208 667 5400, Fax: +1 208 667 8787, www.empirecoe.com, Mel Spelde. Charter cargo/operates FedEx Feeder flights in western US. 39 x Cessna 208, 3 x Shorts 360, 1 x Faichilld F-27F, 10 x Fokker F27

40-MILE AIR (Q5/MLA/519/Mile Air) PO Box 539, Tok, AK 99780, +1 907 883 5191, Fax: +1 907 883 5194 (main office); PO Box 61116, Fairbanks, AK 99706, +1 907 474 0018, Fax: +1 907 474 8954, Charles Warbelow. Scheduled/charter passenger. 4 x Piper Super Cub, 1 x Cessna 185, 3 x Cessna 206, 2 x Cessna 207, 1 x Piper Navajo, 1 x Otter

FOUR STAR AIR CARGO (HK/FSC/861/Four Star) One Air Cargo Center, St Thomas, VI 00802; +1 340 776 4702, Fax: +1 340 776 5536, Francis J McCarthy Jr. Scheduled/charter cargo. 1 x Aztec, 5 x DC-3, 3 x Convair 440

F S AIR SERVICE (Y7) 6121 South Airpark Place, Anchorage, AK 99502; +1 907 248 9595, Fax: +1 907 243 1247, www.fsair.com, Cindy Aldridge. Scheduled/charter passenger, scheduled cargo. 1 x Seneca, 3 x Navajo Chieftain, 1 x Metro III, 2 x Volpar Turboliner, 1 x CASA 212, 1 x Lear 35

GENAVCO AIR CARGO 38 Lagoon Drive, Honolulu, HI 96819, +1 808 836 3467, Harry Clark. Charter cargo. 2 x DC-3

GRAND AIRE EXPRESS (GAE/Grand Express) PO Box 721, Monroe, MI 48161; +1 734 457 1730, Fax: +1 734 457 1733, Tahir Cheema. Charter cargo. 4 x Aerostar, 8 x Metro II, 4 x Hansa Jet, 12 x Falcon 20

GRAND CANYON AIRLINES (CVU/Canyon View) PO Box 3038, Grand Canyon, AZ 86023; +1 520 638 2463, Fax: +1 520 638 9461, www.grandcanyonairlines.com, John Seibold. Charter passenger. 6 x DHC-6-300

GRANT AVIATION (GS) PO Box 89, Emmonak, AK 99581; +1 907 949 1715, Fax: +1 907 949 1226 Res, 1 800 478 1944, www.flygrant.com, Mark Hiekel. Scheduled/charter passenger, charter cargo. 1 x Cessna 172, 7 x Cessna 207, 4 x Navajo Chieftain, 1 x Beech 18, 1 x King Air 200

HAGELAND AVIATION SERVICES (H6) PO Box 195, St Mary's, AK 99658; +1 907 438 2246, Fax: +1 907 438 2435, Res: +1 907 543 3900, www.hageland.com, Ron Tweto. Scheduled/charter passenger, charter cargo. 1 x Cessna 185, 1 x Cessna 206, 16 x Cessna 207, 2 x Cessna 402, 1 x Reims-Cessna F406, 4 x Cessna 208, 1 x Commander 690, 1 x Beech 18

HAINES AIRWAYS (7A) PO Box 470, Haines, AK 99827; +1 907 766 2646, Fax: +1 907 766 2780, haines.ak.us/hainesair/, Ken Brewer. Scheduled/charter passenger. 4 x Cherokee Six, 4 x Navajo Chieftain

HARBOR AIRLINES (HB/HAR/495/Harbor) 1302 26th Avenue NW, Gig Harbor, WA 98335; +1 253 851 2381, Fax: +1 253 851 2365, Res: 1 800 359 3220, www.harborair.com, Randall Brink. Scheduled/charter passenger. 8 x Navajo Chieftain/T-1020, 4 x Cessna 208

ILIAMNA AIR TAXI (LS/IAR/Iliamna Air) PO Box 109, Iliamna, AK 99606; +1 907 571 1248, Fax: +1 907 571 1244, Timothy LaPorte. Scheduled/charter passenger. 1 x Cessna 185, 1 x Bonanza, 1 x Cessna 206, 2 x Cessna 207, 1 x Baron, 4 x Beaver, 1 x Chieftain, 1 x Cessna 208

ISLAND AIRLINES (IS/ISA/Island) PO Box 2495, Nantucket, MA 02584; +1 508 228 7575, Fax: +1 508 228 6645, Res: 1 800 248 7779, www.nantucket.net/trans/islandair, William McGrath. Scheduled/charter passenger. 6 x Cessna 402C, 1 x Beech H18

ISLAND EXPRESS (2S/SDY/579/Sandy Isle) 750 SW 34th Street, Ft Lauderdale, FL 33315; +1 954 359 0383, Fax: +1 954 359 7944, Res: +1 954 359 0380, Ruben Acrich. Scheduled passenger. 3 x Cessna 402

KENMORE AIR (M5) PO Box 82064, Kenmore, WA 98028-0064; +1 425 486 1257, Fax: +1 425 486 5471, Res: 1 800 543 9595, www.kenmoreair.com, Robert Munro. Scheduled/charter passenger. 4 x Cessna 180, 10 x Beaver/Turbo Beaver, 5 x Turbo Otter

KEY LIME AIR (LYM/Key Lime) 7625 South Peoria, Suite D15, Englewood, CO 80112; +1 303 768 9626, Fax: +1 303 768 8144. Charter cargo. 4 x Chieftain, 1 x Cessna 404, 5 x Metro, 1 x Lear 25

KITTY HAWK CHARTERS (KFS/Kalitta) 842 Willow Run Airport, Ypsilanti, MI 48197; +1 734 484 7376, Fax: +1 734 487 6420, www.kha.com, Louis Birurakis. Charter passenger/cargo. 3 x MU-2, 11 x Volpar Turboliner, 19 x Lear 23/24/25, 2 x Lear 35/36, 1 x Falcon 20

LAB FLYING SERVICE (JF/LAB/510/Lab) PO Box 272, Haines, AK 99827; +1 907 766 2222, Fax: +1 907 766 2734, Res: 1 800 426 0543, haines.ak.us/lab/, Layton Bennett. Scheduled/charter passenger. 1 x Cherokee, 2 x Helio Courier, 22 x Cherokee Six/Lance/Saratoga, 4 x Piper Seneca, 1 x Aerostar, 2 x Islander, 3 x Navajo Chieftain

LARRY'S FLYING SERVICE (J6) 3822 University Avenue, Fairbanks, AK 99709; +1 907 474 9169, Fax: +1 907 474 8815, www.larrysflying.com, Lawrence Chenaille. Scheduled/charter passenger. 5 x Cherokee Six/Lance/Saratoga, 1 x Cessna 206, 2 x Cessna 207, 1 x Islander, 3 x Navajo Chieftain, 1 x King Air

LAS VEGAS AIRLINES (6G/540) PO Box 15105, Las Vegas, NV 89114; +1 702 647 3056, Fax: +1 702 647 1846, Res: 1 800 634 6851, www.lasvegasair.com, Donald Donohue Jr. Scheduled/charter passenger. 6 x Navajo Chieftain

LORAIR 1002 East Valencia Road, Tucson, AZ 85706; +1 520 294 3136, Fax: +1 520 294 3145, Walter Cole. Charter passenger. 2 x Boeing 737-200

LYNX AIR INTERNATIONAL 5500 NW 21st Terrace, Hangar 24, Ft Lauderdale, FL 33309; +1 954 772 9808, Fax: +1 954 772 1141, www.lynxair.com, Linda Tonks. Charter passenger/cargo. 3 x Metro III

MARTINAIRE (MRA/Martinaire US) 8030 Aviation Place, Suite 2000, Dallas, TX 75235; +1 214 358 5858, Fax: +1 214 350 7979, C Edward Acker. Charter cargo. 20 x Cessna 208B, 8 x Dornier 228, 7 x Metro III

MERLIN EXPRESS (MEI/Avalon) 9623 West Terminal Drive, San Antonio, TX 78216; +1 210 824 2313, Fax: +1 210 826 4415, Ron Stoltz. Charter passenger/cargo. 3 x Metro II, 23 Metro III/Merlin IVC

MIAMI VALLEY AVIATION (OWL/Night Owl) 1707 Run Way, Middletown, OH 45042; +1 937 422 5050, Fax: +1 937 422 1494, Terrence Hogan. Charter passenger/cargo. 3 x Aztec, 3 x Beech 18, 2 x Lear 25, 1 x Lear 35, 6 x DC-3, 1 x Falcon 20

MID-ATLANTIC FREIGHT (MDC/Night Ship) PO Box 35048, Greensboro, NC 27425; +1 336 668 7474, Fax: +1 336 668 3906, Don Godwin. Charter cargo. 19 x Cessna 208

MOUNTAIN AIR CARGO (MTN/Mountain) PO Box 488, Denver, NC 28037; +1 828 464 8741, Fax: +1 828 465 5281, www.mtaircargo.com, William Simpson. Charter cargo/operates FedEx Feeder services in eastern US, Puerto Rico, and Dominican Republic. 44 x Cessna 208, 2 x Shorts 330, 1 x Shorts 360, 22 x F27

MURRAY AVIATION (MUA/Murray Air) 835 Willow Run Airport, Ypsilanti, MI 48918; +1 734 484 4800, Fax: +1 734 484 4875, www.murray-aviation.com, Preston Murray. Charter passenger/cargo. 1 x MU-2, 3 x King Air 90, 1 x Jetstream 31, 4 x CASA 212

NEW ENGLAND AIRLINES (EJ/NEA/367/New England) 56 Airport Road, Westerly, RI 02891; +1 401 596 2460, Fax: +1 401 596 7366, Res: 1 800 243 2460, www.block-island.com/nea/, William Bendokas. Scheduled/charter passenger. 4 x Cherokee Six, 2 x Islander

NORTH STAR AIR CARGO 4340 Satellite Drive, Anchorage, AK 99502; +1 907 243 4340, Fax: +1 907 243 6545, Baxter Snider. Charter cargo. 1 x Cessna 337, 1 x Commander 681, 5 x Skyvan

OLSON AIR SERVICE (4B) PO Box 142, Nome, AK 99762; +1 907 443 3625, Fax: +1 907 443 5017, Margaret Olson. Scheduled/charter passenger. 2 x Cessna 207, 2 x Cessna 402

PACIFIC WINGS (LW/NMI/568/Tsunami) PO Box 930, Paia, HI 96779; +1 808 873 0877, Fax: +1 808 873 7920, Res: 1 888 575 4546, Myron Caplan. Scheduled/charter passenger. 1 x Cessna 172, 5 x Cessna 402

PRO MECH AIR (P9) 1515 Tongass Avenue, Ketchikan, AK 99901; +1 907 225 3845, Fax: +1 907 247 3875, Res: 1 800 860 3845, Kevin Hack. Scheduled/charter passenger. 3 x Cessna 185, 5 x Beaver

REDWING AIRWAYS (RX/RWG/Redwing Air) RR 6, Kirksville Municipal Airport, Kirksville, MO 63501; +1 660 665 6607, Fax: +1 660 665 6061, James Kelsey. 1 x Cessna 401, 1 x Cessna 402, 1 x Queen Air

RENOWN AVIATION (RGS/Renown) 3940 Mitchell Road, Santa Maria, CA 93455; +1 805 934 2484, Fax: +1 805 934 2007, Terry Cedar. Charter passenger/cargo. 3 x Convair 240, 1 x Convair 340, 3 x Convair 440, 3 x Convair 580, 6 x Lockheed Electra

RHOADES INTERNATIONAL (RDS/Rhoades Express) Columbus Municipal Airport, Columbus, IN 47203; +1 812 372 1819, Fax: +1 812 378 2708, Jack Rhoades. Charter cargo. 1 x Cessna 310, 1 x Cessna 402, 2 x Cessna 421, 2 x Lear 25, 1 x DC-3, 2 x Convair 240, 1 x Convair 340, 1 x Convair 440, 2 x Convair 640

RIO GRANDE AIR (GRN/Grande) PO Box 2219, El Prado, NM 87526, +1 505 758 4995, Fax: +1 505 751 4038. Timothy Woodridge. Scheduled/charter passenger. 1 x Cessna 207, 1 x Cessna 208

ROYAL AIR FREIGHT (RAX/Air Royal) 2141 Airport Road, Waterford, MI 48327; +1 248 666 3070, Fax: +1 248 666 4719, William Kostich. Charter cargo. 6 x Cessna 310, 2 x Cessna 402, 1 x Navajo Chieftain, 3 x MU-2, 5 x Bandeirante, 7 x Lear 23/24/25

SABER CARGO AIRLINES (SBR/854/Freighter) 4825 Express Drive, Charlotte, NC 28219; +1 704 359 8456, Fax: +1 704 359 8275, Michael Dockery. Charter cargo. 1 x Cessna 402, 1 x Beech 18, 5 x DC-3

SIERRA WEST AIRLINES (PKW/Platinum West) 4511 W Cheyenne, #401, Las Vegas, NV 89030; +1 702 638 0144, Fax: +1 702 638 0156, Deborah Robinson. Charter passenger/cargo. 4 x Metro II/Merlin IV, 6 x Metro III/Merlin IVC, 1 x Lear 23, 1 x Lear 25, 2 x Lear 35, 1 x Westwind

SKAGWAY AIR SERVICE (7J/SGY/493/Skagway Air) PO Box 357, Skagway, AK 99840; +1 907 983 2218, Fax: +1 907 983 2948, www.ptialaska.net/~skagair, Ben Lingle. Scheduled/charter passenger. 7 x Cherokee Six/Saratoga, 1 x Piper Seneca, 1 x Islander, 1 x Piper T-1020

SKYWAY ENTERPRISES (SKZ/Skyway Inc) 3031 West Patrick, Kissimmee, FL 34741; +1 407 847 9095, Fax: +1 407 932 4600, Thomas Loumakin. Charter passenger/cargo. 2 x Lear 23, 2 x Shorts 330, 3 x Shorts 360

SOUTHCENTRAL AIR (XE/SCA/301/South Central) 135 Granite Point Court, Kenai, AK 99611; +1 907 283 7064, Fax: +1 907 283 3678, James Munson. Charter passenger, scheduled/charter cargo. 1 x Cherokee Six, 1 x Islander, 3 x Navajo Chieftain, 3 x Piper T-1040, 1 x DC-3

SPECIALIZED TRANSPORT INTERNATIONAL 1383 General Aviation Drive, Melbourne, FL 32935; +1 321 235 0209, Fax: +1 321 235 0039, Marc Oltramare. Charter cargo. 3 x CASA 212

SUBURBAN AIR FREIGHT (SUB/Sub Air) PO Box 19090, Omaha, NE 68119; +1 402 344 4100, Fax: +1 402 344 0415, James Armstrong. Charter cargo. 1 x Commander 500, 9 x Commander 680FL, 5 x Cessna 402, 4 x Beech 99, 2 x Beech 1900

SUNRISE AIRLINES (OQ/AAE/876/Arizona) 2635 East Airlane, Phoenix, AZ 85034; +1 602 244 1851, Res: 1 800 245 8668, Fax: +1 602 244 8308, www.sunriseair.net, Clifford Langness. Scheduled/charter passenger, charter cargo. 4 x Cessna 206, 5 x Cessna 210, 1 x Piper Seneca, 14 Cessna 207/T207, 3 x Cessna 208, 1 x CATPASS 250, 6 x Jetstream 31. Freight services operated as Express Air

SUPERIOR AVIATION (AB/HKA/Spend Air) Ford Airport, Iron Mountain, MI 49801; +1 906 774 0400, Fax: +1 906 774 1645, www.superioraviation.com, Stephen Van Beek. Charter passenger/cargo. 1 x Beech Travel Air, 4 x Cessna 402, 12 x Cessna 404, 1 x Cessna 441, 11 x Cessna 208, 12 Metro II/Merlin IV, 2 x Metro III

TANANA AIR SERVICE (4E/TNR/Tan Air) 3730 University Avenue South, Fairbanks, AK 99709; +1 907 474 0301, Fax: +1 907 474 9311, www.fairbankschamber.org/tanair.htm, Harold Esmailka. Scheduled/charter passenger. 7 x Cherokee Six/Lance, 1 x Navajo.

TAQUAN AIR SERVICE (K3/TQN/Taquan) 1007 Water Street, Ketchikan, AK 99901; +1 907 225 1010, Fax: +1 907 247 9031, Res: 1 800 770 8800, www.taquanair.com, Jerry Scudero. Scheduled/charter passenger. 3 x Cessna 185, 2 x Cessna 206, 1 x Cessna 207, 1 x Cessna 208, 11 x Beaver, 6 x Otter/Turbo Otter, 2 x Jetstream 32EP

TATONDUK FLYING SERVICE (3K) PO Box 61680, Fairbanks, AK 99706; +1 907 474 4697, Fax: +1 907 474 4687, Robert Everts. Scheduled/charter passenger. 2 x Cessna 206, 4 x Piper Lance, 2 x Cessna 208

TELFORD AVIATION (TEL/Telford) 100 Airport Road, Waterville, ME 04901; +1 207 872 5555, Fax: +1 207 872 6794, www.telfordaviation.com, Telford Allen. Charter passenger/cargo. 1 x JetRanger, 1 x Cessna 206, 1 x Piper Malibu, 1 x Navajo Chieftain, 7 x Cessna 208, 2 x Beech 99, 1 x King Air F90, 2 x BAe 125-700A

TMC AIRLINES (TMM/Willow Run) 836 Willow Run Airport, Ypsilanti, MI 48198-0836; +1 734 485 8907, Fax: +1 734 481 9182, James Loree. Charter cargo. 3 x Electra, 2 x DC-8F-55.

TOLAIR SERVICES (TOL/Tol Air) PO Box 37670, San Juan, PR 00937-0670; +1 787 791 5235, Fax: +1 787 791 8385, Jorge Toledo. Charter passenger/cargo. 1 x Cherokee Six, 1 x Beech Baron, 1 x Aerostar, 3 x Cessna 402, 3 x Beech 18, 4 x DC-3, 1 x Convair 240

TRANS FLORIDA AIRLINES (TFA/Trans Florida) PO Box 10150, Daytona Beach, FL 32120-0150; +1 904 252 3053, Fax: +1 904 252 0037, Robert Willman. Charter passenger/cargo. 6 x Convair 240

VIEQUES AIR LINK (VI/VES/381/Vieques) PO Box 487, Vieques, PR 00765; +1 787 741 3266, Fax: +1 787 741 0545, Osvaldo Gonzalez. Scheduled/charter passenger. 6 x Islander, 3 x Trislander

WARBELOW'S AIR VENTURES (4W/VNA/Ventairc) 3750 University Avenue South, Fairbanks, AK 99709; +1 907 474 0518, Fax: +1 907 479 5054, www.akpub.com/fhwag/warbe.html, Arthur Warbelow. Scheduled/charter passenger. 2 x Super Cub, 1 x Cessna 206, 2 x Cessna 207, 9 x Navajo Chieftain

WEST ISLE AIR (7Y/590) 4000 Airport Road, Suite A, Anacortes, WA 98221; +1 360 293 4691, Fax: +1 360 293 0517, Res: 1 800 474 4434, www.rockisland.com/~wia/, James Burton. Scheduled/charter passenger. 3 x Cessna 172, 4 x Cessna 206, 2 x Cessna 207

WESTAIR (PCM/Pac Valley) 5005 East Anderson, Fresno, CA 93727; +1 559 454 7843, Fax: +1 559 454 7840, Beth Wood. Charter cargo./operates FedEx Feeder flights in western USA. 35 x Cessna 208, 2 x Metro III

WESTERN AIR EXPRESS (WAE/Western Express) 815 Park Boulevard, Suite 330, Boise, ID 83712; +1 208 343 2756, Fax: +1 208 343 2878, www.westernairexpress.com, Eugene Heil. Charter cargo. 3 x Cessna 402, 3 x Metro II

WIGGINS AIRWAYS (WIG/Wiggins) One Garside Way, Manchester, NH 03108; +1 603 644 5132, Fax: +1 603 644 5505, David Ladd. Charter cargo./operates FedEx Feeder flights in northeastern US. 32 x Cessna 208, 7 x Beech 99, 1 x Twin Otter

WINGS OF ALASKA (K5/WAK/Wings Alaska) 8421 Livingston Way, Juneau, AK 99801; +1 907 789 9863, Fax: +1 907 789 2021, www.alaskaone.com, Robert Jacobsen. Scheduled/charter passenger. 4 x Cessna 206, 3 x Cessna 207, 6 x Beaver, 5 x Otter, 2 x Cessna 208

WRIGHT AIR SERVICE (8V) PO Box 60142, Fairbanks, AK 99706; +1 907 474 0502, Fax: +1 907 474 0375, Robert Bursiel. Scheduled/charter passenger. 1 x Cessna 185, 2 x Helio Courier, 1 x Cessna 206, 1 x Bonanza, 2 x Cessna 207, 4 x Navajo/Chieftain, 4 x Cessna 208B

YUTE AIR ALASKA (4Y/UYA/Yute Air) PO Box 190169, Anchorage, AK 99519; +1 907 243 1011, Fax: +1 907 243 2811, www.yuteair.com, Jeff Pereira. Scheduled/charter passenger, charter cargo. 1 x Cherokee Six, 3 x Cessna 206, 10 x Cessna 207, 2 x Chieftain, 2 x Cessna 208

NOTES:

BRITISH AEROSPACE 146-200A

AIR BC

IATA: ZX   **ICAO:** ABL   **IATA/ARC:** 742   **RADIO:** Air Coach

CONTACTS:

Mail
5520 Miller Road
Richmond, BC
V7B 1L9

Telephone/Fax
Admin: +1 604 224 2675
Fax: +1 604 244 2675
Res: 1 800 663 3721
Res: 1 800 332 1080
Res: 1 800 776 3000 (US)

OPERATION:

Type: Scheduled/charter passenger
Cities Served: Canada: YCD YCG YDQ YEG YLL YLW YMM YQL YQR YQT YQZ YVR YWG YWL YXC YXE YXH YXJ YXS YXT YYC YYF YYJ **US:** DEN PDX SEA
All service operated as Air Canada Connector using only AC flight numbers (1500-1684, 1811-1899, 1936-1999)
FFP: Aeroplan

HISTORY/STRUCTURE:

Founded: 1980
Start Date: December 1980
Chairman: Mel Cooper
CEO: Al Thompson
Ownership: Air Canada (100%)

FLEET:

Type	No	Seats	Engines
DHC-8-100	9	Y37	PWC PW120A
DHC-8-300	6	Y50	PWC PW123
BAe 146-200A	5	J8Y68	ALF502R-5

BOEING 747-400

AIR CANADA

IATA: AC   **ICAO:** ACA   **IATA/ARC:** 014   **RADIO:** Air Canada

CONTACTS:

Mail
PO Box 14000
7373 Cote Vertu W
St Laurent, QC H4Y 1H4
Internet: www.aircanada.ca

Telephone/Fax
Admin: +1 514 422 5000
Fax: +1 514 422 7741
Res: 1 800 776 3000 (US)

OPERATION:

Type: Scheduled/charter passenger/cargo
Cities Served: Canada: YEG YFC YHZ YOW YQB YQM YQR YQT YSJ YUL YVR YWG YXE YYC YYG YYT YYZ (seasonal: YYJ) **US:** ATL BNA BOS CLE CLT DCA DEN EWR FLL HNL IAD IAH LAS LAX LGA MCI MCO MIA MKE MSP MSY OGG ORD PHX PIT RDU SAN SEA SFO SJC STL TPA (seasonal: PBI RSW) **Caribbean:** ANU BDA BGI FDF KIN MBJ NAS PAP POS PTP UVF **Europe:** CDG CPH FRA GLA LHR MAN ZRH **Asia:** HKG KIX SEL TLV TPE
Global Alliance: Star
Code-Share: Air Canada Connector (Air Alliance, Air BC, Air Nova, Air Ontario), Air Creebec, Air Jamaica, Air New Zealand, Alberta Citylink, All Nippon Airways, Ansett Australia, British Midland, Central Mountain Air, EVA Air, First Air, Lufthansa, Mexicana, Royal Jordanian, SAS, Singapore Airlines, THAI International, United Airlines/United Express, VARIG
FFP: Aeroplan

HISTORY/STRUCTURE:

Founded: April 10, 1937 (as Trans-Canada Air Lines)
Start Date: September 1, 1937
Chairman: John F Fraser
Vice chairman/CEO: R Lamar Durrett
President/COO: Robert A Milton
Ownership: Publicly held (75% Canadian)

AIRBUS A340-313

FLEET:

Type	No	Seats	Engines
Canadair RJ 100ER	25	Y50	GE CF34-3A1/3B1
DC-9-32	17	J12Y80	PW JT8D-7A
Airbus A319-100	35	J16Y96	CFM56-5A4
Airbus A320-200	34	J24Y108	CFM56-5A1
Boeing 767-200	9	J36Y159	PW JT9D-7R4D
Boeing 767-200ER	14	J25Y152	PW JT9D-7R4D
Boeing 767-300ER	6	J35Y168	PW4060
Airbus A340-300	12	J32Y252	CFM56-5C4
Boeing 747-400 (SCD)	3	J37Y262	PW4056
Ordered			
Canadair RJ 100ER	24 options		
Airbus A320-200	6		
Airbus A330-300	6 plus 20 options		
Airbus A340-300	2 plus 8 options		
Airbus A340-500	2 plus 10 options		
Airbus A340-600	3		

NOTES:

RAYTHEON BEECH 1900D

AIR CREEBEC

IATA: YN   **ICAO:** CRQ   **IATA/ARC:** 219   **RADIO:** Cree

CONTACTS:

Mail	Telephone/Fax
PO Box 430	Admin: +1 819 825 8355
Val D'Or, QC	Fax: +1 819 825 0885
J9P 4P4	Res: 1 800 567 6567
Email: info@aircreebec.ca	
Internet: www.aircreebec.ca	

OPERATION:

Type: Scheduled/charter passenger/cargo
Cities Served: YAT YFA YGL YHF YKQ YKU YMO YMT YNC YNS YPO YPX YRJ YTS YUL YVO YYU ZEM ZKE
Code-Share: Air Canada
FFP: Aeroplan

HISTORY/STRUCTURE:

Founded: June 1982
Start Date: July 1, 1982
CEO: Albert Diamond
Ownership: Privately held (100% Cree)

FLEET:

Type	No	Seats	Engines
EMB-110P1 Bandeirante	2	Y14	PWC PT6A-34
Beech 1900D	2	Y18	PWC PT6A-67D
DHC-8-100	1	Y37	PWC PW120A
HS 748-2A	3	Y32/Combi	RR Dart 534-2

AIR GEORGIAN
(dba ONTARIO REGIONAL AIRLINES)

IATA: none   **ICAO:** GGN   **IATA/ARC:** none   **RADIO:** none

CONTACTS:

Mail
2450 Derry Road East
Mississauga, ON L5S 1B2

Telephone/Fax
Admin: +1 905 676 2555
Fax: +1 905 676 1151
Res: 1 800 665 1177

Internet: www.ontarioregional.com

OPERATION:

Type: Scheduled/charter passenger
Cities Served: YQG YSB YYZ YZR
All scheduled service (with Beech 1900Ds) operated as Canadian Partner
using only CP flight numbers (2600-2678)
FFP: Canadian Plus

HISTORY/STRUCTURE:

Founded: 1994
Start Date: 1994
CEO: Paul Mulrooney
Ownership: Western Regional Airlines (100%)

FLEET:

Type	No	Seats	Engines
Cessna 208	1	Y9/Freighter	PWC PT6A-114
Cessna 208B	6	Y9/Freighter	PWC PT6A-114/114A
King Air F90	1	Y9	PWC PT6A-135
Beech 1900C-1	1	Y19	PWC PT6A-65B
Beech 1900D	10	Y19	PWC PT6D-67D

Also wet-leases Beech 1900Ds to Inter-Canadien. Plans to establish Western
Regional Airlines at Calgary as a Canadian Partner

CANADA

BRITISH AEROSPACE (HAWKER SIDDELEY) 748 SERIES 2A (SCD)

AIR INUIT (Air Iniut (1985))

IATA: 3H   **ICAO:** AIE   **IATA/ARC:** 875   **RADIO:** Air Inuit

---

CONTACTS:

Mail	Telephone/Fax
1985 55 Avenue	Admin: +1 514 636 9445
Dorval, QC	Fax: +1 514 636 8916
H9P 1G9	Res: 1 800 361 2965
	Res: 1 800 661 5850 (charters)

Internet: www.sae.ca/abt/airinuit

OPERATION:

Type: Scheduled/charter passenger/cargo
Cities Served: AKV XGR YGL YGW YKG YPH YPJ YPX YQB YSK YTE YTQ YUD YUL YVP YWB YZG
All scheduled service operated using only First Air flight numbers (7F0400-0499)
Code-Share: First Air

HISTORY/STRUCTURE:

Founded: 1979
Start Date: 1979
CEO: Mark T Gordon
Ownership: Makivik Corporation

FLEET:

Type	No	Seats	Engines
DHC-6-300	4	Y18	PWC PT6A-27
DHC-8-100	1	Y37	PWC PW120A
HS 748-2A	4	Y40/Freighter	RR Dart 534-2
Convair 580 (operated on behalf of Hydro-Québec)	5	Y36/Y49	AN 501-D13

AIR LABRADOR (LABRADOR AIRWAYS)

IATA: WJ **ICAO:** LAL **IATA/ARC:** 927 **RADIO:** Lab Air

CONTACTS:

Mail
PO Box 13485
Station A
St John's, NF A0P 1S0
Email: sales@airlabrador.com
Internet: www.airlabrador.com

Telephone/Fax
Admin: +1 709 896 6730
Fax: +1 709 896 8905
Res: 1 800 665 1177

OPERATION:

Type: Scheduled/charter passenger/cargo
Cities Served: YAY YBI YBX YDF YDI YDP YFX YHA YHG YHO YMH YMN YPD YQX YRF YRG YSO YWK YYR YYT
Some scheduled service operated as Canadian Partner using CP flight numbers in 2400 range
FFP: Canadian Plus

HISTORY/STRUCTURE:

Founded: 1948 (as Newfoundland Airways)
Start Date: 1948
CEO: Roger W Pike
Ownership: Provincial Investments (Pike family)

FLEET:

Type	No	Seats	Engines
DHC-3T Otter	1	Y9/Freighter	PWC PT6A-135A
Cessna 208B	1	Freighter	PWC PT6A-114
Beech 1900D	4	Y18	PWC PT6A-67D
DHC-6-100	1	Y19/Combi	PWC PT6A-20
DHC-6-300	3	Y19/Combi	PWC PT6A-27
Shorts 330 (300)	1	Freighter	PWC PT6A-45R

CANADA

AIR MONTRÉAL

IATA: F8   **ICAO:** AMO   **IATA/ARC:** none   **RADIO:** none

CONTACTS:

Mail	Telephone/Fax
10105 Ryan Ave	Admin: +1 514 631 2111
Dorval, QC	Fax: 1 888 561 3943
H9P 1A2	Res: 1 888 631 2111
Email: jfay@airmontreal.com	
Internet: www.airmontreal.com	

OPERATION:

Type: Scheduled/charter passenger/cargo
Cities Served: YBC YBG YGR YND YQB YUL YUY YVB YVO YYY YZV

HISTORY/STRUCTURE:

Founded: 1982
Start Date: 1982
CEO: Peter L Overing
Ownership: The Troppus Group

FLEET:

Type	No	Seats	Engines
Metro II	1	Y19	GA TPE331-3UW-303G
Metro III	4	Y19	GA TPE331-11U-611G/612G
Ordered			
EMB-120ER Brasilia	5		

BRITISH AEROSPACE (HAWKER SIDDELEY) 748 SERIES 2A

AIR NORTH (Air North Charter & Training)

IATA: 4N **ICAO:** ANT **IATA/ARC:** 287 **RADIO:** Air North

---

CONTACTS:

Mail	Telephone/Fax
PO Box 4998	Admin: +1 867 668 2228
Whitehorse, YT	Fax: +1 867 668 6224
Y1A 4S2	Res: 1 800 661 0407 (Canada)
Email: airnorth@yknet.yk.ca	Res: 1 800 764 0407 (US)
Internet: www.airnorth.yk.net	

OPERATION:

Type: Scheduled/charter passenger/cargo
Cities Served: YDA YEV YOC YXY **US:** FAI JNU

HISTORY/STRUCTURE:

Founded: 1977
Start Date: January 17, 1986 (scheduled)
CEO: Joseph T Sparling
Ownership: Joseph T Sparling & Thomas Wood

FLEET:

Type	No	Seats	Engines
PA-31-310 Navajo	1	Y/Combi	LY TIO-540-A1A
Queen Air B80	1	Y/Combi	LY IGSO-540-A1D
Beech 99	1	Y14	PWC PT6A-20
DC-3	4	Y/Combi	PW R-1830
HS 748-2A	2	Y44	RR Dart 534-2

BRITISH AEROSPACE 146-200A

AIR NOVA

IATA: QK   **ICAO:** ARN   **IATA/ARC:** 983   **RADIO:** Nova

CONTACTS:

Mail
310 Goudey Drive
Enfield, NS
B2T 1E4

Internet: www.airnova.ca

Telephone/Fax
Admin: +1 902 873 5000
Fax:　　+1 902 873 4901
PR:　　 +1 902 873 5094
Res:　　1 800 776 3000 (US)

OPERATION:

Type: Scheduled/charter passenger/cargo
Cities Served: Canada: YDF YFC YHZ YOW YQB YQI YQM YQX YQY YSJ YSL YUL YWK YYG YYR YYT ZBF **US:** BOS EWR (seasonal: PWM)
All service operated as Air Canada Connector using only AC flight numbers (8100-8299, 8700-8899)
FFP: Aeroplan

HISTORY/STRUCTURE:

Founded: 1985
Start Date: July 14, 1986
Chairman: Angus Bruneau
CEO: Joseph Randell
Ownership: Air Canada (100%)

FLEET:

Type	No	Seats	Engines
Beech 1900D	5	Y18	PWC PT6A-67D
DHC-8-100	24	Y37/Freighter	PWC PW120A
BAe 146-200A	5	J10Y67	ALF502R-5

NOTES: Air Nova and Air Ontario are expected to be merged

BOMBARDIER DHC-8-301 DASH 8

AIR ONTARIO

IATA: GX **ICAO:** ONT **IATA/ARC:** 368 **RADIO:** Ontario

CONTACTS:

Mail
1000 Air Ontario Drive
London, ON
N5V 3S4

Telephone/Fax
Admin: +1 519 453 8440
Fax: +1 519 453 0063
PR: +1 519 659 5696
Res: 1 800 776 3000 (US)

OPERATION:

Type: Scheduled/charter passenger/cargo
Cities Served: Canada: YAM YGK YOW YQG YSB YTS YTZ YUL YXU YYB YYZ YZR **US:** ABE BDL BWI CLE CMH MDT PVD RIC SYR
All service operated as Air Canada Connector using only AC flight numbers (1200-1499)
FFP: Aeroplan

HISTORY/STRUCTURE:

Founded: 1961
Start Date: 1961
Chairman: David R McCamus
CEO: Joseph Randell
Ownership: Air Canada (100%)

FLEET:

Type	No	Seats	Engines
DHC-8-100	21	Y37	PWC PW120A
DHC-8-300	6	Y50	PWC PW123

NOTES: Air Ontario and Air Nova are expected to be merged

BRITISH AEROSPACE 3112 JETSTREAM 31

AIR SASK AVIATION (1991)
(La Ronge Aviation dba)

IATA: 7W   **ICAO:** ASK   **IATA/ARC:** 094   **RADIO:** Air Sask

CONTACTS:

Mail	Telephone/Fax
PO Box 320	Admin: +1 306 425 2382
La Ronge, SK	Fax: +1 306 425 2455
S0J 1L0	Res: 1 800 665 7275

OPERATION:
Type: Scheduled/charter passenger
Cities Served: YBE YNL YPA YQR YSF YVC YXE ZFD ZWL
Code-Share: Northern Dene Airways

HISTORY/STRUCTURE:
Founded: 1958
Start Date: 1958
CEO: Pat Campling Sr
Ownership: Privately held

FLEET:

Type	No	Seats	Engines
Cessna A185F	3	Y3	CO IO-520-D
DHC-2 Beaver	2	Y4	PW R-985
Baron E55	1	Y5	CO IO-470-L
Baron 58	1	Y5	CO IO-520-C
PA-31-310 Navajo	2	Y7	LY TIO-540-A2C
PA-31-325 Navajo	1	Y7	LY TIO-540-F2BD
PA-31-350 Chieftain	2	Y9	LY TIO-540-J2BD
DHC-3 Otter	1	Y8	PW R-1340
MU-2N	1	Y9	GA TPE331-5-252M
Beech 99A	1	Y14	PWC PT6A-27
DHC-6-100	2	Y14	PWC PT6A-20
Jetstream 31	4	Y19	GA TPE331-10UG-513H

AIRBUS A330-242

AIR TRANSAT

IATA: TS **ICAO:** TSC **IATA/ARC:** 649 **RADIO:** Transat

CONTACTS:

Mail
11600 Cargo Road A1
Mirabel International Airport
Mirabel, QC J7N 1G9

Telephone/Fax
Admin: +1 514 476 1011
Fax: +1 514 476 1038
Res: 1 800 470 1011

Internet: www.airtransat.com

OPERATION:

Type: Scheduled/charter passenger
Cities Served: Canada (some seasonal): YHZ YMX YQB YQX YUL YVR YYC YYT YYZ **Caribbean** (some seasonal): CMW HOG SCU VRA **Europe** (some seasonal): CDG LYS MRS NTE
Additional seasonal service to points in the US, Caribbean, Europe, and Asia
Code-Share: ALITALIA

HISTORY/STRUCTURE:

Founded: December 1986
Start Date: November 14, 1987
CEO: Philippe Sureau
Ownership: Transat AT

FLEET:

Type	No	Seats	Engines
Boeing 737-400	2	Y170	CFM56-3C1
(leased from Virgin Express in northern winter season)			
Boeing 757-200	5	Y228	RR RB211-535E4
L-1011-1	2	J19Y343	RR RB211-22B
L-1011-100	3	J19Y343	RR RB211-22B
L-1011-150	5	J19Y343	RR RB211-22B
L-1011-500	4	J19Y296	RR RB211-524B4-02
Airbus A330-200	2	J21Y336	RR Trent 772B-60
Ordered			
Airbus A330-300	1		

BRITISH AEROSPACE 3212 JETSTREAM 32EP

ALBERTA CITYLINK (Palliser Air)

IATA: none   **ICAO:** ABK   **IATA/ARC:** none   **RADIO:** none

CONTACTS:

Mail	Telephone/Fax
PO Box 161	Admin: +1 403 527 3328
Medicine Hat, AB	Fax: +1 403 527 4721
T1A 7E8	Res: 1 800 332 1080

OPERATION:
Type: Scheduled passenger
Cities Served: YLL YPR YQL YQU YXC YXH YYC
All service operated as Air Canada Connector using only AC flight numbers
Code-Share: Air BC, Air Canada
FFP: Aeroplan

HISTORY/STRUCTURE:
Founded: 1996
Start Date: July 15, 1996
CEO: Les N Little
Ownership: Bar XH Aviation

FLEET:

Type	No	Seats	Engines
Jetstream 31	2	Y19	GA TPE331-10UG-513H
Jetstream 32EP	2	Y19	GA TPE331-12UAR-705H

BOEING 727-200 (ADVANCED) (F)

ALL CANADA EXPRESS

IATA: none　　**ICAO:** CNX　　**IATA/ARC:** none　　**RADIO:** Canex

CONTACTS:

Mail
#603 50 Burnhamthorpe Road West
Mississauga, ON
L5B 3C2
Email: ace@allcanada.com

Telephone/Fax
Admin: +1 905 896 7175
Fax:　　+1 905 896 1549

OPERATION:

Type: Charter cargo
Cities Served: Canada: YHM YMX YVR YWG YYC YYZ **US:** CVG TOL
Operates service on behalf of UPS, DHL, BAX

HISTORY/STRUCTURE:

Founded: 1992
Start Date: 1992
CEO: John MacKenzie
Ownership: Privately held

FLEET:

Type	No	Engines
Boeing 727-100F	2	PW JT8D-7B
Boeing 727-200F (Advanced)	6	PW JT8D-17R

RAYTHEON BEECH 1900D

ATHABASKA AIRWAYS

IATA: 9T   **ICAO:** ABS   **IATA/ARC:** 909   **RADIO:** Athabaska

CONTACTS:

Mail
PO Box 100
Prince Albert, SK
S6V 5R4
Email: ken.g.9t@skisympatica.ca
Internet: www.thechamberofcom.com/athabaskaair

Telephone/Fax
Admin: +1 306 764 1404
Fax: +1 306 763 1313
Res: 1 800 667 9356

OPERATION:

Type: Scheduled/charter passenger/cargo
Cities Served: YBE YBR YEG YNL YPA YQR YSF YVC YWG YXE ZFD ZWL

HISTORY/STRUCTURE:

Founded: 1955
Start Date: 1955
CEO: Floyd R Glass
Ownership: Floyd Glass

FLEET:

Type	No	Seats	Engines
Cessna A185F	3		CO IO-520-D
DHC-2 Beaver	1		PW R-985
Cessna 310R	2		CO IO-520-M
Cessna 402C	2		CO TSIO-520-VB
Piper PA-31-350	3		LY TIO-540-J2BD
DHC-3 Otter	1		PW R-1340
DHC-3T Otter	1		PWC PT6A-135A
Cessna 441	1		GA TPE331-8-401S
DHC-6-100/200	3		PWC PT6A-20
Beech 1900C-1	2	Y19	PWC PT6A-65B
Beech 1900D	4	Y18	PWC PT6A-67B

CANADA

PILATUS PC-12/45

BEARSKIN AIRLINES (Bearskin Lake Air Service)

IATA: JV   **ICAO:** BLS   **IATA/ARC:** 632   **RADIO:** Bearskin

CONTACTS:

Mail
1475 W Walsh Street
Thunder Bay, ON
P7E 4X6

Email: rhell@bearskin-airlines.com
Internet: www.bearskin-airlines.com

Telephone/Fax
Admin: +1 807 577 1141
Fax: +1 807 474 2610
Res: 1 800 465 5039 (Canada)
Res: 1 800 465 2327 (US)
Cargo: 1 800 465 5039

OPERATION:

Type: Scheduled/charter passenger/cargo
Cities Served: KIF MSA SUR WNN XBE XKS YAC YAG YAM YAX YER YFH YFO YGQ YHD YHP YLH YNO YOW YPL YPM YQD YQK YQT YRL YSB YTL YTS YVZ YWG YWP YXL YXZ YYB ZPB ZRJ ZSJ
FFP: Aeroplan

HISTORY/STRUCTURE:

Founded: July 17, 1963 (as Bearskin Lake Air Service)
Start Date: 1963
CEO: Harvey Friesen
Ownership: Privately held

FLEET:

Type	No	Seats	Engines
PA-23 Aztec	2	Y3	LY IO-540-C4B5
Pilatus PC-12	4	Y9	PWC PT6A-67B
King Air A100	4	Y12	PWC PT6A-28
Beech 99	5	Y14	PWC PT6A-28
Metro III	5	Y19	GA TPE331-11U-612G
Metro 23	2	Y19	GA TPE331 12U 701G

CANADA

SAAB 340B*PLUS*

CALM AIR INTERNATIONAL

IATA: MO   **ICAO:** CAV   **IATA/ARC:** 622   **RADIO:** Calm Air

CONTACTS:

Mail	Telephone/Fax
90 Thompson Drive	Admin: +1 204 778 6471
Thompson, MB	Fax: +1 204 778 6954
R8N 1Y8	Res: 1 800 839 2256
Email: calmair@gatewest.net	
Internet: www.calmair.com	

OPERATION:

Type: Scheduled/charter passenger
Cities Served: KES XLB XPK XSI XTL YBK YBT YCS YEK YFO YGX YHD YLR YQD YQR YQT YRT YTH YUT YWG YXE YXN YYL YZS ZJG ZTM
All service operated as Canadian Partner using CP flight numbers (1550-1599)
FFP: Canadian Plus

HISTORY/STRUCTURE:

Founded: 1962
Start Date: 1976 (scheduled service)
CEO: C Arnold L Morberg
Ownership: Canadian Regional Airlines (45%)

FLEET:

Type	No	Seats	Engines
PA-31-350 Chieftain	1	Y9	LY TIO-540-J2BD
DHC-6-100/200	2	Y19	PWC PT6A-20
SAAB 340B	4	Y34	GE CT7-9B
HS 748-2A/2B	6	Y36	RR Dart 534-2/536-2

AIRBUS A330-202

CANADA 3000 AIRLINES

IATA: 2T   **ICAO:** CMM   **IATA/ARC:** 570   **RADIO:** Elite

CONTACTS:

Mail
27 Fasken Drive
Toronto, ON
M9W 1K6

Email: travel@canada3000.com
Internet: www.canada3000.com

Telephone/Fax
Admin: +1 416 674 0257
Fax: +1 416 674 0256
Res: 1 888 226 3000
Res: +1 416 259 1118

OPERATION:

Type: Scheduled/charter passenger
Cities Served: Canada: YEG YHZ YMX YOW YQM YVR YWG YXY YYC YYJ YYT YYZ US (many seasonal): ANC FLL FMY HNL KOA LAS LAX LIH MCO OGG PHX PSP RSW TPA México (many seasonal): ACA CUN CZM HUX MZT PVR SJD ZIH ZLO Caribbean (many seasonal): ANU GCM GND MBJ NAS POP SDQ SKB UVF Central America (seasonal): BZE LIR SJO Europe (many seasonal): AMS BFS BHX BRU CDG CPH DUB DUS EMA GLA HAM KEF LGW MAN MUC PDL SNN STR VIE Oceania (seasonal): NAN SYD
Operates on behalf of Canada 3000 Holidays, Sunquest, and Alba Tours

HISTORY/STRUCTURE:

Founded: April 1, 1988 (as Air 2000 Airlines)
Start Date: December 1, 1988
Chairman: John M S Lecky
CEO: Angus J Kinnear
Ownership: Resource Funding

FLEET:

Type	No	Seats	Engines
Airbus A320-200	6	Y168	CFM56-5A3
Boeing 757-200	6	Y226 or J38Y167	RR RB211-535E4
Airbus A330-200	3	Y340	GE CF6-80E1A4

BOEING 747-400

CANADIAN AIRLINES
(Canadian Airlines International)

IATA: CP   **ICAO:** CDN   **IATA/ARC:** 018   **RADIO:** Canadian

---

CONTACTS:

Mail	Telephone/Fax
615 18th Street SE	Admin: +1 403 294 2000
Calgary, AB	Fax: +1 403 294 2066
T2E 6J5	Res: 1 800 665 1177
Internet: www.cdnair.ca	Res: 1 800 426 7000 (US)

OPERATION:

Type: Scheduled/charter passenger/cargo
Cities Served: Canada: YCB YEG YEV YFB YHZ YOW YRB YRT YTH YUL YVQ YVR YXY YYC YYZ YZF **US:** BOS DFW HNL LAX LGA MIA MCO ORD SFO **México/South America:** EZE GRU MEX MTY **Europe:** FCO LHR **Asia:** BKK HKG MNL NGO NRT PEK TPE
Global Alliance: oneworld
Code-Share: Air Alma, Air Georgian, Air New Zealand, Air Pacific, Air St-Pierre, Aklak Air, ALITALIA, American, American Eagle, BritishAirways, Calm Air, Canadian Regional, Helijet Airways, Inter-Canadien, Japan Airlines, LAN Chile, Malaysia, Mandarin Airlines, Pacific Coastal, QANTAS, Regionnair, Reno Air
FFP: Canadian Plus

HISTORY/STRUCTURE:

Founded: July 1, 1942 (as Canadian Pacific Air Lines)
Start Date: March 27, 1987 (as Canadian)
Chairman: Harold R Steele
CEO: Kevin Benson
Ownership: Canadian Airlines Corp (67%), Aurora Airline Investments (AMR) (33%)

BOEING 767-300 (ER)

FLEET:

Type	No	Seats	Engines
Boeing 737-200C (Advanced) (operated for Canadian North)	2	Y112/Combi	PWJT8D-17/17A
Boeing 737-200/200C (Advanced)	42	J12Y88	PW JT8D 9A/17/17A
Airbus A320-200	13	J24Y108	CFM56-5A1/5A3
Boeing 767-300ER	12	J30Y180	GE CF6-80C2B6/2B6F/2B4F
DC-10-30	8	J28Y228	GE CF6-50C2/C2B
Boeing 747-400	4	J48Y379	GE CF6-80C2B1F
Ordered			
Airbus A320-200	10		
Boeing 767-300ER	4		

NOTES:

CANADA

CANADIAN REGIONAL AIRLINES

IATA: KI   **ICAO:** CDR   **IATA/ARC:** none   **RADIO:** Canadian Regional

CONTACTS:

Mail
8050 22 Street NE
Calgary, AB
T2E 7H6

Telephone/Fax
Admin: +1 403 974 2300
Fax: +1 403 974 7760
Res: 1 800 665 1177
Res: 1 800 426 7000 (US)

OPERATION:

Type: Scheduled/charter passenger
Cities Served: Canada: YCG YEG YKA YLW YMM YMX YOJ YOP YOW YPE YPR YQB YQD YQL YQR YQT YQU YTH YVR YWG YXC YXE YXH YXJ YXS YXT YYC YYD YYE YYF YYJ YYZ YZP **US:** BOS LGA RDU
All service operated as Canadian Partner using only CP flight numbers (1100-1459, 1551-1691)
Code-Share: Reno Air
FFP: Canadian Plus

HISTORY/STRUCTURE:

Founded: 1966 (as Lethbridge Air Services)
Start Date: January 1991 (as Canadian Regional)
CEO: Robert W Reding
Ownership: Canadian Airlines (100%)

FLEET:

Type	No	Seats	Engines
DHC-8-100	10	Y37	PWC PW120A
DHC-8-300	14	Y50	PWC PW123
F28 Mk 1000	30	J10Y45	RR Spey 555-15/15N
F28 Mk 3000	1	J10Y45	RR Spey 555-15H

RAYTHEON BEECH 1900D

CENTRAL MOUNTAIN AIR

IATA: 9M　　**ICAO:** GLR　　**IATA/ARC:** 634　　**RADIO:** Glacier

CONTACTS:

Mail
PO Box 998
Smithers, BC
V0J 2N0

Internet: www.cmair.bc.ca

Telephone/Fax
Admin: +1 250 877 5000
Fax:　　+1 250 847 3744
Res　　1 800 663 3905 (Canada)
Res　　1 800 776 3000 (US)

OPERATION:

Type: Scheduled/charter passenger
Cities Served: Canada: YCD YCG YDQ YKA YLW YQQ YQU YQZ YVR YWL YXC YXJ YXS YYC YYD YYF US: GEG
All service operated as Air Canada Connector using only AC flight numbers
FFP: Aeroplan

HISTORY/STRUCTURE:

Founded: 1987
Start Date: 1987
CEO: Neil Blackwell
Ownership: Privately held

FLEET:

Type	No	Seats	Engines
CATPASS 200	1	EMS	PWC PT6A-41
Beech 1900C-1	3	Y19	PWC PT6A-65B
Beech 1900D	11	Y18	PWC PT6A-67D
Ordered			
Beech 1900D	10 options		

BRITISH AEROSPACE (HAWKER SIDDELEY) 748 SERIES 2B

FIRST AIR (BRADLEY AIR SERVICES dba)

IATA: 7F   **ICAO:** FAB   **IATA/ARC:** 245   **RADIO:** First Air

CONTACTS:

Mail	Telephone/Fax
3257 Carp Road	Admin: +1 613 839 3340
Carp, ON K0A 1L0	Fax: +1 613 839 5690
Email: reservat@firstair.ca	Res: 1 800 267 1247
Internet: www.firstair.ca	

OPERATION:

Type: Scheduled/charter passenger/cargo
Cities Served: Canada: YBB YCB YCO YCY YEG YFB YFS YGT YHI YHK YHY YIO YLC YOW YRB YSM YSR YTE YUL YUX YVM YVP YWG YXP YXY YYH YZF YZS **Greenland:** SFJ
Code-Share: Air Canada (AC8950-8999), Air Inuit, Greenlandair
FFP: Aeroplan

HISTORY/STRUCTURE:

Founded: 1946
Start Date: 1946
CEO: Robert Davis
Ownership: Makivik Corporation

FLEET:

Type	No	Seats	Engines
DHC-2 Beaver	2	Y5	PW R-985
King Air A100	1	Y11	PWC PT6A-28
Beech 99	1	Y15	PWC PT6A-20
DHC-6-300	9	Y19	PWC PT6A-27
Gulfstream 1C	1	Y33	RR Dart 529-8X
HS 748-2A/2B	7	Y43/Combi	RR Dart 534/535-3
DHC-7-150	1	Ice Patrol Surveyor	PWC PT6A-50
Boeing 737-200C (Adv)	3	Combi	PW JT8D-9A
Lockheed L-100-30	1	Freighter	AN 501-D22A
Boeing 727-100C	3	Y129/Combi/Freighter	PW JT8D-7B
Boeing 727-200F	2	Freighter	PW JT8D-7B/-15
Boeing 727-200C (Adv)	1	Y170/Combi/Freighter	PW JT8D-15

DE HAVILLAND CANADA DHC-6-300 TWIN OTTER

HARBOUR AIR SEAPLANES

IATA: H3   **ICAO:** none   **IATA/ARC:** 458   **RADIO:** Harbour

---

CONTACTS:

Mail
4760 Inglis Drive
Richmond, BC
V7B 1W4

Telephone/Fax
Admin: +1 604 278 3478
Fax: +1 604 278 5271
Res: 1 800 665 0212

Internet: www.harbour-air.com

OPERATION:

Type: Scheduled/charter passenger/float aircraft only
Cities Served: CXH YAJ YAQ YAV YBQ YBW YGG YKK YPI YTB YVR YWH YZP ZMT ZQS ZSW

HISTORY/STRUCTURE:

Founded: 1981 (as Windoak Air Service)
Start Date: 1981
CEO: Greg McDougall
Ownership: Privately held

FLEET:

Type	No	Seats	Engines
Cessna A185F	4	Y3	CO IO-520-D
DHC-2 Beaver	17	Y7	PW R-985
DHC-3 Otter	1	Y9	PW R-1340
DHC-3T Otter	2	Y15	PWC PT6A-135A
DHC-6-100/200/300 (leased from Kenn Borek as required)	9	Y19	PWC PT6A-20/-27

SIKORSKY S-76A

HELIJET AIRWAYS

IATA: JB   **ICAO:** JBA   **IATA/ARC:** 613   **RADIO:** Helijet

CONTACTS:

Mail
5911 Airport Road South
Richmond, BC
V7B 1B5
Email: info@helijet.com
Internet: www.helijet.com

Telephone/Fax
Admin: +1 604 273 4688
Fax: +1 604 273 5301
Res: 1 800 665 4354

OPERATION:

Type: Scheduled/charter passenger
Cities Served: Canada: CXH YVR YWH **US:** BFI
Code-Share: Canadian

HISTORY/STRUCTURE:

Founded: September 1986
Start Date: November 27, 1986
Chairman: Alistair MacLennan
CEO: Danny Sitnam
Ownership: Publicly traded company (VSE: WMH)

FLEET:

Type	No	Seats	Engines
S-76A	5	Y12	AN 250-C30S

Other helicopters carry the titles of Vancouver Helicopters, a charter division of
Helijet Airways

AIRBUS A300B4-200 (F)

ICC CANADA (International Cargo Charters Canada)

IATA: none   **ICAO:** CIC   **IATA/ARC:** none   **RADIO:** Air Trader

---

CONTACTS:

Mail
780 Magenta Blvd
Farnham, QC
J2N 1B8

Telephone/Fax
Admin: +1 450 293 3656
Fax: +1 450 293 5169

OPERATION:

Type: Scheduled/charter cargo, primarily contract work for Emery Worldwide
Cities Served: Canada: YVR YYC YYZ **US:** DAY

HISTORY/STRUCTURE:

Founded: 1986 (as ACS Canada)
Start Date: 1998
President/CEO: Edward C C Peagram
Ownership: Privately held

FLEET:

Type	No	Seats	Engines
A300B4-200 (F)	3	Freighter	GE CF6-50C2

AI(R) ATR42-300

INTER-CANADIEN (Inter-Canadien (1991))

IATA: QB   **ICAO:** ICN   **IATA/ARC:** none   **RADIO:** Inter-Canadien

CONTACTS:

Mail	Telephone/Fax
795 Stuart Graham Blvd N	Admin: +1 514 631 9802
Dorval, QC	Fax: +1 514 631 2129
H4Y 1E4	Res: 1 800 665 1177

OPERATION:

Type: Scheduled/charter passenger
Cities Served: Canada: YAM YAY YBC YBX YCH YCL YDF YFC YGK YGL YGP YGR YGV YGW YHR YHZ YJT YNA YOW YQB YQM YQX YQY YSJ YUL YUY YVO YWK YXU YYG YYR YYT YYY YYZ YZV **US:** BOS
All service operated as Canadian Partner using only CP flight numbers (2201-2404)
FFP: Canadian Plus

HISTORY/STRUCTURE:

Founded: 1946 (as Air Rimouski)
Start Date: 1987 (as Inter-Canadien)
Ownership: Canadian Investors Corporation
CEO: Robert Myhill

FLEET:

Type	No	Seats	Engines
ATR42-300	17	Y44	PWC PW120
Aircraft interchange frequently with those of Canadian Regional; Beech 1900Ds wet-leased from Air Georgian (Ontario Regional) for YYZ–YAM route			
Ordered			
EMB-145	6 plus 6 options		

BOEING 727-200 (F)

KELOWNA FLIGHTCRAFT AIR CHARTER

IATA: **ICAO:** KFA   **IATA/ARC:**   **RADIO:** Flightcraft

CONTACTS:

Mail	Telephone/Fax
1-5655 Kelowna Airport Road	Admin: +1 250 491 5500
Kelowna, BC	Fax: +1 250 765 1489
V1V 1S1	

Internet: www.aiac.ca/guide/profiles/kelowna.html

OPERATION:

Type: Scheduled/charter passenger/cargo
Operates for Purolator Courier

HISTORY/STRUCTURE:

Founded: 1970
Start Date: 1974
President: Barry Lapointe
General Manager: Jim Rogers
Ownership: Barry Lapointe & Jim Rogers

FLEET:

Type	No	Seats	Engines
Cessna 402B	2	Freighter	CO TSIO-520E
Convair 580	12	Y52/Combi/Freighter	AN 501-D13
Convair 5800	1	Freighter	AN 501-D22G
Boeing 727-100C/F	10	Freighter	PW JT8D-7B/9
Boeing 727-200F	4	Freighter	PW JT8D-7B/9A
Boeing 727-200	5	Y170	PW JT8D-7B/9A

DE HAVILLAND CANADA DHC-6-300 TWIN OTTER

KENN BOREK AIR

IATA: 4K   **ICAO:** KBA   **IATA/ARC:** 652   **RADIO:** Borek Air

CONTACTS:

Mail
290 McTavish Road NE
Calgary, AB
T2E 7G5
Email: borekair@cadvisive.com

Telephone/Fax
Admin: +1 403 291 3300
Fax: +1 403 250 6908

OPERATION:

Type: Scheduled/charter passenger/cargo
Cities Served: YAB YFB YGZ YIO YRB YSR
Contract operations in Arctic and Antarctic and also conducts extensive
worldwide charter and leasing operations

HISTORY/STRUCTURE:

Founded: 1971
Start Date: 1971
CEO: Kenn Borek
Ownership: Privately held

FLEET:

Type	No	Seats	Engines
Cessna A185	1	Y3	CO IO-520-D
Baron B55	1	Y4	CO IO-470-L
Beech 99	3	Y15	PWC PT6A-20
King Air B90/C90	2		PWC PT6A-20
King Air 100/A100	5		PWC PT6A-28
King Air 200	3		PWC PT6A-41
EMB-110P1 Bandeirante	2		PWC PT6A-34
DHC-6-100/200/300	34	Y19/Combi	PWC PT6A-20/-27
Douglas C-117D	1	Freighter	WR R-1820

RAYTHEON BEECH 1900D

MINISTIC AIR (Kistigan)

IATA: none   **ICAO:** MNS   **IATA/ARC:** none   **RADIO:** Ministic

CONTACTS:

Mail
PO Box 42008
Winnipeg, MB
R3J 3X7

Telephone/Fax
Admin: +1 204 832 8550
Fax: +1 204 889 4731

OPERATION:

Type: Scheduled/charter passenger/cargo
Cities Served: YIV YRL YRS YST YWG YXL ZSJ

HISTORY/STRUCTURE:

Founded: 1981 (as Big Hook Air Lines)
Start Date: 1981
CEO: John Briggs
Ownership: Privately held

FLEET:

Type	No	Seats	Engines
Cessna U206	1	Y5/Freighter	CO IO-520-F
PA-31-310 Navajo	1	Y7	LY TIO-540-A1A
PA-31-350 Chieftain	3	Y8	LY TIO-540-J2BD
King Air 100	2	EMS	PWC PT6A-28
Dornier 228-200	2	Y19	GA TPE331-5-252D
Beech 1900C	1	Y19	PWC PT6A-65B
Beech 1900D	2	Y19	PWC PT6A-67D

BRITISH AEROSPACE 3101 JETSTREAM 31

NORTH VANCOUVER AIR

IATA: VL   **ICAO:** NRV   **IATA/ARC:** none   **Radio:** Norvan

CONTACTS:

Mail	Telephone/Fax
#311 5360 Airport Road South	Admin: +1 604 278 1608
Richmond, BC	Fax: +1 604 278 2608
V7B 1B4	Res: 1 800 228 6608
Email: travelinfo@northvanair.com	
Internet: www.northvanair.com	

OPERATION:

Type: Scheduled/charter passenger
Cities Served: Canada: CFQ YAZ YVR ZNL **US:** BFI
Founded: 1994
Start Date: 1994
CEO: Zoltan Kunn
Ownership: Privately held

FLEET:

Type	No	Seats	Engines
Cessna U206	1	Y5	CO IO-520-F
PA-31-310 Navajo	2	Y6	LY TIO-540-A2B
PA-31-350 Chieftain	2	Y8	LY TIO-540-J2BD
King Air 100	2	Y9/11	PWC PT6A-28
Jetstream 31	4	Y19	GA TPE331-10UG-513H

CANADA

NORTHWESTERN AIR (Northwestern Air Lease)

IATA: J3   **ICAO:** PLR   **IATA/ARC:** 325   **RADIO:** Polaris

CONTACTS:

Mail	Telephone/Fax
PO Box 23	Admin: +1 867 872 2216
Fort Smith, NWT	Fax: +1 867 872 2214
X0E 0P0	
Email: nwal@auroranet.nt.ca	
Internet: www.auroranet.nt.ca/nwal	

OPERATION:

Type: Scheduled/charter passenger
Cities Served: YHY YOJ YQU YSM YZF

HISTORY/STRUCTURE:

Founded: 1965
Start Date: 1965
CEO: Terry Harrold
Ownership: Privately held

FLEET:

Type	No	Seats	Engines
Cessna 337G	1	Y4	CO IO-360-G
Cessna 401	1	Y4	CO TS10-520-E
Cessna 402	1	Y7	CO TSIO-520-E
Beech 99	2	Y15	PWC PT6A-20
Jetstream 31	2	Y19	GA TPE331-10UGR-514H

CANADA

CESSNA 208B GRAND CARAVAN

NORTH-WRIGHT AIRWAYS

IATA: HW   **ICAO:** NWL   **IATA/ARC:** none   **RADIO:** Northwright

CONTACTS:

Mail	Telephone/Fax
Bag Service 2200	Admin: +1 403 587 2288
Norman Wells, NWT	Fax: +1 403 587 2962
X0E 0V0	Res: 1 800 661 0702

OPERATION:

Type: Scheduled/charter passenger
Cities Served: YCK YEV YGH YLE YVQ YWJ YZF ZFN
FFP: Canadian Plus

HISTORY/STRUCTURE:

Founded: 1986
Start Date: 1987
CEO: Warren Wright
Ownership: Privately held

FLEET:

Type	No	Seats	Engines
Helio H295	1		LY GO-480-G1D6
Cessna 207	1		CO IO-520-F
Cessna 337C/337D	2		CO IO-360-C/D
PC-6/B1-H2 Porter	1		PWC PT6A-20
BN-2A-26 Islander	1		LY O-540-E4C5
PA-31-350 Chieftain	1		LY TIO-540-J2BD
Cessna 208B	2		PWC PT6A-114
Beech 99	1		PWC PT6A-20
DHC-6-100	1		PWC PT6A-20

CANADA

GRUMMAN G-21A GOOSE

PACIFIC COASTAL AIRLINES

IATA: 8P   **ICAO:** PCO   **IATA/ARC:** 905   **RADIO:** Pasco

CONTACTS:

Mail	Telephone/Fax
117-4440 Cowley Crescent	Admin: +1 604 273 8666
Richmond, BC	Fax: +1 604 273 6864
V7B 1B8	Res: 1 800 663 2872

Email: webmaster@pacific-coastal.com
Internet: www.pacific-coastal.com/

OPERATION:

Type: Scheduled/charter passenger
Cities Served: QBC YAA YCD YHC YPW YRD YRN YVR YZT ZEL
Some service operated as Canadian Partner using CP flight numbers (1460-1479, 2728-2743)
FFP: Canadian Plus

HISTORY/STRUCTURE:

Founded: 1979
Start Date: 1979
CEO: Daryl Smith
Ownership: AirBC/Powell Air

FLEET:

Type	No	Seats	Engines
Cessna A185F	1	Y3	CO IO-520-D
Cessna U206F	1	Y4	CO IO-520-F
DHC-2 Beaver	3	Y6	PW R-985
G-21A Goose	4	Y9	PW R-985
BN-2A Islander	1	Y9	LY IO-540-K1B5
King Air 200	1	Y13	PWC PT6A-41
EMB-110P1 Bandeirante	4	Y15	PWC PT6A-34
Beech 1900C	1	Y19	PWC PT6A-65B
Shorts 360 (300)	4	Y30	PWC PT6A-65AR

FAIRCHILD SA226-TC METRO II

PERIMETER AIRLINES (INLAND)

IATA: UW   **ICAO:** PAG   **IATA/ARC:** 711   **RADIO:** Perimeter

CONTACTS:

Mail	Telephone/Fax
626 Ferry Road	Admin: +1 204 786 7031
Winnipeg, MB	Fax: +1 204 783 7911
R3H 0T7	Res: 1 800 665 8986
	Res: +1 204 783 8000

OPERATION:

Type: Scheduled/charter passenger/cargo, MEDEVAC
Cities Served: YBR YBV YCR YDN YGO YIV YNE YOH YRS YST YWG ZGI

HISTORY/STRUCTURE:

Founded: 1960
Start Date: 1960
CEO: William J Wehrle
Ownership: Perimeter Aviation

FLEET:

Type	No	Seats	Engines
Merlin IV	1	Y18	GA TPE331-10UA-511G
Metro II	13	Y18	GA TPE331-1OUA-511G

RAYTHEON BEECH 1900D

REGIONNAIR

IATA: RH   **ICAO:** GIO   **IATA/ARC:** 256   **RADIO:** Gionnair

CONTACTS:

Mail	Telephone/Fax
CP29	Admin: +1 418 787 2001
Chevery, QC	Fax: +1 418 787 2004
G0G 1G0	

OPERATION:

Type: Scheduled/charter passenger
Cities Served: YBX YGV YHR YIF YNA YPN YZV ZGS ZKG ZLT
Some service operated as Canadian Partner using CP flight numbers (2500-2520)

HISTORY/STRUCTURE:

Founded: 1992
Start Date: 1992
President/CEO: Guy Marcoux
Ownership: Privately held

FLEET:

Type	No	Seats	Engines
PA-31-310 Navajo	1	Y7	LY TIO-540-A2C
King Air 90	1	Y7	PWC PT6A-20
Cessna 208B	1	Y9	PWC PT6A-114A
DHC-6-200	1	Y18	PWC PT6A-20
Beech 1900C	1	Y19	PWC PT6A-65B
Beech 1900D	2	Y19	PWC PT6A-67D

AIRBUS A310-304

ROYAL AVIATION

IATA: QN   **ICAO:** ROY   **IATA/ARC:** 498   **RADIO:** Roy

---

CONTACTS:

Mail
685 BL Stuart Graham North
Dorval, QC
H4Y 1E4

Telephone/Fax
Admin: +1 514 828 9000
Fax: +1 514 828 9096

OPERATION:

Type: Charter passenger/cargo
Cities Served: Canada: Main Bases: YEG YHZ YMX YUL YVR YWG YYC YYZ
(seasonal): YDF YFC YOW YQG YQM YQR YQT YQX YQY YSJ YTH YXE YXS
YXU YXY YYJ YYT YZF **USA** (some seasonal): EWR FLL LAS MCO PIE
Caribbean (some seasonal): ANU HOG MBJ POP VRA **México** (some season-
al): CUN LTO MZT SJD ZIH ZLO **Europe** (seasonal): AMS BHX CDG GLA LGW
MAN MUC SXF VIE ZRH
Primarily operates for Signature Vacations and Sunflight Holidays

---

HISTORY/STRUCTURE:

Founded: August 3, 1979
Start Date: April 29, 1992
CEO: Michel LeBlanc
Ownership: Publicly traded company (TSE: ROY)

FLEET:

Type	No	Seats	Engines
Boeing 737-200C	3	Y122/Freighter	PW JT8D-9A
Boeing 737-200F (Advanced)	2	Freighter	PW JT8D-9A
Boeing 727-100C	1	Freighter	PW JT8D-9A
Boeing 727-200 (Advanced)	1	Y187	PW JT8D-17
Boeing 757-200	7	Y228/233	RB211-535E4
(four 757s leased from Air 2000 during northern winter season)			
Airbus A310-300	4	Y256	GE CF6-80C2A2

AIRBUS A320-212

SKYSERVICE

IATA: S2   **ICAO:** SSV   **IATA/ARC:** 884   **RADIO:** Skytour

CONTACTS:

Mail
9785 Ryan Avenue
Dorval, QC
H9P 1A2

Telephone/Fax
Admin: +1 514 636 3300
Fax: +1 514 636 4855

Internet: www.Skyservice.com

OPERATION:

Type: Charter passenger
Cities Served: Canada: YYZ **US** (seasonal): LAS RNO **Caribbean** (seasonal): ANU AUA MBJ NAS UVF VRA **México** (seasonal): ACA CUN HUX LTO SJD ZLO **Europe** (seasonal): ATH BCN BFS CIA MXP PSR SUF VCE
Also operates MEDEVAC services using a fleet of turboprops and biz-jets

HISTORY/STRUCTURE:

Founded: 1985
Start Date: 1989
CEO: L Russell Payson
Ownership: Privately held

FLEET:

Type	No	Seats	Engines
Boeing 727-200	2	C50-70/F20Y102	PW JT8D-9A
(operated for SportHawk International Airlines)			
Airbus A320-200	5	Y179/180	CFM56-5A3/IAE V2527-A5
(two A320s leased from Monarch during northern winter season)			
Airbus A330-300	1	J32Y345	PW4168

DE HAVILLAND CANADA DHC-7-102 DASH 7

TRANS-CAPITAL AIR

IATA: none   **ICAO:** none   **IATA/ARC:** none   **RADIO:** none

CONTACTS:

Mail
Hangar #1
Toronto City Centre Airport
Toronto, ON M5V 1A1

Telephone/Fax
Admin: +1 416 203 1144
Fax: +1 416 203 1120

OPERATION:

Type: Charter passenger

HISTORY/STRUCTURE:

Founded: 1994
Start Date: 1994
CEO: Victor P Pappalardo
Ownership: Privately held

FLEET:

Type	No	Seats	Engines
DHC-7-100	2	Y50	PWC PT6A-50

DE HAVILLAND CANADA DHC-7-102 DASH 7

VOYAGEUR AIRWAYS

IATA: 4V   **ICAO:** VAL   **IATA/ARC:** 908   **RADIO:** Voyageur

CONTACTS:

Mail
PO Box 1734
CFB North Bay
Hornell Heights, ON
P0H 1P0
Email: info@VoyageurAirways.com
Internet: www.voyageurairways.com

Telephone/Fax
Admin: +1 705 476 1750
Fax: +1 705 476 6773
Res: 1 800 461 1636

OPERATION:

Type: Scheduled/charter passenger/cargo; operates emergency
medical service in Canada/US
Cities Served: YSB YYB

HISTORY/STRUCTURE:

Founded: 1968
Start Date: 1974
CEO: Max Shapiro
Ownership: Voyageur Airport Services

FLEET:

Type	No	Seats	Engines
King Air 100/A100	8	Y9/EMS	PWC PT6A-28
King Air 200C	3	Y9/EMS	PWC PT6A-42
DHC-7-100	8	Y48	PWC PT6A-50

NOTES: Plans to form a subsidiary called Air Connexion to operate 12 Beech 1900Ds

BRITISH AEROSPACE (HAWKER SIDDELEY) 748 SERIES 2A (F)

WASAYA AIRWAYS

IATA: WG   **ICAO:** WSG   **IATA/ARC:** 093   **RADIO:** Wasaya

CONTACTS:

Mail
PO Box 360
100 Princess St
Thunder Bay, ON
P7J 4T9
Email: information@wasaya.com
Internet: www.wasaya.com

Telephone/Fax
Admin: +1 807 473 1200
Fax: +1 807 577 0432
Res: 1 800 423 3393

OPERATION:

Type: Charter passenger/cargo

HISTORY/STRUCTURE:

Founded: 1986 (as Kelner Airways)
Start Date: 1986
CEO: Tom Kam
Ownership: Wasaya Corporation

FLEET:

Type	No	Seats	Engines
Cessna 208B	6	Y9/Freighter	PWC PT6A-114A
CATPASS 200	2	Y11	PWC PT6A-41
Beech 1900D	1	Y18	PWC PT6A-67D
HS 748-2A/B	5	Y40/Combi/Freighter	RR Dart 534/536/550-2

DE HAVILLAND CANADA DHC-6-100 TWIN OTTER

WEST COAST AIR

IATA: 8O **ICAO:** none **IATA/ARC:** 222 **RADIO:** Coast Air

CONTACTS:

Mail
900 - 1188 W Georgia Street
Vancouver, BC
V6E 4A2

Telephone/Fax
Admin: +1 604 606 6800
Fax: +1 604 606 6820
Res: 1 800 347 2222

Internet: www.westcoastair.com/

OPERATION:

Type: Scheduled/charter passenger
Cities Served: CXH YWH

HISTORY/STRUCTURE:

Founded: 1995
Start Date: January 25, 1996
CEO: Al Baydala
Ownership: Privately held

FLEET:

Type	No	Seats	Engines
DHC-2 Beaver	1	Y6	PW R-985
DHC-6-100	3	Y18	PWC PT6A-20
DHC-6-200	1	Y18	PWC PT6A-20

FAIRCHILD F-27F

WESTEX AIRLINES (WESTERN EXPRESS AIR LINES)

IATA: none   **ICAO:** WES   **IATA/ARC:** none   **RADIO:** Westex

CONTACTS:

Mail	Telephone/Fax
Box 24259	Admin: +1 604 273 1500
Vancouver APO	Fax: +1 604 273 3863
BC V7B 1Y4	Res: 1 877 882 2746

Internet: www.westex.ca

OPERATION:

Type: Scheduled/charter cargo
Cities Served: Canada: YCD YKA YLW YXT YXY YYJ **US:** BFI
Operates for DHL & Purolator Courier

HISTORY/STRUCTURE:

Founded: 1995
Start Date: 1995
President/CEO: David Oliver
Ownership: Privately held

FLEET:

Type	No	Engines
Metro III	2	GA TPE331-1-151G
F-27F	1	RR Dart 529-7E
F27 Mk 300M	1	RR Dart 514-7
F27 Mk 400	1	RR Dart 532-7

BOEING 737-200 (ADVANCED)

WESTJET

IATA: M3   **ICAO:** WJA   **IATA/ARC:** none   **RADIO:** Westjet

CONTACTS:

Mail
35 McTavish Place NE
Calgary, AB
T2E 7J7

Telephone/Fax
Admin: +1 403 735 2600
Fax: +1 403 571 5367
Res: 1 800 538 5696

Internet: www.westjet.com

OPERATION:

Type: Scheduled/charter passenger
Cities Served: YEG YLW YQR YQT YVR YWG YXE YXS YXX YYC YYJ

HISTORY/STRUCTURE:

Founded: 1995
Start Date: February 29, 1996
Chairman: Clive Beddoe
CEO: Stephen C Smith
Ownership: Privately held

FLEET:

Type	No	Seats	Engines
Boeing 737-200	2	Y125	PW JT8D-9A
Boeing 737-200C	1	Y120	PW JT8D-9A
Boeing 737-200 (Advanced)	12	Y125	PW JT8D-9A/15/17

CANADA

Canada Addenda

AIR ALMA (4L/AAJ/248/Air Alma) CP 577, 345 Chemin de L'Aéroport, Alma, QC G8B 5W1; +1 418 668 5566, Fax: +1 418 668 7711, Res: 1 800 463 9660, Email: adm@airalma.com, Jacques Simard. Scheduled/charter passenger/cargo; all scheduled service operated as Canadian Partner using only CP flight numbers. 1 x Navajo, 1 x Cessna 404, 3 x Bandeirante

AIR NUNAVUT (BFF/Air Baffin) PO Box 1239, Iqaluit, NWT X0A 0H0; +1 867 979 4018, Fax: +1 867 979 4318, Email: airnuna@nunanet.com, Jeff Mahoney. Scheduled/charter passenger. 1 x Navajo, 1 x CATPASS 200

AIR RAINBOW PO Box 1451, 3050 Spit Rd, Campbell River, BC V9W 5C7; +1 250 287 8371, Fax: +1 250 287 8366, Email: dir.ops@air-rainbow.com, reservations@air-rainbow.com, www.air-rainbow.com, Murray LeSage. Scheduled/charter passenger. 1 x Cessna 185, 9 x Beaver

AIR SATELLITE (ASJ) ADroport Baie-Comeau, Pointe Lebel, QC G5C 2S6; +1 418 589 8923, Fax: +1 418 589 7416, Res: 1 800 463 8512, Email: airsat@globetrotter.qc.ca, www.air-satellite.com, Jean Fournier. Scheduled/charter passenger/cargo. 1 x Cessna 337, 2 x Cessna 310R, 1 x Cessna 335, 4 x Cessna 402, 1 x Trislander, 1 x Bandeirante

AIR SCHEFFERVILLE PO Box 1540, Schefferville, QC G0G 2T0; +1 418 585 3475, Fax: +1 418 585 3630, www.airschefferville.com, John Bogie. Scheduled/charter passenger (scheduled service operated as Canadian Partner using CP flight numbers (1700 series)). 2 x Otter, 1 x Beech 99

AIR TINDI (8T/744) PO Box 1693, Yellowknife, NWT X1A 2P3; +1 867 669 8200, Fax: +1 867 669 8250, Email: airtindi@ssimicro.com, www.airtindi.com, Alex Arychuk. Scheduled/charter passenger/cargo. 3 x Cessna A185F, 1 x Beaver, 1 x Turbine Otter, 1 x Cessna 208, 2 x Cessna 208B, 1 x King Air C90, 1 x King Air B200C, 5 x Twin Otter

AIR WAVE TRANSPORT (AWV) 2450 Derry Road East, Mississauga, ON L5S 1B2; +1 905 405 8622, Fax: +1 905 405 9228, Chris Dunn. 2 x Chieftain, 2 x Gulfstream I, 1 x Convair 580

AIR WEMINDJI CP 307, Aeroport La Grande Rivière, Radisson, QC J0Y 2X0; +1 819 638 3392, Fax: +1 819 638 3746, Chief Walter Hughboy. Scheduled/charter passenger. 1 x PC-12, 3 x Cessna 208

AKLAK AIR (6L/AKK/709/Aklak) PO Box 1190, Inuvik, NWT X0E 0T0; +1 873 777 2419, Fax: +1 873 777 3256, Res: 403 979 3777, Email: dbethune@irc.inuvialuit.com, www.inuvialuit.com/aklak, David Bethune. Scheduled/charter passenger (joint venture with Kenn Borek, commercial agreement with Canadian). 2 x Beech 99, 2 x Twin Otter

ALTA FLIGHTS (CHARTERS) (ALZ) PO Box 9831, Edmonton International Airport, Edmonton, AB T5J 2T2; +1 403 890 7676, Fax: +1 403 890 7042, www.altaflights.com, Christine Robertson. Charter passenger. 2 x Cessna 402C, 1 x Cessna 404, 3 x Chieftain, 1 x Metro III

AVIATION BOREAL CP 1390, Val d'Or, QC J9P 5Y8; +1 819 825 0405, Fax: +1 819 825 1260, Blandine Arsenault. Charter cargo. 1 x Navajo, 2 x DC-3

AVIATION QUEBEC LABRADOR (QLA) CP 575, Sept Îles, QC G4R 4K7; 418 962 7901, Fax: +1 418 962 9202, Res: 1 800 361 8620, Jacques Cleary. Passenger scheduled/charter (scheduled flights with Bandeirante operated as Air Canada Connector using AC flight numbers). 2 x Chieftain, 1 x Twin Otter, 3 x Bandeirante

BAXTER AVIATION (6B) PO Box 1110, Nanaimo, BC V9R 6E7; +1 250 754 1066, Fax: +1 250 754 1075, Res: 1 800 661 5599, Tom Baxter. Scheduled/charter passenger. 2 x Cessna A185F, 9 x Beaver

BUFFALO AIRWAYS (J4/BFL/Buffalo) 1000 Buffalo Drive, Hay River Airport, NWT X0E 0R9; +1 867 874 3333, Fax: +1 867 874 3572, Joe W C McBryan. Scheduled/charter passenger/cargo. 2 x Cessna A185, 3 x Travel Air, 1 x Norseman, 10 x DC-3, 4 x PBY-5A Canso, 4 x CL-215, 2 x Curtiss C-46, 4 x DC-4

CONTACT AIR (Air Mikisew) (V8) PO Box 5175, Fort McMurray, AB T9H 3G3; +1 780 743 8218, Fax: +1 780 743 8225, Ray McKenzie. Scheduled/charter passenger. 1 x Cessna A185F, 1 x Cessna U206G, 2 x Cessna 207A, 2 x Beaver, 2 x Chieftain, 1 x Beech 99A, 1 x King Air A100, 1 x Jetstream 31

CORPORATE EXPRESS (CPB/Penta) 575 Palmer Road NE, Calgary, AB T2E 7G4, +1 403 216 4050; Fax: +1 403 216 4055, www.corpxair.com, Gordon Peariso. Charter/contract passenger. 4 x Jetstream 31

HAWKAIR AVIATION SERVICES RR 4, Site 166, Comp 5, Bristol Road, Terrace, BC V8G 4V2; +1 250 635 4295, Fax: +1 250 635 4295, Paul Hawkins. Charter/contract cargo. 1 x Bristol 170, 1 x Carvair

KD AIR (XC/KDC/Kaydee) RR #2, Site 225, C-11, Port Alberni, BC V9Y 7L6; +1 250 752 5884, Fax: +1 250 752 5750, Email: kdair@naniamo.ark.com, Kathy Banke. Scheduled/charter passenger. 1 x Cessna 172, 1 x Navajo, 1 x Chieftain

KEYSTONE AIR SERVICES (BZ/KEE/921/Keystone) PO Box 2140, Swan River, MB R0L 1Z0; +1 204 734 9351, Fax: +1 204 734 9181, Res: 1 800 665 3975, Clifford Arlt. Scheduled/charter passenger. 1 x Seneca, 1 x Navajo, 2 x Chieftain, 1 x Beech 99

KNIGHTHAWK AIR EXPRESS (KNX/Knight Flite) #1601 55 York Street, Toronto, ON M5J 1R7; +1 416 214 4880, Fax: +1 416 214 4883, Hugh MacMillan. Charter/contract cargo (operates for FedEx and Dynamex). 1 x Beech 1900C, 4 x Falcon 20

LITTLE RED AIR SERVICE (LRA/Little Red) PO Box 584, Fort Vermilion, AB T0H 1N0; +1 403 927 4630, Fax: +1 403 927 3667, Henry Grandjambe. Scheduled/charter passenger/cargo. 1 x Cessna A185F, 3 x Cessna U206F, 1 x Chieftain, 1 x Beaver, 2 x Islander, 2 x King Air 100

MORNINGSTAR AIR EXPRESS (ME/MAL/Morningstar) Building 16, 29 Airport Road, Edmonton, AB T5G 0W6; +1 403 471 3022, Fax: +1 403 474 9093, Donald Wheaton. Charter/contract cargo (operates as a FedEx Feeder). 2 x Cessna 208B, 4 x Boeing 727-100F

NAKINA OUTPOST CAMPS & AIR SERVICE PO Box 126, Nakina, ON P0T 2H0; +1 807 329 5341, Fax: +1 807 329 5876, Don & Millie Bourdignon. Scheduled/charter passenger/cargo. 1 x Beaver, 1 x Turbine Otter, 1 x PC-12, 2 x Cessna 208B, 1 x Twin Otter

NORTH AMERICAN AIRLINES (NTM/Northam) Box 630, 1441 Aviation Park NE, Calgary, AB T2E 8M7; +1 403 275 7700, Fax: +1 403 275 5947, www.northamericanairlines.com, D G Hollier. Charter passenger/cargo. 2 x Navajo, 2 x Chieftain, 3 x Metro III, 1 x BAe 125-700A, 1 x Falcon 20, 1 x Gulfstream I

NORTH CARIBOO FLYING SERVICE (5N/NCB/North Cariboo) PO Box 6789, Fort St John, BC V1J 4J2; +1 250 787 0311, Fax: +1 250 787 6086, Email: ncfs@pris.bc.ca, Dan O Wuthrich. Charter passenger/cargo for oil and geological exploration companies. 3 x Cessna U206, 1 x Baron, 1 x Navajo, 1 x King Air B90, 1 x King Air 100, 2 x Twin Otter, 1 x Beech 1900C

NORTHERN SKY AVIATION PO Box 205, High Level, AB T0H 1Z0; +1 403 926 3672, Fax: +1 403 926 4460, Email: nsky@telusplanet.et, David Steer. Scheduled/charter passenger. 1 x Navajo, 1 x PC-12

NORTHERN THUNDERBIRD AIR (NT Air) (4R/NTA/Thunderbird) RR#8, Site 10, Comp 29, Prince George, BC V2N 4M6; +1 604 963 9611, Fax: +1 604 963 8427, Email: ntair@netbistro.com, www.pgweb.com/ntair, Vernon Martin. Scheduled/charter passenger. 1 x Cessna 337, 2 x Commander 500, 2 x Chieftain, 1 x Beech 18, 1 x King Air 100, 2 x CATPASS 200, 1 x Twin Otter

NORTHWAY AVIATION (NAL/Northway) PO Box 70, Arnes, MB R0C 0C0; +1 204 276 2045, Fax: +1 204 276 2069. Jim Johnson. Scheduled/charter passenger/cargo. 1 x Cessna A185E, 1 x Cessna U206F, 1 Cessna 207A, 1 x Beaver, 1 x Navajo, 1 x Chieftain, 1 x Islander, 1 x Otter, 1 x Cessna 208

PEACE AIR PO Box 6036, Peace River, AB T8S 1S1; +1 403 624 3060, Fax: +1 403 624 3063, Res: 1 800 563 3060, Albert Cooper. Scheduled/charter passenger. 1 x Cessna 210L, 1 x Seneca, 1 x Chieftain, 1 x Merlin IIB

PEM-AIR (PD/PEM/329/Pem Air) RR #6, Pembroke Municipal Airport, Pembroke, ON P0H 1P0; +1 613 687 8130, Fax: +1 613 687 5166, Res: 1 800 267 3131, D A O'Brien. Scheduled/charter passenger. 2 x Chieftain, 1 x King Air E90, 1 x King Air 100; subsidiary Trillium Air Operates Scheduled service with a Jetstream

POINTS NORTH AIR Bag 7000, La Ronge, SK S0J 1L0; +1 306 633 2137, Fax: +1 306 633 2152, George Eikel. Charter passenger/cargo. 1 x Cessna A185F, 1 x Beaver, 2 x Cessna 402, 3 x Otter, 1 X Cessna 208B, 1 x DC-3

PRINCE EDWARD AIR (CME/Comet) 250 Brackley Point Road, Box 3, Charlottetown, PEI C1A 6Y9; +1 902 566 4488, Fax: +1 902 368 3573, Res: 1 800 656 5359, Email: peairyg@aurora.com, www.peair.com, Robert M Bateman. Scheduled/charter passenger/cargo. 4 x Chieftain, 1 x Cessna 208, 1 x PC-12, 1 x Beech 99, 1 x Beech 1900C

PROPAIR (6P/PRO/Propair) Building GR 20, RR #1, Rouyn, QC J9X 5B7; +1 819 762 0811, Fax: +1 819 762 1852, Jean Pronovost. Charter passenger/cargo. 1 x Cessna A185F, 2 x Beaver, 3 x Otter, 4 x King Air A100, 1 x King Air 200, 1 x Merlin IVA, 1 x Gulfstream I

PROVINCIAL AIRLINES (Inter-Provincial) (AG/PAL/967) Hangar #2, PO Box 29030, St John's, NF A1B 5B5; +1 709 576 1800, Fax: +1 709 576 1802, Res: 1 800 563 2800, www.provair.com, Gus Ollerhead. Scheduled/charter passenger/cargo and maritime surveillance (scheduled passenger service operated as Interprovincial Airlines under a commercial agreement with Air Canada/Air Nova). 1 x Islander, 5 x Navajo, 2 x Chieftain, 4 x King Air 200, 3 x Metro II, 1 x Merlin IV, 1 x Twin Otter, 3 x Metro III

SAMARITAN AIR SERVICE (Keeshig Airlines) (HLO/Halo) 2450 Derry Road East, Hangar #6, Mississauga, ON L5S 1B2; +1 905 672 2226, Fax: +1 905 672 2229, Adam Keller. Scheduled/charter passenger and EMS. 2 x PC-12, 1 x Beech 18, 4 x MU-2, 1 x Lear 24, 2 x Lear 25C, 3 x Jetstream 31, 1 x Jetstream 32

SHUSWAP AIR (3S/SFC) PO Box 1887, Salmon Arm, BC V1E 4P9; +1 250 832 8830, Fax: +1 250 832 2825, Res: 1 800 663 4074, www.shuswapair.com, Stephen Raffel. Scheduled/charter passenger. 1 x Navajo, 1 x King Air 100

SKYLINK EXPRESS 1027 Yonge Street #300, Toronto, ON M4W 2K9; +1 416 925 4530, Fax: +1 416 925 2975, Dan Rocheleau. Charter/contract cargo. 2 x Cessna 208B, 7 x Beech 1900C

SKYWARD AVIATION (K9/SGK/470/Skyward) PO Box 562, Rankin Inlet, NT X0C 0G0; +1 867 645 3200, Fax: +1 867 645 3208, Res: 1 800 476 1873, Email: skyward@arctic.ca, Frank P Behrendt. Scheduled/charter passenger. 2 x Cessna U206, 1 x Cessna 207A, 2 x Cessna 310R, 1 x Cessna 414, 2 x Cessna 402, 1 x Islander, 1 x Cessna 421C, 2 x Cessna 208B, 1 x King Air 100, 4 x Bandeirante, 1 x CATPASS 200

SOWIND AIR (SOW/Sowind) 101-501 Airline Road, St Andrews, MB R1A 3P4; +1 204 338 5429, Fax: +1 204 338 5431, Oliver Owen. Charter passenger/cargo. 2 x Cessna A185F, 1 x Beaver, 1 x Navajo, 3 x Chieftain, 1 x Otter, 2 x Cessna 208B

SUNWEST INTERNATIONAL AVIATION SERVICES (CNK/Chinook) 230 Aviation Place NE, Calgary, AB T2E 7G1; +1 403 275 8121, Fax: +1 403 275 4637, www.sunwest.ab.ca, Gordon Laing. Charter passenger/cargo. 1 x Cessna A185F, 3 x Navajo, 2 x Chieftain, 2 x King Air B100, 4 x Metro II, 2 x Metro III, 1 x Cessna 550, 2 x Lear 35

THUNDER AIRLINES (THU/Air Thunder) 310 Hector Dougall Way, Thunder Bay, ON P7E 6M6; +1 807 475 4211, Fax: +1 807 475 5841, Info: 1 800 803 9943, Email: tairltd@baynet.net, www.thunderair.com, Ken Bittle. Charter passenger/cargo. 2 x PC-12, 1 x Cessna 208B, 3 x King Air A100, 1 x Shorts 330

NOTES:

BOEING 757-200

GRØNLANDSFLY (GREENLANDAIR)

IATA: GL	**ICAO:** GRL	**IATA/ARC:** 631	**RADIO:** Greenlandair

CONTACTS:

Mail
PO Box 1012
DK-3900 Nuuk
Greenland
Email: glsales@greenlandair.gl
Internet: www.greenland-guide.dk/gla/

Telephone/Fax
Admin: +299 34 34 34
Fax: +299 32 72 88

OPERATION:

Type: Scheduled/charter passenger
Cities Served: Greenland: AGM CNP GOH JAV JCH JEG JFR JGO JGR JHS
JJU JNN JNS JSU JUV KUS NAQ OBY SFJ THU UAK UMD **Europe:** CPH REK
Service to Canada operated in cooperation with First Air (Bradley Air Services)

HISTORY/STRUCTURE:

Founded: November 7, 1960
Start Date: 1963
Chairman: Peter Groenvold Samuelsen
Ownership: Greenland government (37.5%), SAS-Scandinavian (37.5%),
Danish government (25%)

FLEET:

Type	No	Seats	Engines
MD 500D	4	Y4	AN 250-C20B
AS350B2	6	Y6	TU Arriel 1D1
Bell 407	1	Y6	AN 250-C47
Beech 200	1	Y7	PWC PT6A-41
Bell 212	4	Y9	PWC PT6T-3B
DHC-6-300	2	Y18/Combi	PWC PT6A-27
Sikorsky S-61N	4	Y25	GE CT58-140-2
DHC-7-103	5	Y50/Combi	PWC PT6A-50
Boeing 757-200	1	CY209	RB211-535E4

(additional helicopters leased during northern summer season)

GREENLAND

ATR42-320

AIR SAINT-PIERRE

IATA: PJ   **ICAO:** SPM   **IATA/ARC:** 638   **RADIO:** Saint Pierre

---

CONTACTS:

Mail
BP 4225
18 rue Albert Briand
F-95700 Saint-Pierre et Miquelon
Email: asp@cancom.net
Internet: http:// 209.205.50.254/aspweb

Telephone/Fax
Admin: +508 41 47 18
Fax: +508 41 23 36

OPERATION:

Type: Scheduled/charter passenger
Cities Served: FSP **Canada:** YHZ YQY YUL YYT
All scheduled service operated as Canadian Partner using only CP
flight numbers (2500 range)
Code-Share: Canadian Airlines

HISTORY/STRUCTURE:

Founded: 1958
CEO: Rémy L Briand

Start Date: 1958
Ownership: Briand family

FLEET:

Type	No	Seats	Engines
PA-31-350 Chieftain	1	Y8	LY TIO-540-J2BD
ATR42-320	1	Y42 or Y34	PWC PW121

DOUGLAS DC-9-32

AERO CALIFORNIA

IATA: JR   **ICAO:** SER   **IATA/ARC:** 078   **RADIO:** Aerocalifornia

CONTACTS:

Mail	Telephone/Fax
Aquiles Serdán 1995	Admin: +52 112 5 9002
La Paz, BCS 23000	Fax: +52 112 3 5343
	Res: 5 207 1392 (Mexico City)
	Res: 01 800 237 6225 (México)
	Res: 1 800 237 6225 (US/Can)

Email: interline@aerocalifornia@uabcs.mx
100447.657@compuserve.com

OPERATION:

Type: Scheduled passenger
Cities Served: México: AGU CEN CJS CLQ CUL CUU CVM DGO GDL HMO LAP LMM LTO MAM MEX MTY MZT PBC SJD SLP TIJ TPQ TRC ZLO
US: LAX TUS
Code-Share: American Airlines
FFP: Club Altus

HISTORY/STRUCTURE:

Founded: 1960
Start Date: 1960
President/CEO: Raul A Aréchiga
Ownership: Privately held

FLEET:

Type	No	Seats	Engines
DC-9-14	5	CY85	PW JT8D-7A/7B
DC-9-15	6	CY85	PW JT8D-7A/7B
DC-9-32	8	CY104	PW JT8D-9A/15

CESSNA 208B GRAND CARAVAN DE LUXE

AEROCARIBE

IATA: QA   **ICAO:** CBE   **IATA/ARC:** 723   **RADIO:** Aerocaribe

CONTACTS:

Mail	Telephone/Fax
Avenida Coba 5, Local B1 y B3	Admin: +52 98 87 4002
Plaza América, Cancún, QR 77500	Fax: +52 98 84 9996
Xola 535, 28Fl, Col del Valle	Admin: +52 5 682 0230
México, DF 03100	Fax: +52 5 543 3382
	Res: +52 98 84 2000
Email: info@aerocaribe.com.mx	Res: 01 800 502 2000 (México)
Internet: www.aerocaribe.com	Res: 1 800 531 7921 (US/Can)

OPERATION:

Type: Scheduled/charter passenger
Cities Served: México: ACA CME CTM CUN CZA CZM HUX MEX MID MTT MTY OAX PCM PQM PXM SCRIS TAP TGZ VER VSA **Central America/ Caribbean:** BZE FRS HAV VAR
All scheduled service operated as Mexicana Inter using only MX flight numbers (7000 range). Some flights operated by associated company Aerocozumel
Code-Share: AeroMexico, Mexicana

HISTORY/STRUCTURE:

Founded: 1975
Start Date: July 12, 1975
President/CEO: Jaime Valenzuela
Ownership: CINTRA Holdings (IPC: CINTRA)

FLEET:

Type	No	Seats	Engines
Cessna 208B	2	Y13	PWC PT6A-114A
Jetstream 32EP	5	Y19	GA TPE331-12UAR-704H
Fairchild F-27J	3	Y44	RR Dart 532-7
DC-9-14	3	Y83 or Y85	PW JT8D-7B
DC-9-15	2	Y83	PW JT8D-7B

BRITISH AEROSPACE 320I JETSTREAM 32EP

AERO CUAHONTE

IATA: none   **ICAO:** CUO   **IATA/ARC:** none   **RADIO:** Cuahonte

---

CONTACTS:

Mail	Telephone/Fax
Aeropuerto Federal de Uruapan	Admin: +52 452 40 032
60160 Uruapan	Fax: +52 452 49 360

OPERATION:

Type: Scheduled/charter passenger
Cities Served: CLQ GDL LZC MLM UPN ZIH

HISTORY/STRUCTURE:

Founded: 1957
Start Date:
President: Enrique Amezua Cuahonte
Ownership: Privately held

FLEET:

Type	No	Seats	Engines
Cessna T210N	1	Y3	CO TSIO-520-R
Cessna 402C	1	Y5	CO TSIO-520-VB
Metro II	1	Y19	GA TPE331-10UA-511G
Jetstream 32EP	1	Y19	GA TPE331-12UAR-704H

BOEING 727-100

AEROLINEAS INTERNACIONALES

IATA: N2   **ICAO:** LNT   **IATA/ARC:** 440   **RADIO:** Lineaint

CONTACTS:

Mail
Concepción Beistegui 815
Col del Valle, México, DF 03100

Telephone/Fax
Admin: +52 5 543 1223
Fax: +52 5 536 1549
Res: 01 800 990 9100 (México)

Email: aeroint@iwm.com.mx
Internet: www.iwm.com.mx/foroemp/aerint.html

OPERATION:

Type: Scheduled/charter passenger
Cities Served: AGU CUL MEX TIJ REX
Charter operations to Mexican resort areas
FFP: Exclusive Card

HISTORY/STRUCTURE:

Founded: June 24, 1993
Start Date: March 25, 1994
President/CEO: Jorge Luis Rodriguez
Ownership: Privately held

FLEET:

Type	No	Seats	Engines
DC-9-14	1		PW JT8D-7A
Boeing 727-100	2		PW JT8D-7B
Boeing 727-200	1		PW JT8D-9

FAIRCHILD SA227-DC METRO 23

AEROLITORAL (Servicios Aéreos Litoral)

IATA: none   **ICAO:** SLI   **IATA/ARC:** 297   **RADIO:** Costera

CONTACTS:

Mail
Carretera Miguel Alemán Km 22.8
Apodaca, NL 66601

Telephone/Fax
Admin: +52 8 386 2070
Fax: +52 8 368 1601
Res: 01 800 021 4000 (México)
Res: 1 800 247 6639 (US/Can)

Email: comentarios@aerolitoral.com.mx
Internet: www.aerolitoral.com.mx

OPERATION:

Type: Scheduled passenger
Cities/Areas Served: México: AGU BJX CEN CJS CUL CUU DGO GDL GUB GYM HMO LAP LMM LOV LTO MAM MLM MTY MXL MZT PAZ PDS PVR QRO SJD SLP SLW TAM TIJ VER VSA ZIH ZLO **US:** DFW ELP IAH PHX SAT TUS
All service operated on behalf of AeroMexico using only AM flight numbers
Code-Share: AeroMexico, Mexicana

HISTORY/STRUCTURE:

Founded: May 1989
Start Date: July 1989
President/CEO: Carlos Trevi'o
Ownership: CINTRA Holdings (IPC: CINTRA)

FLEET:

Type	No	Seats	Engines
Metro III	14	Y19	GA TPE331-11U-611G
Metro 23	12	Y19	GA TPE331-12U-701G
SAAB 340B	6	Y33	GE CT7-9B

ATR42-512

AEROMAR (Transportes Aeromar)

IATA: VW   **ICAO:** TAO   **IATA/ARC:** 590   **RADIO:** Trans Aeromar

CONTACTS:

Mail
Hangar 7, Zona E Aviación General
Aeropuerto Internacional
Cd de México, México, DF 15620

Internet: www.aeromar-air.com

Telephone/Fax
Admin: +52 5 627 0205
Fax: +52 5 756 0174
Res: 5 627 0207 (Mexico City)
Res: 01 800 704 2900 (México)
Res: 1 210 829 7482 (US)

OPERATION:

Type: Scheduled passenger/cargo
Cities/Areas Served: México: AGU BJX CLQ CVM DGO GDL HUX LZC MEX MLM MTY PAZ PBC QRO SCX SLP UPN ZCL ZLO **US:** IAH SAT
Code-Share: Mexicana, AeroMexico, United Airlines

HISTORY/STRUCTURE:

Founded: January 29, 1987
Start Date: November 7, 1987
President/CEO: Juan Ignacio Steta
Ownership: Autrey Group

FLEET:

Type	No	Seats	Engines
ATR42-320	6	Y48	PWC PW121
ATR42-500	4	Y48	PWC PW127E

McDONNELL DOUGLAS DC-9-82 (MD-82)

AEROMEXICO (Aerovías de México)

IATA: AM   **ICAO:** AMX   **IATA/ARC:** 139   **RADIO:** Aeromexico

CONTACTS:

Mail
Paseo de la Reforma 445
México, DF 06500

Internet: www.aeromexico.com

Telephone/Fax
Admin: +52 5 133 4000
Fax: +52 5 133 4628
Res: 5 133 4010 (Mexico City)
Res: 01 800 021 4010 (México)
Res: 1 800 237 6639 (US/Can)

OPERATION:

Type: Scheduled passenger
Cities Served: México: ACA AGU BJX CEN CJS CPE CUL CUN CUU DGO GDL GYM HMO LAP LMM MAM MEX MID MTY MZT OAX PVR REX SJD TAP TIJ TRC VER VSA ZIH **US:** ATL DFW IAH JFK LAX MIA MSY PHX SAN **South America:** EZE GRU LIM SCL **Europe:** CDG MAD
Code-Share: Aerocaribe, Aerolitoral, Aeromar, Air France, Austrian Airlines, Delta Air Lines, El Al, LAN Chile, Mexicana, Swissair
FFP: Club Premier

HISTORY/STRUCTURE:

Founded: 1934 (as Aeronaves de México)
Start Date: May 15, 1934
Chairman/President: Alfonso Pasquel
CEO: Arturo Barahona
Ownership: CINTRA Holdings (IPC: CINTRA)

BOEING 757-200

FLEET:

Type	No	Seats	Engines
DC-9-31	2	J12Y85	PW JT8D-17
DC-9-32	15	J12Y85	PW JT8D-17
MD-82	12	J12Y130	PW JT8D-217A/-217C
MD-83	7	J12Y130	PW JT8D-219
MD-87	3	J12Y100	PW JT8D-219
MD-88	10	J12Y130	PW JT8D-219
Boeing 757-200	9	J24Y156	PW PW2037 or RR RB211-535E4
Boeing 767-200ER	2	J21Y160	PW PW4056
Boeing 767-300ER	3	J21Y188	PW PW4060/4062

BOEING 727-200 (ADVANCED) (F)

AEROMEXPRESS

IATA: QO   **ICAO:** MPX   **IATA/ARC:** 976   **RADIO:** Aeromexpress

CONTACTS:

Mail
Ave Texcoco esq Av Tahel
Col Pe'on de los Ba'os
México, DF 15620

Telephone/Fax
Admin: +52 5 537 0203
Fax: +52 5 237 2226
Info: 01 800 706 9300 (México)

Internet: www.aeromexpress.com.mx

OPERATION:

Type: Scheduled/charter cargo
Cities Served: México: BJX GDL MEX MID SJO **US:** DFW LAX MIA
Code-Share: Aerolitoral, AeroMexico, Mexicana

HISTORY/STRUCTURE:

Founded: 1989
Start Date: December 1, 1989
President/CEO: Javier Elizalde
Ownership: CINTRA Holdings (IPC: CINTRA)

FLEET:

Type	No	Engines
Boeing 727-200F	2	PW JT8D-17

DOUGLAS DC-9-14

ALLEGRO AIR (Líneas Aéreas Allegro)

IATA: LL   **ICAO:** GRO   **IATA/ARC:** 902   **RADIO:** Allegro

CONTACTS:

Mail
Jose Benitez 2709
Col Obispado
64060 Monterrey

Telephone/Fax
Admin: +52 83 33 9938
Fax: +52 83 33 9940

Internet: http://www.traveldiscounts.com/discount/suntrips/allegro_profile.htm

OPERATION:

Type: Charter passenger
Areas Served: North and South America and Caribbean

HISTORY/STRUCTURE:

Founded: 1992
Start Date: December 26, 1992
President: Fernando Padilla
Ownership: Privately held

FLEET:

Type	No	Seats	Engines
DC-9-14	1	Y90	PW JT8D-7B
Boeing 727-200	9	Y167-Y182	PW JT8D-9A/15/17A/217C
Ordered			
Boeing 727-200	5		

DOUGLAS DC-9-15

AVIACSA (Aviación de Chiapas)

IATA: 6A　　**ICAO:** CHP　　**IATA/ARC:** 095　　**RADIO:** Aviacsa

CONTACTS:

Mail	Telephone/Fax	
Hangar No 13, Zona D	Admin:	+52 5 756 0650
Aeropuerto Internacional	Fax:	+52 5 700 3852
Ciudad de México	Res:	5 716 9004 (Mexico City)
Aviación General	Res:	01 800 006 22 00 (México)
México, DF 15520	Res:	1 800 237 6396 (US/Can)

OPERATION:

Type: Scheduled/charter passenger
Cities Served: México: CTM CUN GDL MID MEX MTY OAX TAP TGZ TIJ VSA
US: IAH LAS
FFP: AviacsaPass

HISTORY/STRUCTURE:

Founded: May 1990
Start Date: September 1990
President/CEO: Eduardo Morales
Ownership: Privately held (Consorcio Aviacsa)

FLEET:

Type	No	Seats	Engines
DC-9-15	3	Y90	PW JT8D-7A/7B
Boeing 727-200 (Advanced)	8	Y164	PW JT8D-15

MAGNICHARTERS

IATA: none   **ICAO:** GMT   **IATA/ARC:** none   **RADIO:** Grupomonterrey

CONTACTS:

Mail	Telephone/Fax
La Barca 1128	Admin: +52 8 369 0855
Col Mitras Sur 4	Fax: +52 8 369 0977
64020 Monterrey	

OPERATION:

Type: Charter passenger
Areas Served: North and South America and Caribbean

HISTORY/STRUCTURE:

Founded: 1994
Start Date: January 1995
President:
Ownership: Magnitur (Grupo Turisto Magno)

FLEET:

Type	No	Seats	Engines
Boeing 737-200	4	Y122 or Y130	PW JT8D-7B/9A

DOUGLAS DC-8-71F

MASAIR CARGO (Aerotransportes Mas de Carga)

IATA: MY **ICAO:** MAA **IATA/ARC:** 865 **RADIO:** Mas Carga

---

CONTACTS:

Mail
Almacen 22, Aduana Interior
Aeropuerto Internacional
Ciudad de México, México, DF 15520

Telephone/Fax
Admin: +52 5 786 9555
Fax: +52 5 786 9543

OPERATION:

Type: Scheduled/charter cargo
Cities Served: México: GDL MEX **US:** LAX MIA
Charter operations to BOG CCS EZE GRU JFK LIM MVD SCL VCP

HISTORY/STRUCTURE:

Founded: September 13, 1990
Start Date: April 29, 1992
President/CEO: Luis Sierra
Ownership: Promotor Aéreo Latinoamericano, International Aviation
Services

FLEET:

Type	No	Engines
Boeing 707-300C	1	PW JT3D-3B
DC-8-71F	1	CFM56-2C

AIRBUS A320-231

MEXICANA (Corporación Mexicana de Aviación)

IATA: MX   **ICAO:** MXA   **IATA/ARC:** 132   **RADIO:** Mexicana

CONTACTS:

Mail	Telephone/Fax
Xola 535, Col del Valle	Admin: +52 5 448 3000
México, DF 03100	Fax: +52 5 523 2364
	Res: 5 448 0990 (Mexico City)
	Res: 01 800 502 2000 (México)
Internet: www.mexicana.com	Res: 1 800 531 7921 (US/Can)

OPERATION:

Type: Scheduled passenger
Cities/Areas Served: México: ACA BJX CME CUN CZM GDL HMO HUX MEX MID MLM MTT MXL MZT NLD OAX PVR PXM SJD SLW TAM TIJ VER VSA ZCL ZIH ZLO **Caribbean:** HAV **Central America/South America:** BOG EZE GUA SCL SJO **US:** DEN EWR LAS LAX MCO MIA ORD SAT SFO SJC **Canada:** YMX YYZ
Code-Share: Aerocaribe, Aerolitoral, Aeromar, AeroMexico, Air Canada, Lufthansa, SERVIVENSA, United Airlines
FFP: Frecuenta

HISTORY/STRUCTURE:

Founded: July 12, 1921
Start Date: July 12, 1921
President/CEO: Fernando Flores
Ownership: CINTRA Holdings (IPC: CINTRA)

FLEET:

Type	No	Seats	Engines
Fokker 100	12	J8Y93	RR Tay 650-15
Airbus A320-200	14	J12Y138 or Y174	IAE V2500-A1
Boeing 727-200 (Advanced)	23	J12Y138 or Y156	JT8D-17/17R
Boeing 757-200	5	J12Y170/171	PW2040

BOEING 727-100

TAESA (Transportes Aéreos Ejecutivos)

IATA: GD   **ICAO:** TEJ   **IATA/ARC:** 838   **RADIO:** Transejecutivos

CONTACTS:

Mail
Aviación General
Zona de Hangares C, No 27
Aeropuerto Intl Cd de México
PO Box 9-212
México, DF 15001

Email: taecaal@taesa.com.mx
Internet: www.taesa.com.mx

Telephone/Fax
Admin: +52 5 227 0727
Fax: +52 5 227 4044
Res: 5 227 0700 (Mexico City)
Res: 01 800 904 6300 (México)
Res: 1 800 328 2372 (US/Can)
PR: +52 5 227 4017

OPERATION:

Type: Scheduled/charter passenger/cargo
Cities Served: México: ACA AGU BJX CUN CJS CUL GDL HMO MID MEX MLM MTY MXL PVR TAP TIJ UPN ZCL **US:** LRD OAK ORD
TAESA operates worldwide charters and wet-leasing services, conducts air taxi and third party work, and has an FBO at Mexico City and Toluca
FFP: Viajero Frecuente

HISTORY/STRUCTURE:

Founded: April 27, 1988
Start Date: February 12, 1991 (scheduled)
President/CEO: Alberto Abed Shekaiban
Ownership: Abed family

FLEET:

Type	No	Seats	Engines
DC-9-14	2	Y83	PW JT8D-7A/7B
DC-9-15	3	Y83	PW JT8D-7A/7B
DC-9-31F	1	Y117/Freighter	PW JT8D-7B
Boeing 737-200 (Advanced)	4	Y133	PW JT8D-15
Boeing 737-300	4	Y148	CFM56-3B1/3B2
Boeing 737-400	1	Y170	CFM56-3C1
Boeing 727-100/100C	5	Y131	PW JT8D-7B
Boeing 727-200 (Advanced)	1	Y173	PW JT8D-15
Boeing 757-200	1	Y223	RR RB211-535E4
DC-10-30F	1	Freighter	GE CF6-50C2

México Addenda

AEROCOZUMEL (AZM/686/Aerocozumel) Aeropuerto Internacional, Apartado Postal 322, 77600 Cozumel (Quintana Roo); +52 987 23 456, Fax: +52 987 20 503, Jaime V Tamariz. Scheduled/charter passenger, all scheduled service operated as Mexicana Inter in cooperation with Aerocaribe using only MX flight numbers (7000 range). 2 x Trislander

AEROFERINCO Calle 3 Sur s/n, Esquina Con 15 Av, 77710 Playa del Carmin (Quintana Roo); +52 987 31 919, Fax: +52 987 30 574, Cap Fernando Quintin Vargas. Scheduled/charter passenger. 2 x Dornier 28D-2, 3 x Let 410

AVIOQUINTANA (Aviones de Renta de Quintana Roo) (AQT/Avioquintana) Av Juarez 90, Centro, 77000 Chetumal (Quintana Roo); +52 983 20 664, Fax: +52 983 28 597, Cap Mario A Hermosillo Torres. Scheduled/charter passenger. 1 x Seneca, 2 x Metro II, 5 x Metro III

MAYAIR (MYI/Mayair) Calle 11 Sur No 598, Col Gonzalo Guerrera, 77663 Cozumel (Quintana Roo); +52 987 20 433, Fax: +52 987 21 044. 1 x Let 410

SUDPACIFICO (Aero Sudpacifico) (SDP/Sudpacifico) Manuel Perez Coronado 94, 60080 Uruapan (Michoacan); +52 452 37 937, Fax: +52 452 44 773, Cap Manuel Arguelles Mejia. Scheduled/charter passenger. 1 x Seneca, 2 x Islander, 2 x Metro II

TACSA (Transportes Aereos de Coahuila) (Transcoahuila) Carretera Saltillo-Monterrey Km 30, 5, 25900 Saltillo (Coahuila); +52 84 88 1890, Fax: +52 84 88 1811. 1 x Cessna 208B, 1 x Metro II

TANSA (Transportes Aereos de Nayarit) Apartado Postal 221, 63190 Tepic (Nayarit); +52 321 33 111, Fax: +52 321 33 117, Cap P A Alberto Velasco Navarro. Scheduled/charter passenger. 1 x Cessna 402B, 2 x DC-3

NOTES:

ILYUSHIN IL-18V

AEROCARIBBEAN

IATA: CR   **ICAO:** CRN   **IATA/ARC:** none   **RADIO:** Aerocaribbean

CONTACTS:

Mail
No 64 esq P Vedado
Plaza de la Revolución
Ciudad de La Habana, Cuba
Email: aerocarvpcr@iacc3.6et.cma.net

Telephone/Fax
Admin: +53 7 33 4543
Fax: +53 7 33 5016

OPERATION:

Type: Charter passenger/cargo
Code-Share: Cubana

HISTORY/STRUCTURE:

Founded: 1982
Start Date: December 2, 1982
Chairman: Julian Alvarez Infiesta
CEO: Arturo Mirabal
Ownership: Cuban government

FLEET:

Type	No	Seats	Engines
Yakovlev Yak-40	2	Y32/Freighter	IV AI-25
Ilyushin Il-14M	1	Y40	ASh-82T
ATR42-300	2	Y46	PWC PW120
Antonov An-24B	1	Y50	IV AI-24-II
Antonov An-26	4	Freighter	IV AI-24-VT
Ilyushin Il-18D/V	4	Y100/Freighter	IV AI-20M

ATR42-300

AEROGAVIOTA

IATA: none   **ICAO:** GTV   **IATA/ARC:** none   **RADIO:** Gaviota

CONTACTS:

Mail
Avenida 47, Playa, 2814
Reparto Kolhy, Playa
Ciudad de La Habana, Cuba

Telephone/Fax
Admin: +53 7 29 4990
Fax: +53 7 33 2621

OPERATION:
Type: Charter passenger/cargo

HISTORY/STRUCTURE:
Founded: 1994
Start Date: 1994
Ownership: Cuban government

FLEET:

Type	No	Seats	Engines
PZL An-2	1	Y11	ASh-621R
Mil Mi-8/8P/8T	15	Y24/Cargo	KL TV2-117A
Yakovlev Yak-40	4	Y32	IV AI-25
ATR42-300	2	Y46	PWC PW120
Antonov An-26/26B	22	Combi	IV AI-24-VT
Antonov An-30	2	Survey	IV AI-24T
All operated by Cuban Air Force			

BOMBARDIER DHC-8-311 DASH 8

AIR ALM (ALM 1997 Airline)

IATA: LM   **ICAO:** ALM   **IATA/ARC:** 119   **RADIO:** Antillean

CONTACTS:

Mail
Aeropuerto Hato
Curaçao, Netherlands Antilles
Email: airalm@ibm.net
Internet: www.airalm.com/

Telephone/Fax
Admin: +599 833 8888
Fax: +599 833 8300
Res: 1 800 327 7230

OPERATION:

Type: Scheduled/charter passenger
Cities Served: Caribbean: AUA BON CUR KIN PAP POS SDQ SJU SXM
South America: CCS MAR PBM VLN **US:** ATL MIA
Code-Share: Air Aruba, ASERCA, KLM, Martinair, SLM, Surinam Airways,
United, Winair
FFP: Mileage Plus (MIA flights only)

HISTORY/STRUCTURE:

Founded: 1964 (as Antilliaanse Luchtvaart Maatschappij)
Start Date: August 1, 1964
Chairman: K Chong
President: Drs P (Armand) Kariembaks
Ownership: Netherlands Antilles government (75%), KLM (25%)

FLEET:

Type	No	Seats	Engines
DHC-8-300	4	Y48 or Y50	PWC PW123
MD-82	3	C8Y131	PW JT8D-217/-217C

BOEING MD-90-30

AIR ARUBA

IATA: FQ   **ICAO:** ARU   **IATA/ARC:** 276   **RADIO:** Aruba

CONTACTS:

Mail	Telephone/Fax	
PO Box 1017	Admin:	+297 8 30005
Oranjestad, Aruba	Fax:	+297 8 38138
	Res:	1 800 882 7822
	Admin (US):	1 800 858 8028

Internet: www.airaruba.com

OPERATION:

Type: Scheduled/charter passenger
Cities Served: Caribbean: AUA BON CUR **South America:** BOG CCS
MDE **US:** BWI EWR MIA PHL TPA
Code-Share: Air ALM ASERCA, KLM, SAM

HISTORY/STRUCTURE:

Founded: September 1986
Start Date: August 18, 1988
Chairman: E R Arends
CEO: Simeon R Garcia
Ownership: ASERCA (70%), Aruban government (30%)

FLEET:

Type	No	Seats	Engines
DC-9-32	1	C8Y95	PW JT8D-9A
MD-88	2	C8Y135	PW JT8D-219
MD-90-30	2	C12Y143	IAE V2525-D5

SHORTS SD3-60 VARIANT 300

AIR CALYPSO

IATA: none   **ICAO:** KLY   **IATA/ARC:** none   **RADIO:** Dancing Bird

CONTACTS:

Mail
Aéroport du Raizet
Zone Sud
F-97139 Abymes, Guadeloupe

Telephone/Fax
Admin: +590 89 27 69
Fax: +590 93 73 14
Res: +590 89 27 69

OPERATION:

Type: Scheduled/charter passenger
Cities Served: FDF PTP SFG

HISTORY/STRUCTURE:

Founded: 1997
Start Date: December 9, 1997
CEO: Simon Hayot
Ownership: Privately held

FLEET:

Type	No	Seats	Engines
Shorts SD3-60 (300)	3	Y36	PWC PT6A-67R

BOEING 737-200 (ADVANCED)

AIR CARIBBEAN

IATA: C2   **ICAO:** CBB   **IATA/ARC:** 189   **RADIO:** Ibis

CONTACTS:

Mail
PO Box 1021
Port of Spain, Trinidad

Internet: http://aircaribbean.com

Telephone/Fax
Admin: +1 868 627 5109
Fax: +1 868 627 4519
Res: +1 868 623 2500

OPERATION:

Type: Scheduled passenger/cargo
Cities Served: Caribbean: BGI GND POS **South America:** GEO

HISTORY/STRUCTURE:

Founded: November 26, 1991
Start Date: August 8, 1993
Executive CEO: Leslie Lucky-Samaroo
GM: Nelson Tomyew
Ownership: Luxsam Holdings (50%), Medishi Investments (50%)

FLEET:

Type	No	Seats	Engines
YS-11A-500	5	Y60	RR Dart 542-10
YS-11A-600	1	Freighter	RR Dart 542-10
Boeing 737-200 (Advanced)	3	Y122 or Y124	PW JT8D-9A/15/15A
Ordered			
Boeing 737-200	2		

The side tab reads: CARIBBEAN

BOEING 737-200 (ADVANCED)

AIR GUADELOUPE (Société Martinique Aéronautique)

IATA: TX   **ICAO:** FWI   **IATA/ARC:** 427   **RADIO:** French West

---

CONTACTS:

Mail
Immeuble Le Caducet
Aéroport du Raizet
F-97139 Abymes, Guadeloupe
Email: airguadeloupe@show-voyage.com
Internet: www.show-voyage.com/air-guadeloupe.htm

Telephone/Fax
Admin: +590 82 47 22
Fax: +590 83 70 03
Res: +590 91 53 44

OPERATION:

Type: Scheduled passenger/charter
Cities Served: Caribbean: ANU BGI DOM DSD FDF GBJ LSS PAP PTP SBH SDQ SFG SJU SLU SVD SXM UNI **South America:** CAY
Code-Share: Air France, Air Saint Barthélemy, Air Saint Martin

---

HISTORY/STRUCTURE:

Founded: 1969 (as Société Antillaise de Transport Aérien/Air Guadeloupe)
Start Date: August 1994
CEO: François Paneole
Ownership: Caribéenne de Transport Aérien

FLEET:

Type	No	Seats	Engines
DHC-6-300	1	Y19	PWC PT6A-27
Dornier 228-200	8	Y19	GA TPE331-5/-5A
ATR42-300	1	Y50	PWC PW120
ATR42-500	2	Y46	PWC PW127E
ATR72-200	2	Y70	PWC 124B
Boeing 737-200 (Advanced)	1	Y120	PW JT8D-15

Some aircraft wear the titles of Air Martinique, a subsidiary and member of Groupe Air Guadeloupe

---

AIRBUS A321-211

AIR JAMAICA

IATA: JM   **ICAO:** AJM   **IATA/ARC:** 201   **RADIO:** Juliette Mike

CONTACTS:

Mail
72-76 Harbour Street
Kingston, Jamaica

Internet: www.airjamaica.com

Telephone/Fax
Admin: +1 876 922 3460
Fax: +1 876 922 0107
Res: 1 800 523 5585

OPERATION:

Type: Scheduled passenger/cargo
Cities Served: Caribbean: BGI GCM GND HAV KIN MBJ NAS SLU
US: ATL BWI EWR FLL JFK LAX MCO MIA ORD PHL **Europe:** LHR
Code-Share: Air Canada, Delta Air Lines
FFP: 7th Heaven

HISTORY/STRUCTURE:

Founded: October 1968
Start Date: April 1, 1969
Chairman: Gordon (Butch) Stewart
CEO: Christopher Zacca
President: Albert P Chappell
Ownership: Air Jamaica Acquisition Group (70%), Jamaican government (25%), employees (5%)

FLEET:

Type	No	Seats	Engines
MD-83	2	F12Y135	PW JT8D-219
Airbus A320-200	6	F12Y138	CFM56-5A3/5B4
Airbus A321-200	3	F12Y175	CFM56-5B3/P
Airbus A310-300 (ET)	4	F18Y200	PW4152/4156
Airbus A340-300	1	F12C35Y254	CFM56-5C3

Air Jamaica wet-leases a DC-8F for cargo operations

SHORTS SD3-60 VARIANT 300

AIR JAMAICA EXPRESS

IATA: JQ   **ICAO:** JMX   **IATA/ARC:** 100   **RADIO:** Jamaica Express

---

CONTACTS:

Mail	Telephone/Fax
Kingston Tinson Pen Aerodrome	Admin: +1 876 923 9498
Kingston 11	Fax: +1 876 937 3807
Jamaica	Res: 1 800 523 5585
Email: jmxpress@bellsouth.net	+1 876 922 4661
Internet: www.airjamaica.com/express.html	

OPERATION:

Type: Scheduled passenger
Cities Served: KIN MBJ NEG OCJ POT
All service operated for Air Jamaica using only JM flight numbers
FFP: 7th Heaven

HISTORY/STRUCTURE:

Founded: 1973 (as Jamaica Air Taxi)
Start Date: April 18,1996
Chairman: Gordon (Butch) Stewart
CEO: David Taylor
Ownership: Air Jamaica Acquisition Group, DT Brown, John Cooke, Jamaican government

---

FLEET:

Type	No	Seats	Engines
Dornier 228-200	2	Y19	GA TPE331-5/-252D
Shorts 360 (300)	2	Y36	PWC PT6A-67R

AIR SANTO DOMINGO (Aerolíneas Santo Domingo)

IATA: EX   **ICAO:** SDO   **IATA/ARC:** 309   **RADIO:** Aero Domingo

---

CONTACTS:

Mail	Telephone/Fax
Edificio JP, Ave 27 de Febrero 272	Admin: +1 809 683 8428
Esq Calle Seminario	Fax: +1 809 683 8436
Santo Domingo, Dominican Republic	Res: +1 809 683 8428
Email: info.air_sdo@g.air_europa.ca	
Internet: www.g-air-europa.es	

OPERATION:

Type: Scheduled passenger
Cities Served: EPS HEX LRM POP PUJ SDQ STI

HISTORY/STRUCTURE:

Founded: 1996
Start Date: 1996
CEO: Juan José Hidalgo Acera
Ownership: Air Europa

FLEET:

Type	No	Seats	Engines
Let 410	4	Y19	WA M-601D/E

BOEING 737-200 (ADVANCED)

BAHAMASAIR

IATA: UP   **ICAO:** BHS   **IATA/ARC:** 111   **RADIO:** Bahamas

CONTACTS:

Mail
PO Box N4881
Nassau, Bahamas

Internet: www.bahamasair.com

Telephone/Fax
Admin: +1 242 377 8451
Fax: +1 242 377 8550
Res: 1 800 222 4262

OPERATION:

Type: Scheduled passenger
Cities Served: Caribbean: ASD ATC AXP BIM CRI ELH FPO GGT GHB IGA LGI MAY MHH MYG PLS RSD SAQ SML TBI TCB TZN ZSA **US:** FLL MCO MIA PBI
Code-Share: Congo Air, Sky Unlimited

HISTORY/STRUCTURE:

Founded: 1973
Start Date: June 7, 1973
Chairman: Anthony C Miller
Managing Director: Glenn Pickard
Ownership: Bahamasair Holdings (Bahamas government)

FLEET:

Type	No	Seats	Engines
Shorts 360 (200)	3	Y36	PWC PT6A-65AR
DHC-8-300	5	Y50	PWC PW123
Boeing 737-200	3	Y120	PW JT8D-9A

BOMBARDIER DHC-8-311 DASH 8

BWIA INTERNATIONAL AIRWAYS

IATA: BW   **ICAO:** BWA   **IATA/ARC:** 106   **RADIO:** West Indian

CONTACTS:

Mail
Administration Building
Golden Grove Road
PO Box 604
Piarco International Airport
Port of Spain, Trinidad
Email: bwiapr@wow.net
Internet: www.bwee.com

Telephone/Fax
Admin: +1 868 669 3000
Fax: +1 868 664 3535
Res: 1 800 538 2942

OPERATION:

Type: Scheduled passenger
Cities Served: Caribbean: ANU BGI GND KIN POS SLU SXM TAB **South America:** CCS GEO **US:** MIA JFK **Canada:** YYZ **Europe:** LHR
FFP: BWIA Frequent Flyer

HISTORY/STRUCTURE:

Founded: 1939 (as British West Indian Airways)
Start Date: November 27, 1940
Chairman: Lawrence Duprey
CEO: Conrad Aleong
Ownership: Private investors (51%); Trinidad & Tobago government (33.5%), employees (15.5%)

FLEET:

Type	No	Seats	Engines
DHC-8-300 operated as BWee Express	2	Y50	PWC PW123
MD-83	5	F12Y108	PW JT8D-219
Boeing 737-700	1	F20Y118	CFM56-7B24
L-1011-500	4	F28Y210	RR RB211-524B4
Ordered			
Boeing 737-800	6		

DORNIER 228-201

CARAIBES AIR TRANSPORT (AIR CARAIBES)

IATA: WS   **ICAO:** ISB   **IATA/ARC:** none   **RADIO:** Island Bird

CONTACTS:

Mail
Aéroport de Fort-du-France
F-97232 Le Lamentin
Martinique

Telephone/Fax
Admin: +590 51 17 27
Fax: +590 51 39 04

OPERATION:

Type: Charter passenger

HISTORY/STRUCTURE:

Founded: 1987 (as Air Caraibes)
Start Date: 1987
CEO: Jean-Paul Dubeuil
Ownership: Union Stars Aviation (100%)

FLEET:

Type	No	Seats	Engines
King Air C90	1	Y6	PWC PT-6A-21
King Air 200	1	Y8	PWC PT6A-21/41
BN-2A Islander	1	Y9	LY O-540-E4C5
Cessna 208/208B	2	Y9	PWC PT6A-114/114A
DHC-6-300	1	Y18	PWC PT6A-27
Dornier 228-200	4	Y19	GA TPE331-5-252D

CARIBBEAN

BOEING 737-200 (ADVANCED)

CAYMAN AIRWAYS

IATA: KX   **ICAO:** CAY   **IATA/ARC:** 378   **RADIO:** Cayman

---

CONTACTS:

Mail	Telephone/Fax
PO Box 1101	Admin: +1 345 949 8200
Georgetown	Fax: +1 345 949 7607
Grand Cayman, Cayman Islands	Res: 1 800 422 9626

Internet: http://cayman.com.ky/com/cal/index.htm

OPERATION:

Type: Scheduled passenger
Cities Served: Caribbean: CYB GCM KIN **US:** IAH MCO MIA TPA
Code-Share: United Airlines
General Manager: Michael T Adam
FFP: Cayman Airways FFP

HISTORY/STRUCTURE:

Founded: 1955 (as Cayman Brac Airways)
Start Date: July 1968
Chairman: Leonard Ebanks
Ownership: Cayman Islands government (100%)

FLEET:

Type	No	Seats	Engines
Boeing 737-200 (Advanced)	2	Y122	PW JT8D-15A/-17A

AIRBUS 320-231

CUBANA (Cubana de Aviación)

IATA: CU   **ICAO:** CUB   **IATA/ARC:** 136   **RADIO:** Cubana

CONTACTS:

Mail
Calle 23 No 64 esq a Infanta
Vedado, Ciudad de La Habana 1040C, Cuba
Email: ecadcom@iacc3.6et.cma.net
Internet: www.cubana.cu

Telephone/Fax
Admin: +53 33 4949
Fax: +53 33 4056

OPERATION:

Type: Scheduled/charter passenger/cargo. Cubana also operates many flights for the Cuban military.
Cities Served: Caribbean: AVI BCA BYM CCC CMW CUR CYO FDF GAO GER HOG KIN MOA MZO PTP SCU VRA VTU **México/Central America/South America:** BOG CCS CUN EZE GIG GRU GYE LIM MAR MDZ MEX MVD SCL SJO SRZ UIO VVI **Canada:** YMX YYZ **Europe:** BCN BRU CPH FCO FRA IST LGW LIS LPA LYS MAD MAN ORY SCQ SVO SXF
Code-Share: Aerocaribbean, Aeroflot, TAME

HISTORY/STRUCTURE:

Founded: October 8, 1929 (as Compañía Nacional Cubana de Aviación Curtiss)
Start Date: October 30, 1930
Administrator: Heriberto Prieto Musa   **Ownership:** Cuban government

FLEET:

Type	No	Seats	Engines
Antonov An-24RV	5	Y44	IV AI-24-VT
Antonov An-26	1	Freighter	IV AI-24-VT
Yakovlev Yak-42D	4	Y120	IV D-36
F27 Mk 600	5	Y44	RR Dart 532-7
Tupolev Tu-154B-2	3	Y149	NK-8-2U
Tupolev Tu-154M	2	Y149	RM D-30KU-154
Ilyushin Il-62M	8	C12Y150	RM D-30KU
Airbus A320-231 operated by TransAer	2	C18Y150	IAE V2500-A1
Ilyushin Il-76MD	2	Freighter	RM D-30KP

Cubana uses DC-10-30s (C28Y275) operated by AOM (France) and Boeing 767-300s operated by Eurofly (Italy) on many European flights

CARIBBEAN

BEECH 1900C-1 AIRLINER

HELENAIR CARIBBEAN

IATA: 2Y   **ICAO:** HCL   **IATA/ARC:** 687   **RADIO:** Helencorp

CONTACTS:

Mail	Telephone/Fax
GFL Charles Airport	Admin: +1 758 452 1958
PO Box 253	Fax: +1 758 451 7360
Castries, St Lucia	Res: +1 758 453 2777

Email: helenair@candw.lc
Internet: www.stluciatravel.com.lc/helenair.htm

OPERATION:

Type: Scheduled/charter passenger
Cities Served: BGI BQU DOM GND POS SLU SVD UVF

HISTORY/STRUCTURE:

Founded: 1987
Start Date: 1987
CEO: Joaquin A Willie
Ownership: Arthur Neptune, Joaquin Willie, Marie Reyes

FLEET:

Type	No	Seats	Engines
Beech 99	1	Y15	PWC PT6A-20
DHC-6-300	1	Y19	PWC PT6A-27
Beech 1900C-1	3	Y19	PWC PT6A-65B

DE HAVILLAND CANADA DHC-6-300 TWIN OTTER VISTALINER

ISLAND AIR

IATA: G5   **ICAO:** none   **IATA/ARC:** none   **RADIO:** none

CONTACTS:

Mail
PO Box 2433
Georgetown
Grand Cayman, Cayman Islands
Email: iair@candw.ky
Internet: www.cayman.com.ky/com/iair/iair.htm

Telephone/Fax
Admin: +1 345 949 0241
Res: +1 345 949 5252
Fax: +1 345 949 7044

OPERATION:

Type: Scheduled/charter passenger
Cities Served: CYB GCM LYB

HISTORY/STRUCTURE:

Founded: 1989
Start Date: 1989
CEO: Mervyn Cumber
Ownership: Privately held

FLEET:

Type	No	Seats	Engines
PA-31-350 Chieftain	1	Y7	LY TIO-540-J2BD
BN-2A Islander	1	Y8	LY O-540-E4C5
DHC-6-300	1	Y19	PWC PT6A-27

BOEING 727-200 (ADVANCED)

L B LTD

IATA: 7Z   **ICAO:** LBH   **IATA/ARC:** 569   **RADIO:** Laker Bahamas

---

CONTACTS:

Mail	Telephone/Fax
1170 Lee Wagner Boulevard, Suite 200	Admin: +1 954 359 0199
Fort Lauderdale, FL 33315	Fax: +1 954 359 7698
	Res: +1 954 359 0199
	1 800 545 1300

Internet: www.princess-vacations.com/cities.html

OPERATION:

Type: Scheduled/charter passenger, primarily on behalf of Princess Vacations/Grand Bahama Vacations between the Bahamas and the US
Cities Served: Caribbean: FPO **US:** BDL BNA BWI CLE CLT CVG FLL MCO MEM ORD PBI RDU RIC

HISTORY/STRUCTURE:

Founded: 1992 (as Laker Airways [Bahamas])
Start Date: May 18, 1992
CEO: Sir Freddie Laker
Ownership: Sir Freddie Laker (34%), Sir Jack Hayward (33%), Oscar Wyatt (33%)

FLEET:

Type	No	Seats	Engines
Boeing 727-200 (Advanced)	2	Y175	PW JT8D-15

BOMBARDIER DHC-8-110 DASH 8

LIAT (LIAT (1974))

IATA: LI **ICAO:** LIA **IATA/ARC:** 140 **RADIO:** LIAT

CONTACTS:

Mail	Telephone/Fax
PO Box 819	Admin: +1 268 462 0700
V C Bird International Airport	Fax: +1 268 462 3455
Coolidge, Antigua	Res: +1 268 462 0700

Internet: www.liatairlines.com

OPERATION:

Type: Scheduled passenger
Cities Served: Caribbean: ANU AXA BBQ BGI CRU DOM EIS FDF GND NEV POS PTP SJU SKB SLU STI STT STX SVD SXM TAB UNI **South America:** GEO
Code-Share: Airlines of Carriacou, Dominair

HISTORY/STRUCTURE:

Founded: September 20, 1956 (as Leeward Islands Air Transport Services)
Start Date: September 20, 1974
Acting Chairman: David Jardine
CEO: Ray Sayer
Ownership: 11 Caribbean governments (30.8%), BWIA (29.2%), private investors (26.7%), employees (13.3%)

FLEET:

Type	No	Seats	Engines
DHC-6-300	2	Y19	PWC PT6A-27
DHC-8-100	9	Y37	PWC PW120A/121
DHC-8-300	3	Y50	PWC PW123

CARIBBEAN

DE HAVILLAND CANADA DHC-6-300 TWIN OTTER

WINAIR (Windward Islands Airways International)

IATA: WM   **ICAO:** WIA   **IATA/ARC:** 295   **RADIO:** Winair

---

CONTACTS:

Mail
PO Box 2088
Philipsburg
St Maarten, Netherlands Antilles

Telephone/Fax
Admin: +599 5 52568
Fax: +599 5 54229
Res: +599 5 52649/52662/54237

Internet: www.riverland.net.au/~winair/

OPERATION:

Type: Scheduled/charter passenger
Cities Served: AXA EIS EUX NEV SAB SBH SKB
Code-Share: Air ALM

HISTORY/STRUCTURE:

Founded: August 24, 1961 (as Windward Islands Airways)
Start Date: August 5, 1962
Chairman: Michael Ferrier
Ownership: Netherlands Antilles government

FLEET:

Type	No	Seats	Engines
DHC-6-300	3	Y19	PWC PT6A-27

Caribbean Addenda

ABACO AIR Marsh Harbour International Airport, PO Box AB20492, Marsh Harbour, Abaco, Bahamas; +1 242 367 2266, Fax: +1 242 367 3256, Andrew Kelly. Charter passenger. 2 x Commander 500, 1 x Islander

AEROMAR AIRLINES Aeropuerto Internacional Las Américas, Dominican Republic; +1 809 549 0281, Fax: +1 809 542 0152, Email: aeromar@dominicana.com. Scheduled/charter passenger/cargo, uses aircraft wet-leased from US carriers as required.

AEROTAXI (CNI/Seraer) Calle 27, Numero 102, Vedado, Ciudad de La Habana, Cuba; +53 7 32 8127, Fax: +53 7 33 2621, Benigno Miranda. Charter passenger. 40 x An-2, 3 x DC-3

AEROVARADERO (TAME) Calle 23, Numero 64, Vedado, Plaza de la Revolución, Ciudad de La Habana, Cuba; +53 7 33 4949, 2320, Fax: +53 7 33 4126

AEROVIAS CARIBE Calle 23, Numero 64, Vedado, Plaza de la Revolución, Ciudad de La Habana, Cuba; +53 7 33 3621, Fax: +53 7 33 3871

AIR ATLANTIC DOMINICANA (LU) Av 27 de Febrero esq Tiradentes, Apto 105, Plaza Merengue, Santo Domingo, Dominican Republic; +1 809 472 1441, Fax: +1 809 472 1622. Scheduled/charter passenger using aircraft wet-leased from US carriers as required.

AIRLINES OF CARRIACOU (C4/COU/484/Air Carriacou) PO Box 805, St George's, Grenada; +1 809 444 3549, Fax: +1 809 444 2898, Email: beans@caribsurf.com, Arthur W Bain. Scheduled passenger (all flights carry only LIAT's code). 3 x Islander

AIR NEGRIL PO 1, PO Box 477, Montego Bay, Jamaica; + 1 876 940 7747, 1 800 678 1300, Fax: +1 876 940 6491, Email: info@caribbean-travel.com, caribbean-travel/airnegril/. Charter passenger. 1 x Cessna T210N, 2 x Cessna U206, 1 x Islander

AIR SAINT BARTHÉLEMY (Société Commerciale Aéronautique) (OJ/BTH/981/Barths) St Jean, F-97133, Saint Barthélemy, Guadeloupe; +590 27 71 90, Fax: +590 27 67 03, Res: +590 27 71 90, Eric Koury. Scheduled passenger (Groupe Air Guadeloupe). 2 x Twin Otter

AIR SAINT MARTIN (SCTA - Société Caribéenne Aéronautique) (S6/ASM/707/Air Saint Martin) Immeuble Le Lieu No 1 &11, F-97139 Les Abymes, Guadeloupe; +590 82 96 63, Fax: +590 91 49 69, Res: +590 82 96 63, Raphael Koury. Scheduled passenger (Groupe Air Guadeloupe). 8 x Cessna 208B

APA INTERNATIONAL AIR (7P/APY/917/APA International) PO Box 524039, Miami, FL 33152-4039 USA; +1 305 526 3304, Fax: +1 305 871 4012, Rafael Trujillo. Scheduled/charter passenger/cargo using wet-leased equipment from US carriers.

CARDINAL AIRLINES (NN/DCF/855/Cardinal Air) 26 King George V Street, Roseau, Dominica; +1 767 449 8922, Fax: +1 767 449 8923, John Tomlinson. Scheduled passenger. 2 x Beech C99

CARIBAIR Avenida Luperon, Aeropuerto Internacional de Herrera, Santo Domingo, Dominican Republic; +1 809 567 2394, Fax: +1 809 567 7033, Rafael Rosado Fermin. Charter passenger. 1 x PA-32 Lance, 1 x PA-34 Seneca, 2 x Navajo, 1 x Islander, 4 x Let 410

CARIB AVIATION (K7/DEL/Red Tail) PO Box 318, St John's, Antigua; +1 268 462 3452, Fax: +1 268 462 3125, Email: carib@candoo.com, www.candoo.com, Frank S Delisle. Charter passenger. 3 x P.68C, 3 x Islander, 1 x Queen Air, 1 x Cessna 402, 1 x DHC-6 Twin Otter

CAT ISLAND AIR PO Box CB-11150, Nassau, Bahamas; +1 242 377 3318, Fax: +1 242 377 3320, Albert Rolle. Charter passenger. 1 x Bandeirante

CONGO AIR (CAK) PO Box SS-6046, Nassau, Bahamas; +1 242 377 8329, Fax: +1 242 377 7413, Anthony Davis. Charter passenger. 1 x Metro II

DOMINAIR (Aerolíneas Dominicanas) (YU/ADM) Apde 202, Calle el Sol No 62, Santiago, Dominican Republic; +1 809 247 410, Fax: +1 809 582 5074, Armando J Bermudez. Wet-leases Dash 8s from LIAT.

FLY BVI PO Box 3347, Roadtown, Tortola, British Virgin Islands; 1 800 435 9284 (US), +1 284 495 1747, Fax: +1 284 495 1973, Email: flybvi@caribsurf.com, www.fly_bvi.com, Nikki Abrams. Charter passenger. 2 x Aztec, 1 x Islander, 1 x Cessna 404, 2 x Cessna 172

INTER-CUBA Office Grupo TACA, Habana Libre Hotel, Ciudad de La Habana, Cuba. Scheduled passenger. Cessna 208B

INTERISLAND AIRWAYS Provo, Turks & Caicos Islands, BWI; +1 941 793 7157, 1 800 645 1179, www.fortmyers.com/turks/interisl.html. Charter passenger. 2 x Aztec, 1 x Chieftain

MUSTIQUE AIRWAYS (Q4/MAW/Mustique) PO Box 1232, Kingstown, St Vincent & The Grenadines; +1 784 458 4380, Fax: +1 784 456 4586, Res: +1 784 458 4380, www.caribisles.com/mustique-air, Jonathan Palmer. Scheduled passenger. 1 x Commander 500, 2 x Islander, 1 x Bandeirante

NEVIS EXPRESS (D4) Newcastle Airport, Nevis, St Kitts & Nevis, WI 0265; +1 869 469 9065, Fax: +1 869 469 9751, Res: +1 869 469 9755/9756, Email: express1@caribsurf.com, www.nevisexpress.com, Allen Haddadi. Scheduled/charter passenger/cargo. 3 x Islander

REGION AIR CARIBBEAN (Spice) Point Salines Intl Airport, St George's, Grenada; +1 473 444 1117, Fax: +1 473 444 1114, www.skyviews.com/grenada/regionair.html. Scheduled/charter passenger. 1 x Cessna 402B, 1 x Islander

SAP (Servicios Aéreos Profesionales) Aeropuerto de Herrera, Avenida Luperon, Santo Domingo, Dominican Republic; +1 809 565 2448, Fax: +1 809 540 4667, Email: sap.air@codetel.net.do, www.sapair.com, José Miguel Patin Hernandez. Charter/contract passenger. 1 x Cessna U206, 1 x Cessna 210, 1 x Islander, 2 x Twin Otter, 7 x Let 410, 1 x Beech 1900D, 2 x Shorts 360, 1 x Gulfstream I

SKY UNLIMITED PO Box N-10859, Nassau, Bahamas; +1 242 377 8993, Fax: +1 242 377 8910, Heuter Rolle. Charter passenger. 2 x Beech C99

ST BARTH COMMUTER (PV/Commuter) Aéroport Gustave III, F-97133 St Barthélemy, Guadeloupe; +590 27 54 54, Fax: + 590 27 54 58, Bruno Masens. Scheduled/charter passenger. 3 x Islander

SVG AIR (St Vincent & The Grenadines Air) PO Box 39, Kingstown, St Vincent; +1 457 5124, Fax: +1 784 457 5077, Email: info@svgair.com, www.svgair.com, Martin Barnard. Charter passenger. 1 x Cessna 402B , 2 x Commander 500S, 1 x Islander

TAINO AIR PO Box F4006, Freeport Intl Airport, Bahamas; +1 242 352 8885, Fax: +1 242 352 5175, John Doherty. Charter passenger. 2 x Bandeirante

TCI SKYKING (RU/Skyking) PO Box 398, Providenciales, Turks & Caicos Islands; +1 649 941 5464, Fax: +1 649 941 5127, Email: king@tciway.tc, www.skyking.tc, Charles Harold. Scheduled/charter passenger. 2 x Aztec, 1 x Cessna 402B/C, 1 x Cessna 404, 1 x Shorts 360

TRANS ANGUILLA PO Box 1329, Wallblake Airport, Anguilla; +1 264 497 8690, Fax: +1 264 497 8689, Email: transang@anguillanet.com, www.trans.ai, Lincoln Gumbs. Scheduled/charter passenger. 2 x Islander, 1 x Twin Otter, 1 x King Air 200

TRANSCARAIBES AIR INTERNATIONAL (DZ/NOE/French Hopper) Les terrasses de St Jean, F-97133 St Barthélemy; +590 27 9336, Fax: +590 27 9338, www.st-barths.com/transcaraibes/index.html. Charter passenger. 1 x Cessna 207A, 1 x P.68B

TRANS ISLAND AIR (TRD/Trans Island) South Ramp, Grantley Adams International Airport, Christ Church, Barbados; +1 246 428 1651, Fax: +1 246 428 0916, Herbert Yearwood. Charter passenger. 3 x Islander, 1 x Bandeirante, 1 x Twin Otter

TURKS & CAICOS AIRWAYS (QW/TCI/254/Turk National) PO Box 114, Providenciales, Turks & Caicos Islands; +1 809 946 4255, Fax: +1 809 946 5388, A V Butterfield. Scheduled/charter passenger. 1 x Aztec, 2 x Islander

TYDEN AIR SERVICES PO Box 107, The Valley, Anguilla; +1 264 497 3419, Fax: +1 264 497 3079, Lesley Lloyd. Charter passenger. 2 x Islander

NOTES:

DE HAVILLAND CANADA DHC-6-300 TWIN OTTER

AEROPERLAS (AEROLÍNEAS PACIFICO ATLÁNTICO)

IATA: WL   **ICAO:** APP   **IATA/ARC:** 828   **RADIO:** Aeroplan

CONTACTS:

Mail
Apartado 6-3596
El Dorado (Panamá)
Panamá
Email: iflyap@aeroperlas.com
Internet: www.aeroperlas.com

Telephone/Fax
Admin: +507 315 0303
Fax: +507 315 0337
Res: +507 210 9500

OPERATION:

Type: Scheduled/charter passenger
Cities Served: BOC CHX CTO DAV ELE GHE JQE NMG ONX OTD PAC PLP PTY SAX SJO SYP
Some services operated under the name Aerolínas Pacifico Atlantico
Code-Share: LACSA, TACA
FFP: Distancia

HISTORY/STRUCTURE:

Founded: 1969 (as Aerolíneas Islas de las Perlas)
Start Date: June 1970
President/CEO: George F Novey
Ownership: Grupo TACA, private investors

FLEET:

Type	No	Seats	Engines
King Air A100	1	Y10	PWC PT6A-27
DHC-6-300	6	Y20	PWC PT6A-27
Shorts SD3-60 (200)	4	Y36	PWC PT6A-65AR

BOEING 737-200 (ADVANCED)

AVIATECA

IATA: GU   **ICAO:** GUG   **IATA/ARC:** 240   **RADIO:** Aviateca

---

CONTACTS:

Mail	Telephone/Fax
Avenida Hincapié 12-22, Zona 13	Admin: +502 331 8261
Aéropuerto La Aurora	Fax: +502 331 7412
Guatemala City 01013, Guatemala	Res: 1 800 327 9832

Internet: www.grupotaca.com

OPERATION:

Type: Scheduled passenger
Cities Served: México/Central America GUA MGA MEX PTY SAL SJO
US: DFW MIA
Code-Share: American Airlines, Inter, LACSA, TACA
FFP: Distancia, LatinPass

HISTORY/STRUCTURE:

Founded: 1945 (as Compañia Guatemalteca de Avíacíon)
Start Date: March 1946
President/CEO: Ing Julio Obols Gomes
Ownership: Grupo TACA (30%), private investors (70%)

FLEET:

Type	No	Seats	Engines
Cessna 208B	2	Y9	PWC PT6A-114A
operated by Inter (Transportes Aéreos Inter)			
Boeing 737-200 (Advanced)	5	C8Y110 or C8Y113	PW JT8D-9A/-15

BOEING 737-700

COPA AIRLINES (Compañía Panameña de Aviación)

IATA: CM   **ICAO:** CMP   **IATA/ARC:** 230   **RADIO:** Copa

---

CONTACTS:

Mail	Telephone/Fax
Apartado, Postal 1572	Admin: +507 227 2522
Panamá 1 (Panamá)	Fax: +507 227 1952
Panamá	Res: 1 800 359 2672
Email: cserv@mail.copa.com.pa	PR: 1 507 227 0116
Internet: www.copaair.com	

OPERATION:

Type: Scheduled/charter passenger
Cities Served: México/Central America: GUA MEX PTY SJO SAL SAP
Caribbean: HAV KIN MBJ PAP SDQ SJU **South America:** BAQ BOG CCS CLO
CTG GYE LIM MDE SCL UIO **US:** MIA
Code-Share: AVIANCA/SAM, Continental Airlines
FFP: OnePass

HISTORY/STRUCTURE:

Founded: 1944
Start Date: May 5, 1947
CEO: Pedro Heilbron
Ownership: Private investors (51%), Continental Airlines (49%)

FLEET:

Type	No	Seats	Engines
Boeing 737-200C	1	Freighter	PW JT8D-9
Boeing 737-200 (Advanced)	12	C8Y106	PW JT8D-15
Boeing 737-700	2	C12Y112	CFM56-7B24
Ordered			
Boeing 737-700	10		

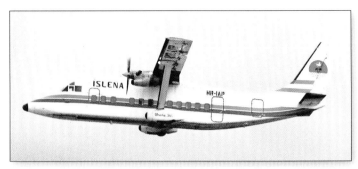

SHORTS SD3-60 VARIANT 100

ISLEÑA AIRLINES (Isleña de Inversiones)

IATA: WC   **ICAO:** ISV   **IATA/ARC:** 282   **RADIO:** none

CONTACTS:

Mail	Telephone/Fax
PO Box 402	Admin: +504 43 0179
Frente Parque Central, Avda San Isidro	Fax:　　+504 43 2739
La Ceiba, Honduras	Res:　　+504 43 0179
Email: islena@caribe.hn	

OPERATION:

Type: Scheduled/charter passenger
Cities Served: México/Central America: BZE CUN FRS GUA LCE LIR MGA MID RTB SAL SAP SJO TGU **Caribbean:** GCM
All service operated using Aviateca, LACSA, or TACA flight numbers
FFP: Distancia, LatinPass

HISTORY/STRUCTURE:

Founded: 1981
Start Date: March 31, 1981
President/CEO: Arturo Alvarado Wood
Ownership: Private investors (80%), Grupo TACA (20%)

FLEET:

Type	No	Seats	Engines
Cessna 208B	1	Y9	PWC PT6A-114A
Let 410	3	Y18	WA M-601D
Shorts 360 (100)	2	Y39	PWC PT6A-65R
ATR42-300	5	Y50	PWC PW120/121

SHORTS SD3-60 VARIANT 200

LA COSTEÑA

IATA: W8   **ICAO:** none   **IATA/ARC:** none   **RADIO:** Lacostena

---

CONTACTS:

Mail	Telephone/Fax	
Aeropuerto Internacional AC Sandino	Admin:	+505 263 1228
Terminal Vuelos Nacionales	Fax:	+505 263 1281
Managua, Nicaragua	Res:	+505 263 1228

OPERATION:

Type: Scheduled/charter passenger
Cities Served: BEF BZA MGA NCR NVG PUZ RNI WSP
Code-Share: TACA
FFP: Distancia

HISTORY/STRUCTURE:

Founded: 1991
Start Date: 1991
President/CEO: Alfredo Caballero
Ownership: Grupo TACA (50%), Caballero/private investors (50%)

FLEET:

Type	No	Seats	Engines
Cessna 208B	4	Y9	PWC PT6A-114A
Shorts SD3-60 (200)	2	Y36	PWC PT6A-65AR

CENTRAL AMERICA

AIRBUS A320-232

LACSA (Lineas Aéreas Costarricenses)

IATA: LR   **ICAO:** LRC   **IATA/ARC:** 133   **RADIO:** Lacsa

CONTACTS:

Mail
Apartado 1531-1000
San José, Costa Rica

Internet: http://www.grupotaca.com

Telephone/Fax
Admin: +506 231 6064
Fax: +506 232 9185
Res: 1 800 225 2272

OPERATION:

Type: Scheduled/charter passenger
Cities Served: México/Central America: CUN MGA MEX PTY SAL SJO
Caribbean: HAV SJU **South America:** BOG CCS GYE LIM SCL UIO
US: LAX MCO MIA MSY JFK
Code-Share: Aeroperlas, American Airlines, Aviateca, Isleña, SAM Colombia, SANSA, TACA
FFP: Distancia, LatinPass

HISTORY/STRUCTURE:

Founded: October 17, 1945
Start Date: June 1, 1946
Chairman: Alonso Lara
President: José G Rojas
Ownership: Private investors, employees, Grupo TACA (10%)

FLEET:

Type	No	Seats	Engines
Boeing 737-200 (Advanced)	6	C8Y113	JT8D-15/-17/-17A
Airbus A320-200	5	C12Y144	IAE V2527-A5/V2527E-A5

BOEING 737-200 (ADVANCED)

NICA (Nicaraguenses de Aviación)

IATA: 6Y   **ICAO:** NIS   **IATA/ARC:** 930   **RADIO:** Nica

CONTACTS:

Mail
Apartado Postal 6018
KM 10.5, Carretera del Norte
Managua, Nicaragua

Telephone/Fax
Admin: +505 263 1929
Fax: +505 263 1822
Res: 1 800 831 6422

Internet: http://www.grupotaca.com

OPERATION:

Type: Scheduled passenger
Cities Served: Central America: MGA **US:** MIA
Code-Share: Aviateca, LACSA, TACA
FFP: Distancia, LatinPass

HISTORY/STRUCTURE:

Founded: 1992
Start Date: July 10, 1992
President/CEO: Enrique Dreyfus
Ownership: Nicaraguan government (51%), Grupo TACA (49%)

FLEET:

Type	No	Seats	Engines
Boeing 737-200 (Advanced)	1	C8Y108	PW JT8D-15

BOEING 767-300 (ER)

TACA

IATA: TA   **ICAO:** TAI   **IATA/ARC:** 202   **RADIO:** Taca

---

CONTACTS:

Mail
Edificio Caribe, 2 Piso
San Salvador, El Salvador

Internet: www.grupotaca.com

Telephone/Fax
Admin: +503 298 5055
Fax: +503 223 3757
Res: 1 800 535 8780

OPERATION:

Type: Scheduled/charter passenger/cargo
Cities Served: México/Central America: BZE GUA MEX MGA PTY RTB SAL SAP SJO TGU **US:** DFW IAD IAH JFK LAX MCO MIA SFO
Cargo: GUA IAH LAX MGA MIA SAL SAP SJO
Code-Share: American Airlines, Aviateca, Isleña, LACSA
FFP: Distancia, LatinPass

HISTORY/STRUCTURE:

Founded: December 1931 (as Transportes Aéreos Centro-Americanos)
Start Date: March 16, 1932
President/CEO: Federico Bloch
Ownership: Grupo TACA

FLEET:

Type	No	Seats	Engines
Boeing 737-200 (Advanced)	6	C8Y103	PW JT8D-17/-17A
Airbus A320-200	9	C12Y144	IAE V2527E-A5
Airbus A300B4-200 (F)	6	Freighter	GE CF6-50C2
Boeing 767-200ER	1	Y234	GE CF6-80A2
Boeing 767-300ER	2	C16Y254	GE CF6-80C2B4F/B6F
Ordered			
Airbus A319-100	21		
Airbus A320-200	11		
Airbus A300F-200	2		

AERO COSTA SOL (ACS) Grupo Costa Sol, PO Box 7-1880-1000, San José, Costa Rica; +506 239 0033, Fax: +506 239 0210, Res: 1 800 832 0474, 1 800 245 8420 (US/Can), www.costa-sol.co.cr/aero/index.html. Charter passenger. 1 x Aztec, 1 x Navajo, 1 x Lear, 1 x Let 410

AEROLINEAS SOSA (P4/Sosa) Avenida San Isidro, Frente al Parque Central, La Ceiba, Honduras; +504 43 1894, Juan Antonio Sosa B. Charter passenger. 1 x Cessna U206G, 1 x Let 410

CARGO THREE (CTW/413/Third Cargo) AP 2472, Panamá 9A (Panamá), Panamá; +507 238 4091, Fax: +507 238 4417, Francisco Giraldo. Charter cargo. 1 x Convair 580

DHL AERO EXPRESSO (DS/DAE/992) Apartado Aéreo 11491, Panamá City 6 (Panamá), Panamá; +507 238 4206, Fax: +507 238 4149, Steve Getzler. Scheduled cargo. 1 x 727-200F

DHL DE GUATEMALA (Z8/JOS/947) Air Operations Department, Blvd Juan Pablo II, 6-75 Zona 13, Guatemala City 01013, Guatemala; +502 361 7458, Fax: +502 361 7450, Enrique Salazar. Scheduled cargo. 1 x Metro III, 1 x 727-100F

INTER (Transportes Aéreos Inter) (TSP/Transpo-Inter) Hincapié 12-22, Zona 13, Aéropuerto La Aurora, Guatemala City 01013, Guatemala; +502 331 8261, +502 331 7402, www.flylatinamerica.com/ing/inter.html, Julio O Gomes. Scheduled/charter passenger. 2 x Cessna 208B

MAYA AIRWAYS PO Box 458, Municipal Airport, Belize City, Belize; +501 2 35794, Fax: +501 2 30585, Email: mayair@btl.net, www.mayaairways.com/.Scheduled passenger/cargo. 2 x Islander

MAYA ISLAND AIR (Island Air) San Pedro Town, Ambergris Caye, Belize;+1 501 2 62435, 1 800 521 1247, Email: miaspra@btl.net, www.ambergriscaye.com/islandair/index.html, Emanuel Fernando Trejo. Scheduled/charter passenger. 2 x Cessna 207A, 2 x Islander, 1 x Cessna 208B

MAYAN WORLD AIRLINES (EY/MYN/987/Mayan World) Centro Gerencial Las Margaritas, Torre II, 7 Nivel, Diagonal 6, Guatemala City 01001, Guatemala; +502 360 2828, Fax: +502 360 2838, Res: +502 360 2828, Email: mwa@infovia.com.gt, www.mayanworldairlines.com, Santiago de La Rocha. Scheduled/charter passenger. 2 x Yak-40

PACIFIC INTERNATIONAL AIRLINE (PFC/Pacific International) Apartado Postal 1592, Panamá 9A (Panamá), Panamá; +507 226 3211, Fax: +507 226 4012, Guillermo Rodriguez. Charter cargo. 2 x 727-100F

PANAVIA (PNV) Apartado 8140030, Zona 14/1, Panamá City (Panamá), Panamá; +507 238 4503, Fax: +507 238 4509. Charter cargo. 1 x 727-100F

RACSA (Rutas Aéreas Centro Americanas, SA) Avenida Hincapie y 18 Calle, Zona 13, Aeropuerto La Aurora, Guatemala City 01013, Guatemala; +502 332 7470, Fax: +502 334 7935, Res: +502 332 5686, Email: aerovias@tradepoint.org.gt. Fernando Castillo. Scheduled/charter passenger. 1 x Nord 262A

SANSA (RZ/LRS/503) Apartado 999-1007, Centro Colon, San José, Costa Rica; +506 221 9414, Fax:+506 255 2176, 1 800 225 2272, www.crdirect.com/sansa. Scheduled/charter passenger. 7 x Cessna 208B

TRAVELAIR (U3/585) Apartado 8-4920, San José, Costa Rica; +506 220 3054, Fax: +506 220 0413, Res: 1 800 948 3770, Email: travelair@centralamerica.com, www.centralamerica.com/cr/tran/travlair.htm, Charles Warbelow. Charter passenger. 1 x Cessna U206E 1 x Islander, 2 x Trislander, 1 x Let 410

TROPIC AIR (PM/TOS) PO Box 20, San Pedro, Belize; +501 26 2012, Fax: +501 26 2338, tropicair@btl.net, www.tropicair.com, Celi McCorkle. Scheduled/charter passenger. 1 x Cessna 207A, 5 x Cessna 208B

NOTES:

NOTES:

CITY AND AIRPORT DECODE

A

ABE	Allentown, PA
ABI	Abilene, TX
ABQ	Albuquerque, NM
ABR	Aberdeen, SD
ABY	Albany, GA
ACA	Acapulco, México
ACK	Nantucket, MA
ACT	Waco, TX
ACV	Eureka/Arcata, CA
ACY	Atlantic City Intl, NJ
ADK	Adak Island, AK
ADQ	Kodiak, AK
ADZ	Isla de San Andrés, Colombia
AED	Aleneva, AK
AET	Allakaket, AK
AEX	Alexandria, LA
AFW	Fort Worth-Alliance, TX
AGM	Tasiilaq, Greenland
AGS	Augusta, GA
AGT	Ciudad del Este, Brazil
AGU	Aguascalientes, México
AHN	Athens, GA
AIA	Alliance, NE
AKI	Akiak, AK
AKK	Akhiok, AK
AKL	Auckland, New Zealand
AKN	King Salmon, AK
AKP	Anaktuvuk, AK
AKV	Akulivik, QC
ALB	Albany, NY
ALM	Alamogordo, NM
ALO	Waterloo, IA
ALS	Alamosa, CO
ALW	Walla Walla, WA
ALZ	Alitak, AK
AMA	Amarillo, TX
AMS	Amsterdam, Netherlands
ANC	Anchorage, AK
ANI	Aniak, AK
ANU	Antigua, West Indies
AOO	Altoona, PA
AOS	Amook, AK
APF	Naples, FL
ARC	Arctic Village, AK
ARN	Stockholm-Arlanda, Sweden
ART	Watertown, NY
ASD	Andros Town, Bahamas
ASE	Aspen, CO
ASU	Asunción, Paraguay
ATC	Arthur's Town, Bahamas
ATH	Athens, Greece
ATL	Atlanta, GA
ATT	Atmautluak, AK
ATW	Appleton, WI
ATY	Watertown, SD
AUA	Aruba, Aruba
AUG	Augusta, ME
AUS	Austin, TX
AVI	Ciego de Avila, Cuba
AVL	Asheville, NC
AVP	Wilkes-Barre/Scranton, PA
AXA	Anguilla, Leeward Islands
AXP	Spring Point, Bahamas
AZO	Kalamazoo, MI

B

BAQ	Barranquilla, Colombia
BBQ	Barbuda, West Indies
BBR	Basse Terre, French Antilles
BCA	Baracoa, Cuba
BCN	Barcelona, Spain
BDA	Bermuda-Kindley Field
BDL	Bradley Intl, CT
BDR	Bridgeport, CT
BEF	Bluefields, Nicaragua
BEH	Benton Harbor, MI
BET	Bethel, AK
BFD	Bradford, PA
BFF	Scottsbluff, NE
BFI	Seattle-Boeing Field, WA
BFL	Bakersfield, CA
BFM	Mobile, AL
BFS	Belfast, UK
BGI	Barbados, Barbados
BGM	Binghamton, NY
BGR	Bangor, ME
BHB	Bar Harbor, ME
BHM	Birmingham, AL
BHX	Birmingham, UK
BIL	Billings, MT
BIM	Bimini, Bahamas
BIS	Bismarck, ND
BJI	Bemidji, MN
BJX	León/Guanajuato, México
BKK	Bangkok, Thailand
BKW	Beckley, WV
BKX	Brookings, SD
BLF	Bluefield, WV
BLI	Bellingham, WA
BMG	Bloomington, IN
BMI	Bloomington, IL
BNA	Nashville, TN
BOC	Bocas Del Toro, Panamá
BOD	Bordeaux, France
BOG	Bogotá, Colombia
BOI	Boise, ID
BOM	Mumbai, India
BON	Bonaire, Netherlands Antilles
BOS	Boston, MA
BPT	Beaumont/Pt Arthur, TX
BQK	Glynco Jetport, GA
BQN	Aguadilla, PR
BQU	Port Elizabeth, Bequia
BRD	Brainerd, MN
BRL	Burlington, IA
BRO	Brownsville, TX
BRU	Brussels, Belgium
BRW	Barrow, AK
BSL	Basle-Mulhouse, France
BTI	Barter Island, AK
BTM	Butte, MT
BTR	Baton Rouge, LA
BTT	Bettles, AK
BTV	Burlington, VT
BUD	Budapest, Hungary
BUF	Buffalo, NY
BUR	Burbank, CA
BWD	Brownwood, TX
BWI	Baltimore, MD
BYM	Bayamo, Cuba
BZA	Bonanza, San Pedro, Nicaragua
BZE	Belize City, Belize
BZN	Bozeman, MT

C

CAE	Columbia, SC
CAI	Cairo, Egypt
CAK	Akron/Canton, OH
CAP	Cap-Haïtien, Haiti
CAY	Cayenne, French Guiana
CBE	Cumberland, MD
CCC	Cayo Coco, Cuba
CCS	Caracas, Venezuela
CDB	Cold Bay, AK
CDC	Cedar City, UT
CDG	Paris-Charles de Gaulle, France
CDR	Chadron, NE
CDV	Cordova, AK

CEC	Crescent City, CA	CUR	Curaçao, Netherlands Antilles	DXB	Dubai, UAE
CEN	Ciudad Obregon, México	CUU	Chihuahua, México		
CEZ	Cortez, CO	CVG	Cincinnati, OH	**E**	
CFQ	Croston, BC	CVJ	Cuernavaca, México	EAT	Wenatchee, WA
CGI	Cape Girardeau, MO	CVM	Ciudad Victoria, México	EAU	Eau Claire, WI
CGN	Cologne/Bonn, Germany	CVN	Clovis, NM	EDI	Edinburgh, UK
CGX	Meigs Field, IL	CWA	Central Wisconsin, WI	EEK	Eek, AK
CHA	Chattanooga, TN	CWF	Lake Charles, LA	EEN	Keene, NH
CHO	Charlottesville, VA	CWL	Cardiff, UK	EFD	Ellington Field, TX
CHS	Charleston, SC	CXH	Vancouver-Coal Harbour, BC	EGE	Vail, CO
CHX	Changuinola, Panamá			EGX	Egegik, AK
CIA	Rome-Ciampino, Italy	CXL	Calexico, CA	EIS	Tortola, British Virgin Islands
CIC	Chico, CA	CYB	Cayman Brac, West Indies		
CID	Cedar Rapids, IA	CYF	Chefornak, AK	EKO	Elko, NV
CIU	Chippewa County, MI	CYS	Cheyenne, WY	ELD	El Dorado, AR
CIW	Canouan Island, Windward Islands	CYO	Cayo Lago, Cuba	ELE	El Real, Panamá
		CZA	Chichen Itza, México	ELH	North Eleuthera, Bahamas
CJS	Ciudad Juárez, México	CZM	Cozumel, México	ELM	Elmira/Corning, NY
CKB	Clarksburg, WV			ELP	El Paso, TX
CLD	Carlsbad, CA			EMA	East Midlands, UK
CLE	Cleveland, OH	**D**		ENA	Kenai, AK
CLL	College Station, TX	DAB	Daytona Beach, FL	EPS	El Portillo, Dominican Republic
CLM	Port Angeles, WA	DAL	Love Field, Dallas, TX		
CLO	Cali, Colombia	DAV	David, Panamá	ERI	Erie, PA
CLQ	Colima, México	DAY	Dayton, OH	ESC	Escanaba, MI
CLT	Charlotte, NC	DBQ	Dubuque, IA	EUG	Eugene, OR
CME	Ciudad del Carmen, México	DCA	Washington-Ronald Reagan National, DC	EUX	St Eustatius, Netherlands Antilles
CMH	Columbus, OH	DCF	Can Field, West Indies	EVV	Evansville, IN
CMI	Champaign, IL	DDC	Dodge City, KS	EWR	Newark Intl, NJ
CMW	Camaguey, Cuba	DEC	Decatur, IL	EXT	Exeter, UK
CMX	Hancock, MI	DEL	Delhi, India	EYW	Key West, FL
CNF	Belo Horizonte, Brazil	DEN	Denver, CO	EZE	Buenos Aires-Pistarini, Argentina
CNM	Carlsbad, NM	DFW	Dallas/Fort Worth, TX		
CNP	Nerlerit Inaat, Greenland	DGO	Durango, México		
CNS	Cairns, Australia	DHN	Dothan, AL	**F**	
CNW	Waco-Connolly, TX	DIK	Dickinson, ND	FAI	Fairbanks, AK
COD	Cody, WY	DLG	Dillingham, AK	FAR	Fargo, ND
COS	Colorado Springs, CO	DLH	Duluth, MN	FAT	Fresno, CA
COU	Columbia, MO	DOM	Dominica, West Indies	FAY	Fayetteville, NC
CPE	Campeche, México	DPS	Denpasar, Bali, Indonesia	FCA	Kalispell, MT
CPH	Copenhagen, Denmark	DRO	Durango, CO	FCO	Rome-Fiumicino, Italy
CPR	Casper, WY	DRT	Del Rio, TX	FDF	Fort-de-France, Martinique
CRI	Crooked Island, Bahamas	DSD	La Desirade, French Antilles	FHU	Fort Huachuca/Sierra Vista, AZ
CRP	Corpus Christi, TX				
CRU	Carriacou, Windward Islands	DSM	Des Moines, IA	FKL	Franklin, PA
		DTN	Shreveport-Downtown, LA	FLG	Flagstaff, AZ
CRW	Charleston, WV	DTW	Detroit-Metro Wayne County, MI	FLL	Fort Lauderdale, FL
CSG	Columbus, GA			FLO	Florence, SC
CTG	Cartegena, Colombia	DUB	Dublin, Ireland	FMN	Farmington, NM
CTM	Chetumal, México	DUJ	Dubois, PA	FMY	Fort Myers, FL
CTO	Calverton, NY	DUS	Düsseldorf, Germany	FNL	Fort Collins/Loveland, CO
CTS	Sapporo-Chitose, Japan	DUT	Dutch Harbor, AK	FNT	Flint, MI
CUL	Culiacán, México	DVL	Devils Lake, ND		
CUN	Cancún, México				

FOD   Fort Dodge, IA

FOE   Topeka Forbes AFB, KS

FPO   Freeport, Bahamas

FRA   Frankfurt, Germany

FRM   Fairmont, MN

FRS   Flores, Guatemala

FSD   Sioux Falls, SD

FSM   Fort Smith, AR

FSP   St-Pierre et Miquelon

FUK   Fukuoka, Japan

FWA   Fort Wayne, IN

FYU   Fort Yukon, AK

FYV   Fayetteville, AR

G

GAL   Galena, AK

GAO   Guantanamo, Cuba

GBD   Great Bend, KS

GBJ   Marie Galante, French Antilles

GCC   Gillette, WY

GCK   Garden City, KS

GCM   Grand Cayman Island, West Indies

GCN   Grand Canyon, AZ

GDL   Guadalajara, México

GDT   Grand Turk, Turks & Caicos Islands

GDV   Glendive, MT

GDX   Magadan, Russia

GEG   Spokane, WA

GEO   Georgetown, Guyana

GER   Nueva Gerona, Cuba

GFK   Grand Forks, ND

GGG   Longview, TX

GGT   George Town, Bahamas

GGW   Glasgow, MT

GHE   Garachine, Panamá

GHB   Governors Harbour, Bahamas

GIG   Rio de Janeiro-Intl, Brazil

GJT   Grand Junction, CO

GLA   Glasgow, UK

GLD   Goodland, KS

GLH   Greenville, MS

GND   Grenada, Windward Islands

GNU   Goodnews Bay, AK

GNV   Gainesville, FL

GOH   Nuuk, Greenland

GON   New London/Groton, CT

GPT   Gulfport/Biloxi, MS

GPZ   Grand Rapids, MN

GRB   Green Bay, WI

GRI   Grand Island, NE

GRR   Grand Rapids, MI

GRU   São Paulo-Guarulhos, Brazil

GSO   Greensboro/High Pt/ Winston-Salem, NC

GSP   Greenville/Spartanburg, SC

GTF   Great Falls, MT

GTR   Golden Triangle Regional, Columbus, MS

GUA   Guatemala City, Guatemala

GUB   Guerrero Negro, México

GUC   Gunnison, CO

GUM   Guam, Guam

GUP   Gallup, NM

GVA   Geneva, Switzerland

GYE   Guayaquil, Ecuador

GYM   Guaymas, México

H

HAM   Hamburg, Germany

HAV   Havana, Cuba

HDN   Steamboat Springs- Hayden, CO

HEL   Helsinki, Finland

HEX   Santo Domingo-Herrera, Dominican Republic

HGR   Hagerstown, MD

HHH   Hilton Head Island, SC

HIB   Hibbing/Chisholm, MN

HII   Lake Havasu City, AZ

HKG   Hong Kong, China

HKY   Hickory, NC

HLN   Helena, MT

HMO   Hermosillo, México

HNL   Honolulu, HI

HNM   Hana, Maui, HI

HOB   Hobbs, NM

HOG   Holguín, Cuba

HOM   Homer, AK

HON   Huron, SD

HOT   Hot Springs, AR

HOU   Houston, TX

HPB   Hooper Bay, AK

HPN   Westchester County, NY

HRE   Harare, Zimbabwe

HRL   Harlingen, TX

HRO   Harrison, AR

HSL   Huslia, AK

HSV   Huntsville/Decatur, AL

HTS   Huntington, WV

HUF   Terre Haute, IN

HUX   Huatulco, México

HVN   New Haven, CT

HVR   Havre, MT

HYA   Hyannis, MA

HYS   Hays, KS

I

IAD   Washington-Dulles Intl, DC

IAH   Houston-Intercontinental, TX

ICT   Wichita, KS

IDA   Idaho Falls, ID

IFP   Bullhead City, AZ

IGA   Inagua, Bahamas

IGG   Igiugig, AK

IGM   Kingman, AZ

ILE   Killeen, TX

ILG   Wilmington, DE

ILI   Iliamna, AK

ILM   Wilmington, NC

ILN   Wilmington, OH

IMT   Iron Mountain, MI

IND   Indianapolis, IN

INL   International Falls, MN

INT   Winston-Salem/Smith- Reynolds, NC

IPL   El Centro/Imperial, CA

IPT   Williamsport, PA

IQT   Iquitos, Perú

ISN   Williston, ND

ISO   Kinston, NC

ISP   Long Island, MacArthur, NY

IST   Istanbul, Turkey

ITH   Ithaca, NY

ITO   Hilo, HI

IWD   Ironwood, MI

IYK   Inyokern, CA

J

JAC   Jackson Hole, WY

JAN   Jackson, MS

JAV   Ilulissat, Greenland

JAX   Jacksonville, FL

JBR   Jonesboro, AR

JCH   Qasigiannguit, Greenland

JEG   Aasiaat, Greenland

JFK   New York-Kennedy Intl, NY

JFR   Paamiut, Greenland

JGO   Qeqertarsuaq, Greenland

JGR   Kangilinnguit, Greenland

JHM   Kapalua, Maui, HI

JHS   Sisimiut, Greenland

JHW   Jamestown, NY

JJU	Qaqortoq, Greenland
JLN	Joplin, MO
JMS	Jamestown, ND
JND	Johannesburg, South Africa
JNN	Nanortalik, Greenland
JNS	Narsaq, Greenland
JNU	Juneau, AK
JON	Johnstone Island, US
JQE	Jaque, Panamá
JST	Johnstown, PA
JSU	Maniitsoq, Greenland
JUV	Upernavik, Greenland

K

KAL	Kaltag, AK
KCG	Fisheries, AK
KCL	Chignik, AK
KCQ	Chignik, AK
KEF	Keflavík, Iceland
KEK	Ekwok, AK
KES	Kelsey, MB
KGK	Koliganek, AK
KHH	Kaohsiung, Taiwan
KHV	Khabarovsk, Russia
KIB	Ivanof Bay, AK
KIF	Kingfisher Lake, ON
KIJ	Niigata, Japan
KIN	Kingston, Jamaica
KIX	Osaka-Kansai, Japan
KKB	Kitoi Bay, AK
KKH	Kongiganak, AK
KOA	Kona, Hawaii, HI
KOY	Olga Bay, AK
KOZ	Ouzinkie, AK
KPN	Kipnuk, AK
KSA	Kosrae, Caroline Islands
KSM	Saint Marys, AK
KTN	Ketchikan, AK
KTP	Tinson, Jamaica
KUK	Kasigluk, AK
KUL	Kuala Lumpur, Malyasia
KUS	Kulusuk, Greenland
KVC	King Cove, AK
KWA	Kwajalein, Marshall Islands
KWK	Kwigillngok, AK
KWN	Quinhagak, AK
KWP	West Point, AK
KZB	Zachar Bay, AK

L

LAA	Lamar, CO
LAF	Lafayette, IN
LAM	Los Alamos, NM
LAN	Lansing, MI
LAP	La Paz, México
LAR	Laramie, WY
LAS	Las Vegas, NV
LAW	Lawton, OK
LAX	Los Angeles, CA
LBA	Leeds/Bradford, UK
LBB	Lubbock, TX
LBE	Latrobe, PA
LBF	North Platte, NE
LBL	Liberal, KS
LCE	La Ceiba, Honduras
LCH	Lake Charles, LA
LCK	Columbus (Rickenbacker), OH
LEB	Lebanon, NH
LEX	Lexington, KY
LFT	Lafayette, LA
LGA	New York-LaGuardia, NY
LGB	Long Beach, CA
LGI	Deadmans Cay, Long Island, Bahamas
LGW	London-Gatwick, UK
LHR	London-Heathrow, UK
LIH	Lihue, Kauai, HI
LIM	Lima, Perú
LIR	Liberia, Costa Rica
LIS	Lisbon, Portugal
LIT	Little Rock, AR
LMM	Los Mochis, México
LMT	Klamath Falls, OR
LNK	Lincoln, NE
LNS	Lancaster, PA
LNY	Lanai City, Lanai, HI
LOV	Monclova, México
LPA	Las Palmas, Gran Canaria, Spain
LPB	La Paz, Bolivia
LRD	Laredo, TX
LRM	La Romana, Dominican Republic
LRU	Las Cruces, NM
LSE	La Crosse, WI
LSS	Terre-de-Haut, Guadeloupe
LTO	Loreto, México
LWB	Greenbrier, WV
LWS	Lewiston, ID
LWT	Lewistown, MT
LYH	Lynchburg, VA
LYS	Lyon-Satolas, France
LYU	Ely, MN
LZC	Lazáro Cárdenas, México

M

MAD	Madrid, Spain
MAF	Midland/Odessa, TX
MAJ	Majuro, Marshall Islands
MAM	Matamoros, México
MAN	Manchester, UK
MAO	Manaus, Brazil
MAR	Maracaiba, Venezuela
MAY	Mangrove Cay, Bahamas
MAZ	Mayaguez, PR
MBJ	Montego Bay, Jamaica
MBL	Mainstee, MI
MBS	Saginaw, MI
MCE	Merced, CA
MCG	McGrath, AK
MCI	Kansas City, MO
MCK	McCook, NE
MCN	Macon, GA
MCO	Orlando Intl, FL
MCW	Mason City, IA
MDE	Medellín, Colombia
MDS	Middle Caicos, Turks & Caicos Islands
MDT	Harrisburg Intl, PA
MDW	Midway, IL
MDZ	Mendoza, Argentina
MEI	Meridian, MS
MEL	Melbourne, Australia
MEM	Memphis, TN
MEX	Mexico City, México
MFE	McAllen, TX
MFR	Medford, OR
MGA	Managua, Nicaragua
MGM	Montgomery, AL
MGW	Morgantown, WV
MHH	Marsh Harbour, Bahamas
MHK	Manhattan, KS
MHR	Sacramento-Mather, CA
MHT	Manchester, NH
MIA	Miami, FL
MID	Mérida, México
MKC	Kansas City, MO
MKE	Milwaukee, WI
MKG	Muskegon, MI
MKK	Molokai/Hoolehua, HI
MKL	Jackson, TN
MLB	Melbourne, FL
MLI	Moline, IL
MLL	Marshall, AK
MLM	Morelia, México

MLS	Miles City, MT
MLU	Monroe, LA
MNI	Montserrat, Montserrat
MNL	Manila, Philippines
MOA	Moa, Cuba
MOB	Mobile, AL
MOD	Modesto, CA
MOT	Minot, ND
MPB	Miami-Watson Island, FL
MQT	Marquette, MI
MRS	Marseille, France
MRY	Monterey, CA
MSA	Muskrat Dam, ON
MSL	Muscle Shoals, AL
MSN	Madison, WI
MSO	Missoula, MT
MSP	Minneapolis/St Paul, MN
MSS	Massena, NY
MSY	New Orleans, LA
MTH	Marathon, FL
MTJ	Montrose, CO
MTO	Mattoon, IL
MTT	Minatitlán, México
MTY	Monterrey, México
MUC	Munich, Germany
MVD	Montevideo, Uruguay
MVN	Mt Vernon, IL
MVY	Martha's Vineyard, MA
MWA	Marion, IL
MWH	Moses Lake, WA
MXL	Mexicali, México
MXP	Milan-Malpensa, Italy
MYG	Mayaguana, Bahamas
MYR	Myrtle Beach, SC
MYU	Mekoryuk, AK
MZO	Manzanillo, Cuba
MZT	Mazatlán, México

N

NAN	Nadi, Fiji
NAQ	Qaanaaq, Greenland
NAS	Nassau, Bahamas
NBO	Nairobi, Kenya
NCA	North Caicos, Turks & Caicos Islands
NCE	Nice, France
NCL	Newcastle, UK
NCR	San Carlos, Nicaragua
NEG	Negril, Jamaica
NEV	Nevis, Leeward Islands
NGO	Nagoya, Japan
NLD	Nuevo Laredo, México
NLG	Nelson Lagoon, AK

NME	Nightmute, AK
NMG	San Miguel, Panamá
NRT	Tokyo-Narita, Japan
NSB	Bimini North, Bahamas
NTE	Nantes, France
NUE	Nuremberg, Germany
NUI	Nuiqsut, AK
NUL	Nulato, AK
NUP	Nunapitchuk, AK
NVG	Nueva Guinea, Nicaragua

O

OAJ	Jacksonville, NC
OAK	Oakland, CA
OAX	Oaxaca, México
OBY	Ittoqqortoormiit, Greenland
OCJ	Ocho Rios, Jamaica
OFK	Norfolk, NE
OGG	Kahului, Maui, HI
OGS	Ogdensburg, NY
OKC	Oklahoma City, OK
OKJ	Okayama, Japan
OLF	Wolf Point, MT
OLH	Old Harbor, AK
OMA	Omaha, NE
OME	Nome, AK
ONT	Ontario, CA
ONX	Colón, Panamá
OOK	Toksook Bay, AK
ORD	Chicago-O'Hare International, IL
ORF	Norfolk/Virginia Beach/Williamsburg, VA
ORH	Worcester, MA
ORI	Port Lions, AK
ORY	Paris-Orly, France
OSA	Osaka-Metropolitan, Japan
OSH	Oshkosh, WI
OSL	Oslo, Norway
OTD	Contadora, Panamá
OTH	North Bend, OR
OTM	Ottumwa, IA
OTZ	Kotzebue, AK
OWB	Owensboro, KY
OXR	Oxnard, CA

P

PAC	Panama City, Panamá
PAH	Paducah, KY
PAP	Port-au-Prince, Haiti
PAZ	Poza Rica, México
PBC	Puebla, México
PBI	West Palm Beach, FL

PBM	Paramaribo, Suriname
PCM	Playa del Carmen, México
PDL	Ponta Delgada, Portugal
PDS	Piedras Negras, México
PDT	Pendleton, OR
PDX	Portland, OR
PEK	Beijing, China
PEN	Penang, Malaysia
PFN	Panama City, FL
PGA	Page, AZ
PGV	Greenville, NC
PHF	Newport News/Williamsburg, VA
PHL	Philadelphia, PA
PHX	Phoenix, AZ
PIA	Peoria, IL
PIB	Laurel Pine Belt Regional Airport, MS
PID	Nassau Paradise Island, Bahamas
PIE	St Petersburg Intl, FL
PIH	Pocatello, ID
PIK	Prestwick, UK
PIP	Pilot Point, AK
PIR	Pierre, SD
PIT	Pittsburgh, PA
PKA	Napaskiak, AK
PKB	Parkersburg, WV
PKC	Petropavlovsk-Kamchatsky, Russia
PLB	Plattsburgh, NY
PLN	Pellston, MI
PLP	La Palma, Panamá
PLS	Providenciales, Turks & Caicos Islands
PMD	Palmdale/Lancaster, CA
PNC	Ponca City, OK
PNI	Pohnpei, Caroline Islands
PNS	Pensacola, FL
POP	Puerto Plata, Dominican Republic
POS	Port of Spain, Trinidad & Tobago
POT	Port Antonio, Jamaica
POU	Poughkeepsie, NY
PPE	Puerto Penasco, México
PPG	Pago Pago, American Samoa
PPT	Papeete, French Polynesia
PQI	Presque Isle, ME
PQM	Palenque, México
PRC	Prescott, AZ
PRG	Prague, Czech Republic
PSC	Pasco, WA
PSE	Ponce, PR
PSG	Petersburg, AK

PSM	Portsmouth, NH
PSP	Palm Springs, CA
PSR	Pescara, Italy
PTH	Port Heiden, AK
PTP	Pointe-à-Pitre, Guadeloupe
PTU	Platinum, AK
PTY	Panama City, Panamá
PUB	Pueblo, CO
PUJ	Punta Cana, Dominican Republic
PUW	Pullman, WA
PUZ	Puerto Cabezas, Nicaragua
PVD	Providence, RI
PVR	Puerto Vallarta, México
PWM	Portland, ME
PXM	Puerto Escondido, México

Q

QBC	Bella Coola, BC
QRO	Queretaro, México

R

RAP	Rapid City, SD
RBY	Ruby, AK
RDB	Red Dog, AK
RDD	Redding, CA
RDG	Reading, PA
RDM	Redmond, OR
RDU	Raleigh/Durham, NC
REK	Reykjavík, Iceland
REX	Reynosa, México
RFD	Rockford, IL
RHI	Rhinelander, WI
RIC	Richmond/Wmbg, VA
RIW	Riverton, WY
RKD	Rockland, ME
RKS	Rock Springs, WY
RNI	Corn Island, Nicaragua
RNO	Reno, NV
ROA	Roanoke, VA
ROC	Rochester, NY
ROR	Koror, Palau Island
ROW	Roswell, NM
RSD	Rock Sound, Bahamas
RSH	Russian Mission, AK
RST	Rochester, MN
RSW	Southwest Florida Regional
RTB	Roatán, Honduras
RUH	Riyadh, Saudi Arabia
RUI	Ruidoso, NM
RUT	Rutland, VT

RWI	Rocky Mount/Wilson, NC

S

SAB	Saba, Netherlands Antilles
SAF	Santa Fe, NM
SAL	San Salvador, El Salvador
SAN	San Diego, CA
SAP	San Pedro Sula, Honduras
SAQ	San Andros, Bahamas
SAT	San Antonio, TX
SAV	Savannah, GA
SAX	Sambu, Panamá
SBA	Santa Barbara, CA
SBH	St Barthélémy, French Antilles
SBN	South Bend, IN
SBP	San Luis Obispo, CA
SBS	Steamboat Springs, CO
SBY	Salisbury, MD
SCC	Prudhoe Bay/Deadhorse, AK
SCE	State College, PA
SCL	Santiago, Chile
SCM	Scammon Bay, AK
SCQ	Santiago de Compostela, Spain
SCRIS	San Cristóbal de Las Casas, México
SCU	Santiago, Cuba
SCX	Salina Cruz, México
SDF	Louisville, KY
SDJ	Sendai, Japan
SDP	Sand Point, AK
SDQ	Santo Domingo, Dominican Republic
SDY	Sidney, MT
SEA	Seattle/Tacoma, WA
SEL	Seoul, Republic of Korea
SFB	Sanford, FL
SFG	St Martin, French Antilles
SFJ	Kangerlussuaq, Greenland
SFO	San Francisco, CA
SFS	Subic Bay, Philippines
SGF	Springfield, MO
SGU	Saint George, UT
SHA	Shanghai, China
SHD	Shenandoah Valley, VA
SHJ	Sharjah, UAE
SHR	Sheridan, WY
SHV	Shreveport, LA
SIN	Singapore
SIT	Sitka, AK
SJC	San Jose, CA
SJD	San José del Cabo/Los Cabos, México

SJO	San José, Costa Rica
SJT	San Angelo, TX
SJU	San Juan, PR
SKB	St Kitts, Leeward Islands
SLC	Salt Lake City, UT
SLK	Saranac Lake, NY
SLN	Salina, KS
SLP	San Luis Potosí, México
SLU	St Lucia, West Indies
SLW	Saltillo, México
SMF	Sacramento Metropolitan, CA
SML	Stella Maris, Long Island, Bahamas
SMX	Santa Maria, CA
SNA	Orange County, CA
SNN	Shannon, Ireland
SNP	St Paul Island, AK
SOP	Pinehurst, NC
SOW	Show Low, AZ
SPI	Springfield, IL
SPK	Sapporo, Japan
SPN	Saipan, Mariana Islands
SPS	Wichita Falls, TX
SPW	Spencer, IA
SQI	Sterling/Rock Falls, IL
SRQ	Sarasota/Bradenton, FL
SRZ	Santa Cruz, Bolivia
STC	St Cloud, MN
STG	St George Island, AK
STI	Santiago, Dominican Republic
STL	St Louis, MO
STN	London-Stansted, UK
STR	Stuttgart, Germany
STS	Santa Rosa, CA
STT	St Thomas, VI
STX	St Croix, VI
SUF	Lamezia Terme, Italy
SUN	Sun Valley, ID
SUR	Summer Beaver, ON
SUX	Sioux City, IA
SVC	Silver City, NM
SVD	Saint Vincent
SVO	Moscow-Sheremetyevo
SWF	Newburgh, NY
SXB	Strasbourg, France
SXF	Berlin-Schönefeld, Germany
SXM	St Maarten, Netherlands Antilles
SYB	Seal Bay, AK
SYD	Sydney, Australia
SYP	Santiago, Panamá
SYR	Syracuse, NY

T

TAB   Tobago, Trinidad & Tobago
TAL   Tanana, AK
TAM   Tampico, México
TAP   Tapachula, México
TBI   The Bight, Bahamas
TBN   Fort Leonard Wood, MO
TCB   Treasure Cay, Bahamas
TCL   Tuscaloosa, AL
TEX   Telluride, CO
TGU   Tegucigalpa, Honduras
TGZ   Tuxtla Gutierrez, México
THU   Pituffik (Thule), Greenland
TIJ   Tijuana, México
TKK   Truk (Chuuk), Caroline Islands
TLC   Toluca, México
TLH   Tallahassee, FL
TLS   Toulouse, France
TLT   Tuluksak, AK
TLV   Tel Aviv, Israel
TNK   Tununak, AK
TOG   Togiak, AK
TOL   Toledo, OH
TPA   Tampa/St Petersburg, FL
TPE   Taipei, Taiwan
TPQ   Tepic, México
TRC   Torreón, México
TRI   Tri-City Airport, TN
TTN   Trenton, NJ
TUL   Tulsa, OK
TUP   Tupelo, MS
TUS   Tucson, AZ
TVC   Traverse City, MI
TVF   Thief River Falls, MN
TWA   Twin Hills, AK
TWF   Twin Falls, ID
TXK   Texarkana, AR
TXL   Berlin-Tegel, Germany
TYR   Tyler, TX
TYS   Knoxville, TN
TZN   South Andros, Bahamas

U

UAK   Narsarsuaq, Greenland
UCA   Utica, NY
UGB   Ugashik Bay, AK
UGI   Uganik, AK
UIN   Quincy, IL
UIO   Quito, Ecuador
UMD   Uummannaq, Greenland
UNI   Union Island, Windward Islands

UNK   Unalakleet, AK
UPN   Uruapan, México
UTO   Utopia Creek, AK
UUS   Yuzhno-Sakhalinsk, Russia
UVF   Hewanorra, West Indies

V

VAK   Chevak, AK
VAR   Varna, Bulgaria
VCE   Venice, Italy
VCP   São Paulo-Viracopas, Brazil
VCT   Victoria, TX
VDZ   Valdez, AK
VEE   Venetie, AK
VEL   Vernal, UT
VER   Veracruz, México
VIE   Vienna, Austria
VIS   Visalia, CA
VIT   Vitoria, Spain
VKO   Moscow-Vnukovo, Russia
VLD   Valdosta, GA
VLN   Valencia, Venezuela
VPS   Ft Walton Beach, FL
VRA   Varadero, Cuba
VSA   Villahermosa, México
VTU   Victoria de las Tunas, Cuba
VVI   Santa Cruz-Viru Viru, Bolivia
VVO   Vladivostok, Russia

W

WAW   Warsaw, Poland
WBQ   Beaver, AK
WDG   Enid, AK
WMH   Mountain Home, AR
WNA   Napakiak, AK
WNN   Wunnummin Lake, ON
WRG   Wrangell, AK
WRL   Worland, WY
WSP   Waspam, Nicaragua
WTL   Tuntutuliak, AK
WWT   Newtok, AK
WYS   West Yellowstone, MT

X

XBE   Bearskin Lake, ON
XGR   Kangiqsuallujjuang, QC
XKS   Kasabonika, ON
XLB   Lac Brochet, MB

XNA   Northwest Arkansas Regional, AR
XPK   Pukatawagan, MB
XSC   South Caicos, Turks & Caicos Islands
XSI   South Indian Lake, MB
XTL   Tadoule Lake, MB

Y

YAA   Anahim Lake, BC
YAB   Arctic Bay, NWT
YAC   Cat Lake, ON
YAG   Fort Frances, ON
YAJ   Lyall Harbour, BC
YAK   Yakutat, AK
YAM   Sault Sainte Marie, ON
YAP   Yap, Caroline Islands
YAQ   Maple Bay, BC
YAT   Attawapiskat, ON
YAV   Miner's Bay, BC
YAX   Wapekeka/Angling Lake, ON
YAY   St Anthony, NF
YAZ   Tolfino/Ucluelet, BC
YBB   Pelly Bay, NWT
YBC   Baie Comeau, QC
YBE   Uranium City, SK
YBG   Bagotville, QC
YBI   Black Tickle, NF
YBK   Baker Lake, NWT
YBL   Campbell River, BC
YBQ   Telegraph Harbour, BC
YBR   Brandon, MB
YBS   Opapamiska Lake/Musselwhite, ON
YBT   Brochet, MB
YBV   Berens River, MB
YBW   Bedwell Harbor, BC
YBX   Blanc Sablon, QC
YCB   Cambridge Bay, NWT
YCD   Nanaimo, BC
YCG   Castlegar, BC
YCH   Chatham, NB
YCK   Colville Lake, NWT
YCL   Charlo, NB
YCN   Cochrane, ON
YCO   Kugluktuk/Coppermine, NWT
YCQ   Chetwynd, BC
YCR   Cross Lake, MB
YCS   Chesterfield Inlet, NWT
YCY   Clyde River, NWT
YDA   Dawson City, YT
YDF   Deer Lake, NF

YDI	Davis Inlet, NF
YDL	Dease Lake, BC
YDN	Dauphin, MB
YDO	Dolbeau, QC
YDP	Nain, NF
YDQ	Dawson Creek, BC
YEG	Edmonton Intl, AB
YEK	Arviat, NWT
YER	Fort Severn, ON
YEV	Inuvik, NWT
YFA	Fort Albany, ON
YFB	Iqaluit, NWT
YFC	Fredericton, NB
YFH	Fort Hope, ON
YFO	Flin Flon, MB
YFR	Fort Resolution, NWT
YFS	Fort Simpson, NWT
YFX	Fox Harbour, NF
YGG	Ganges Harbor, BC
YGH	Fort Good Hope, NWT
YGK	Kingston, ON
YGL	La Grande, QC
YGO	Gods Narrows, MB
YGP	Gaspe, QC
YGQ	Geraldton, ON
YGR	Îles-de-la-Madeleine, QC
YGT	Igloolik, NWT
YGV	Havre Saint Pierre, QC
YGW	Kuujjuarapik, QC
YGX	Gillam, MB
YGZ	Grise Fiord, NWT
YHA	Port Hope Simpson, NF
YHC	Hakai Pass, BC
YHD	Dryden, ON
YHF	Hearst, ON
YHG	Charlottetown, NF
YHI	Holman Island, NWT
YHK	Gjoa Haven, NWT
YHM	Hamilton, ON
YHO	Hopedale, NF
YHP	Poplar Hill, ON
YHR	Chevery, QC
YHY	Hay River, NWT
YHZ	Halifax, NS
YIB	Atikokan, ON
YIF	Pakuashapi, QC
YIK	Ivujivik, QC
YIO	Pond Inlet, NWT
YIP	Detroit-Willow Run, OH
YIV	Island Lake/Garden Hill, MB
YJT	Stephenville, NF
YKA	Kamloops, BC
YKG	Kangirsuk, QC
YKK	Kikatla, BC
YKM	Yakima, WA
YKN	Yankton, SD
YKQ	Waskaganish, QC
YKU	Chisasibi, QC
YLC	Kimmirut/Lake Harbour, NWT
YLE	Wha Ti/Lac la Matre, NWT
YLH	Lansdowne House, ON
YLL	Lloydminster, AB
YLR	Leaf Rapids, MB
YLS	Lebel-sur-Quevillon, QC
YLW	Kelowna, BC
YMG	Manitouwadge, ON
YMH	Mary's Harbour, NF
YMM	Fort McMurray, AB
YMN	Makkovik, NF
YMO	Moosonee, ON
YMT	Chibougamau, QC
YMX	Mirabel, QC
YNA	Natashquan, QC
YNC	Wemindji, QC
YND	Gatineau, QC
YNE	Norway House, MB
YNG	Youngstown, OH
YNL	Points North Landing, SK
YNO	North Spirit Lake, ON
YNS	Nemaska, QC
YOC	Old Crow, YT
YOG	Ogoki Post, ON
YOH	Oxford House, MB
YOJ	High Level, AB
YOP	Rainbow Lake, AB
YOW	Ottawa, ON
YPA	Prince Albert, SK
YPC	Paulatuk, NWT
YPD	Parry Sound, ON
YPE	Peace River, AB
YPH	Inukjuak, QC
YPI	Port Simpson, BC
YPJ	Aupaluk, QC
YPL	Pickle Lake, ON
YPM	Pikangikum, ON
YPN	Port Meunier, QC
YPO	Peawanuck, ON
YPR	Prince Rupert, BC
YPW	Powell River, BC
YPX	Puvirnituq, QC
YQB	Quebec City, QC
YQC	Quaqtaq, QC
YQD	The Pas, MB
YQG	Windsor, ON
YQI	Yarmouth, NS
YQK	Kenora, ON
YQL	Lethbridge, AB
YQM	Moncton, NB
YQN	Nakina, ON
YQQ	Comox, BC
YQR	Regina, SK
YQT	Thunder Bay, ON
YQU	Grande Prairie, AB
YQX	Gander, NF
YQY	Sydney, NS
YQZ	Quesnel, BC
YRA	Rae Lakes (Gameti), NWT
YRB	Resolute, NWT
YRD	Dean River, BC
YRF	Cartwright, NF
YRG	Rigolet, NF
YRJ	Roberval, QC
YRL	Red Lake, ON
YRN	Rivers Inlet, BC
YRS	Red Sucker Lake, MB
YRT	Rankin Inlet, NWT
YSB	Sudbury, ON
YSF	Stony Rapids, SK
YSG	Lutsel K'e (Snowdrift), NWT
YSJ	Saint John, NB
YSK	Sanikiluak, NWT
YSL	St Leonard, NB
YSM	Fort Smith, NWT
YSO	Postville, NF
YSP	Marathon, ON
YSR	Nanisivik, NWT
YST	Ste Therese Point, MB
YTB	Hartley Bay, BC
YTE	Cape Dorset, NWT
YTF	Alma, QC
YTH	Thompson, MB
YTL	Big Trout Lake, ON
YTQ	Tasiujaq, QC
YTS	Timmins, ON
YTZ	Toronto Island, ON
YUD	Umiujaq, QC
YUL	Dorval, QC
YUM	Yuma, AZ
YUT	Repulse Bay, NWT
YUX	Hall Beach, NWT
YUY	Rouyn-Noranda, QC
YVB	Bonaventure, QC
YVC	La Ronge, SK
YVM	Qikiqtarjuaq (Broughton Island), NWT
YVO	Val d'Or, QC
YVP	Kuujjuaq, QC
YVQ	Norman Wells, NWT
YVR	Vancouver, BC
YVZ	Deer Lake, ON

YWB	Kangigsujuaq, QC	YYF	Penticton, BC	ZEL	Bella Bella, BC
YWG	Winnipeg, MB	YYG	Charlottetown, PEI	ZEM	Eastmain, QC
YWH	Victoria Inner Harbour, BC	YYH	Taloyoak, NT	ZFD	Fond du Lac, SK
YWJ	Deline, NWT	YYJ	Victoria, BC	ZFN	Fort Norman, NWT
YWK	Wabush, NF	YYL	Lynn Lake, MB	ZGI	Gods River, MB
YWL	Williams Lake, BC	YYQ	Churchill, MB	ZGS	Gethsemani, QC
YWP	Webequie, ON	YYR	Goose Bay, NF	ZIH	Ixtapa/Zihuatanejo, México
YWQ	Chute-des-Passes, QC	YYT	St John's, NF	ZJG	Jenpeg, MB
YXC	Cranbrook, BC	YYU	Kapuskasing, ON	ZJN	Swan River, MB
YXD	Edmonton Municipal, AB	YYY	Mont Joli, QC	ZKE	Kaschechewan, ON
YXE	Saskatoon, SK	YYZ	Toronto-Pearson International, ON	ZKG	Kegaska, QC
YXH	Medicine Hat, AB			ZLO	Manzanillo, México
YXJ	Fort St John, BC	YZF	Yellowknife, NWT	ZLT	La Tabatiére, QC
YXL	Sioux Lookout, ON	YZG	Salluit, QC	ZMT	Masset, BC
YXN	Whale Cove, NWT	YZP	Sandspit, BC	ZNL	Nelson, BC
YXP	Pangnirtung, NWT	YZR	Sarnia, ON	ZPB	Sachigo Lake, ON
YXS	Prince George, BC	YZS	Coral Harbour, NWT	ZQS	Queen Charlotte Island, BC
YXT	Terrace, BC	YZT	Port Hardy, BC		
YXU	London, ON	YZV	Sept Îles, QC	ZRH	Zürich, Switzerland
YXX	Abbotsford, BC	YZY	Mackenzie, BC	ZRJ	Round Lake, ON
YXY	Whitehorse, YT			ZSA	San Salvador, Bahamas
YXZ	Wawa, ON	**Z**		ZSJ	Sandy Lake, ON
YYB	North Bay, ON			ZSW	Seal Cove, BC
YYC	Calgary, AB	ZAC	York Landing, MB	ZTM	Shamattawa, ON
YYD	Smithers, BC	ZBF	Bathurst, NB	ZUM	Churchill Falls, NF
YYE	Fort Nelson, BC	ZCL	Zacatecas, México	ZWL	Wollaston Lake, SK

NOTES:

INDEX TO AIRLINES

US = USA, CN = Canada, GR = Greenland, SP = St Pierre, MX = México, CB = Caribbean, CA = Central America

US = USA, CN = Canada, GR = Greenland, SP = St Pierre, MX = México, CB = Caribbean, CA = Central America

T

U

V

W

Y

Z

US = USA, CN = Canada, GR = Greenland, SP = St Pierre, MX = México, CB = Caribbean, CA = Central America

INDEX TO RADIO CALL-SIGNS

INDEX TO AIRCRAFT TYPES

US = USA, CN = Canada, GR = Greenland, SP = St Pierre, MX = México, CB = Caribbean, CA = Central America

PHOTOGRAPH CREDITS

Andrew Abshier . . . . .US 12

Air Caribbean . . . . .CB 6

Airbus Industrie . . . . .cover

AirSask . . . . .CN 12

Michael L Baker . . . . .CN 15

Mickey Bednar . . . . .US 48

Michael Bolden. . . . . .US 10, 17, 23, 29, 57, 68, 99, 110

Carlos Borda . . . . .US 79; CB 11

Scott Brandenburg . . . . . . .US 40

British Aerospace . . . . .US 26; MX 3

Michael Carter/ . . . . .US 6, 60, 64, 118
Aero Pacific Images

Michael J Chew . . . . .US 109

Kevin Cook . . . . .US 95

Jeffrey S DeVore . . . . .US 20, 43, 53, 84; CN 26

Rurik Enriquez Dominguez .MX 15

Greg Drawbaugh . . . . .US 47, 58, 59, 75, 92, 116, 117; MX 1

Peter Duckworth . . . . .US 111; CN 25

EMBRAER . . . . .US 14

Bruno Emmenegger . . . . . .US 5, 9, 11, 55; CN 14; MX 13

Glen Etchells . . . . .CN 43

George Fariñas . . . . .CA 5

Kelli Farraway . . . . .US 33

Lawrence Feir . . . . .US 38

Jens Flunkert . . . . .MX 6

David C Forward . . . . .SP 1

John A Giambone . . . . .US 15

Paul Giannico/ . . . . .US 93;
Pegasus Photography . . . . .CN 17, 27, 29, 40

Antoine J Givaudon . . . . . .CN 9

Robert S Grant . . . . .CN 42

Stephen L Griffin . . . . .US 13, 35, 62, 80

Eddy Gual/Aviation . . . . . . .US 69, 114; CB 8
Photography of Miami

Damiano Gualdoni . . . . . . .CB 1

George W Hamlin . . . . .US 18, 85, 98

James Helbock . . . . .US 39, 72

Bill Hough . . . . .US 19, 22, 25, 30, 37, 46, 94, 106, 107, 112; MX 7, 8, 14; CB 4

Julio C Infante/Aviation . . . .US 49, 70
Photography of Miami

Robert-Jan James . . . . .CB 13

Dale Jellison . . . . .US 8

Gary Jennings . . . . .US 41, 51, 77, 108; CN 2, 38, 39; CA 7

Jeff S Johnson . . . . .CB 7

Mike Keenan . . . . .US 65, 78, 82, 102; CN 5, 41; CA 6

Duncan Kirk . . . . .US 73

Ernst J Koenig . . . . .US 103

P Loeuillet/J Magendie/ . . . .CB 2
Avimage

Brian Losito . . . . .CN 2, 11, 28

Michael Magnusson . . . . . .MX 4, 12; CA 1

Vicki Mills . . . . .CA 2

Ito Noriyuki . . . . .CA 4

North Vancouver Air . . . . . .CN 32

North-Wright Air . . . . .CN 34

Stefano Pagiola . . . . .US 16; CN 1

Perimeter Airlines . . . . .CN 36

Bob Polaneczky . . . . .US 42, 71, 83; CN 10

Patrick Vinot Préfontaine . . .CB 5

Nigel O Prince . . . . .CB 9

Norbert Raith . . . . .MX 10

Raytheon . . . . .US 3; CN 4, 7, 16, 23, 31, 37

Andreas Rohde . . . . .CB 10

Kurt Roth . . . . .US 54; CB 14

SAAB . . . . .US 81; CN 18

Zenon G Sanchez . . . . .MX 2, 9, 11

Darryl J Sarno . . . . .US 115

Bob Shane . . . . .US 45, 50, 56, 66, 67, 96

Robbie Shaw . . . . .US 76, 86; GR 1

Tom Sheridan . . . . .US 28, 97, 104, 105; CN 13; CB 16, 17, 18

Terry Shone . . . . .US 88

Richard Silagi . . . . .US 44

Mike Small . . . . .US 101

Ed Stephens . . . . .US 31, 32; MX 5

John P Stewart . . . . .US 87, 120

Shane Stoffregan . . . . .US 89, 100

Kenneth Swartz . . . . .US 34, CN 8

Gary Tahir . . . . .US 90

Shingo Takahashi . . . . .US 1

Gordon Tan . . . . .CN 20, 21, 22

Henry Tenby . . . . .CN 6, 24, 30, 33, 35, 44

John van den Berg/Carib- . .CB 15, 19, 20
bean Aviation Curaçao

Joe G Walker . . . . .US 2, 4, 7, 61, 74, 91, 113; CA 3, 8

John Wegg . . . . .US 21, 24, 27, 36, 52, 63; CN 19; CB 3

WestJet . . . . .CN 45

Christofer Witt . . . . .CB 12

World Airways . . . . .US 119

US = USA, CN = Canada, GR = Greenland, SP = St Pierre, MX = México, CB = Caribbean, CA = Central America